Mary Magdalene's Words

Other Books by Aliyah Schick

Meditative Coloring Book 1: Angelic Imprints
Meditative Coloring Book 2: Crosses
Meditative Coloring Book 3: Ancient Symbols
Meditative Coloring Book 4: Hearts
Finally, a Book of Poems

Soon to be released:
Meditative Coloring Book 5: Labyrinths

Mary Magdalene's Words

Two Women's Spiritual Journey, Both Truth and Fiction, Both Ancient and Now

by
Aliyah Schick

Artwork and design by Aliyah Schick
Published by Sacred Imprints, Asheville, North Carolina

For more information about this book, Mary Magdalene, and the author please go online to: www.MarysWords.com

ISBN Number: 978-0-9844125-0-1

Table of Contents

PART ONE: AWAKENING

PART TWO: RISING

PART THREE: CALLING

Mary Magdalene

Mary Magdalene and Maggie Blume:
Truth and Fiction

Truth: Mary Magdalene came to me during a meditation, asking me to act as her scribe to write down her story. Much to my surprise, I was able to do that. All of Mary's Words come directly from her, through me, to you.

Fiction: Maggie Blume's story is modern day fiction. It wraps around and weaves through Mary's Words as Maggie engages in the same struggles and life patterns Mary Magdalene faced long ago. The characters and events in Maggie's story are imagined and used fictionally.

Mary Magdalene is speaking to you and me.
Are we listening?

Aliyah Schick
Winter, 2011

PART ONE

AWAKENING

Chapter One: Awakenings

Maggie made it all the way out the big double doors and down three steps, but she stopped, gazed across at the mountains beyond the city, then turned and worked her way back through the departing crowd. A loud sigh slipped loose as she passed between the gaily-painted doors.

At the far end of the room a half dozen people waited under a brilliant blue and gold stained glass window. She joined them and watched the man in the long black robe as her mind scrambled to know what to say to him.

"Thank you for what you do," she began, trying to ease her way into it.

He smiled, lifted his arms tentatively, and asked, "Do you hug?" She nodded, and as they hugged he said, "It's good to meet you."

Meet me? Does he notice me? Maggie studied him as they released from the hug. She took a breath, and began, "If you ever doubt yourself—"

His eyes locked on hers and she froze. What was she doing? She had nothing to say next. This was all there was. They both waited for her to continue, intently watching each other's face.

Maggie brightened and declared, "If you ever doubt yourself, think of me!" What? What does that mean?

He waited, watching her, his expression both startled and curious.

"Because I know," she heard herself begin to explain, but the words stopped again. Know what? What did she know?

"I know that every Sunday you say something important for me to hear."

The tension eased, then suddenly there was more to say. "I think you are why—" Maggie gasped and caught the next words in her throat. She searched his face. Did he understand what was happening? She had been about to say, "I think you are why I came here." How could she say such a thing?

She began again, more cautiously. "I mean, I think what you say, your messages, are why I came here."

That wasn't true. It wasn't his sermons, it was him. She peered into his face again. Could he tell? They stared at each other, then he nodded and thanked her.

Despite the evasion, it felt done. She could leave now. Maggie smiled, more from relief than anything else, and she left as he turned to hug the next person. She didn't see that he watched her go.

Four months earlier Maggie Blume drove into the southern Appalachian Mountains from the flat land of the north, and these ancient, weathered mountains opened their arms to take her in. They were mother; she felt held in ways she'd never imagined. They were sanctuary. After six months of wandering, she found home.

For ten years she had wanted to get here just to visit, drawn by pictures and tales and urgings to the Blue Ridge, the Smokies, and the city of Asheville. Plans never worked out. Now, leaving her marriage and searching for refuge and a new place to live, this was the right time.

She had never even been in the South, warned, by just about everyone she ever knew, about bigotry and backwardness and cruelty. All of that seemed like smokescreen now, to save this place for her for a new start apart from all the past. As she drove into the city, nestled between mountain ranges, she felt possibility and promise rise in her, waking from a long sleep into a new day.

The first apartment Maggie looked at was perfect. Upstairs in an old house on Cumberland Avenue, just north of downtown, its windows looked out on the city and to the mountains beyond. Maggie walked the neighborhood's quiet streets of older houses with flowers in their yards and friendly greetings for a stranger. She walked downtown, through beautiful, old architecture, with added walkways, benches and sculptures, and every kind of shop imaginable.

One day, on a whim, she stopped at a spa for a massage and ended up getting her long, brown hair cut short in a loose, easy style that found its own curves and waves, and showed off high cheekbones and green eyes. She was not pleased that now, with her casual way of dressing, eager demeanor, and the physical ease of a daily walker, she looked yet another five years younger than her age. Maggie had earned those years, and she wanted credit for them. Anyone had to look closely to notice the sprinkle of gray coming into her hair, fine wrinkles around her eyes, and the softening of her jaw line.

Out in the mountains she explored the Blue Ridge Parkway's branching trails and streams, waterfalls, and beautiful vistas. She climbed Mount Pisgah and Sam Knob for panoramic views of western North Carolina, the Balsams and Smokies, and Shining Rock Wilderness Area. Then as November turned toward December the Parkway closed for winter while its roads and hiking paths filled with snow and ice. Maggie walked instead at the Arboretum and Botanical Gardens, and on city sidewalks.

During one of her walks she discovered the Montford Center for Holistic Health Care, offering ancient and new therapies for healing and well-being. After asking around, she decided to approach the director, Teresa Jasper.

"What I do," Maggie explained, "enhances a person's own natural healing process, similar to acupuncture but without the needles. My work compliments any conventional medical care they receive. It's very effective, and fits well with the other modalities you offer here."

Teresa asked how it works and Maggie knew it was time for the twenty-second elevator speech. "I identify any interference within your energy field and remove it in order to reestablish the clear flow of vital energy. Renewed flow enables natural healing. I've seen amazing results, even with long-standing problems. The best way to understand this is to experience it. Can I offer you a treatment as demonstration?"

"Let's give it a try," said Teresa, leading the way to one of the private therapy rooms.

An hour later Teresa declared, "That was great! I feel very relaxed, my headache is gone, and the pain in my shoulder has disappeared, and I didn't even tell you about that. I can think of a half dozen people right off who should have a session with you. When can you start?"

Maggie began working with individual clients at the Montford Center the following week, and soon added classes, too. She was surprised how quickly her reputation drew word-of-mouth referrals. Even though she had always been very successful with clients, a residue of cynical judgment from her husband, family, and friends in her old life still weighed heavily on her self-confidence. This success was very encouraging.

Down the Cumberland Avenue hill from Maggie's house, on the way into downtown, there was a beautiful old church built of mountain stone with a soft green, copper-clad roof and bell tower, and high stained-glass windows along the sanctuary. Wide front steps and brightly painted doors invited

Maggie's curiosity every time she walked by. On Sunday mornings, between services, the yard filled with a diverse, friendly mix of people and the muffled sounds of a pipe organ. The sign said Presbyterian. Maggie's grandparents had all been Presbyterians.

In the opposite direction she walked past a synagogue of modern brick with plain brown doors and a low roof, silent and empty on a weekday morning. She could join its Reform congregation and fit right in, continuing all those years of the Jewish life she had married into. It would be easy to find new friends and contacts there, instant community. But she didn't want to. She wanted to see what it was like in that stone church with the playful, many-colored doors.

On Maggie's first Sunday at the Cumberland Presbyterian Church the minister, Reverend Michael Cairn, preached compellingly about the most basic Jewish prayer, the Shema, and how essential it is to Christian faith. "Hear, oh Israel, the Lord is our God, the Lord is One." In doing this he came to meet Maggie on familiar ground and he earned her trust.

Still, she thought, it's too bad this minister isn't named Madeleine or Monica instead. I'd just as soon not have any man in a position of importance right now. I'd rather not pay attention to one, or want to hear what he says. But then, she wondered, what am I doing in a Jesus place?

Two nights later, a cross woke her in the middle of the night.

Maggie scowled and shook herself awake. "What? What is it?" The image claimed her mind, insistent, unrelenting. "I see it," she muttered. "I won't forget. Please, can I go back to sleep?" Weariness dragged her deep into the pillow, but the image pushed sleep just out of reach. "I'll draw it in the morning," she moaned, "I promise." And she slid once more toward half-sleep.

An hour later, tangled in the covers, she finally gave up. "Okay, okay!" she groaned, pushing herself to the edge of the bed. "I'm doing it."

It was a Jesus cross, the old-fashioned kind with elaborated ends and a wide, sectioned band encircled the crossing point. She had no idea what it meant, but there it was, now held in place on the paper, a line drawing exactly as she'd seen it in her mind. Maggie wrote the message next to it, "Let go of everything." Everything meant everything, she realized, all assumptions and expectations and shoulds, all barriers and fears and hesitation, let go of everything that held her in or held her back, and then listen to spiritual guidance.

"Now can I sleep?" she sighed out loud, wondering what to expect next. Within seconds of clicking off the light she was asleep.

The drawing of the cross was there in the morning. Good thing, too, because she had forgotten all about it. She stared at it while she pulled on sweats and sneakers. She could hear her atheist parents ask with sarcastic sneers, "What's that?" Her Jewish, soon-to-be-ex husband and their grown daughter would both be horrified that she even had it in her home. It did feel uncomfortable. She'd never even touched any kind of cross before. What was she supposed to do with it? She left the drawing on the dresser, and for the next several weeks it seemed to always be in the way. Then it disappeared into a pile of papers, only vaguely remembered.

Maggie went to the stone church nearly every Sunday morning, to organ concerts once a month, and Wednesday evening discussions. She began to learn about Jesus and Christianity through the surprisingly meaningful messages of its minister. While Maggie spent the winter working out her divorce and establishing her new life, Reverend Cairn spoke about finding God in what sends you into pain and fear. Then, at the very first suggestion of spring, as the mountain valleys began to hint of early green and a few bold flowers initiated the first layer of the long spring bloom, his sermon was about expecting to be amazed.

Maggie liked staying on the edges at the church, watching and listening, with no promises and no obligations. She met a few people, but she never spoke at discussions, and she carefully avoided the minister.

Reverend Cairn seemed to Maggie to be a man of contrasts. The starkness of his narrow, bony face and stern, rimless glasses failed to hide lively eyes or overcome a head full of thick, unruly brown and gray curls. The easy posture and long, loose limbs of his five-foot-ten frame appeared more ready to flop at any moment into a comfy armchair to read the latest Grisham novel all afternoon than to wear a somber, dark suit and formal ministerial robes, or deliver a sermon. And although he seemed friendly and open, there was a reserve about him. He mainly spoke with people who approached him first, and did not linger any longer than necessary at the end of services.

One Sunday, during the service, a startling thought invaded Maggie's mind. What if Reverend Cairn doubts himself? What if he doesn't know how good he is at explaining and inspiring? What if he becomes discouraged, even quits or leaves? She had to talk to him, to tell him how valuable his messages are. What if he resigns and she hasn't said anything?

Maggie interrupted this cascade of worry to protest. Hey, nothing he has said this morning suggested self-doubt. And why is this so intense? Oh, she realized, there must be more here than I can see. It's so strong and compelling that this must be spiritual guidance, and it must be important. I better pay attention. But, what would I say?

No words came, only the unrelenting and compelling urge to talk to him.

When the service ended and the pipe organ recessional followed the crowd outside, Maggie tried to leave. Halfway down the front steps she could not go any farther. Leaving felt awful, as if something in the fabric of life would tear if she did, and nothing would ever be what it should have been. There seemed no way around it; she had to talk to him. She went back inside.

*

"Doubt himself?" she wrote in her journal later that afternoon. *"I said that to him? Think of me? We've never even spoken before. What was I thinking? How could I?"* She sighed.

"But how could I leave? The urge to speak with him was so powerful that it definitely came from spirit, not from me. Have I ever experienced guidance that strong?" Maggie stopped and shifted in her seat before writing more. *"Okay then, so it's good I didn't leave. And, that means I also probably shouldn't have held back that second part, saying, 'I think you are why I came here.'"*

After another sigh she added, *"I wonder if he realized that was what I started to say."*

The last thing she wanted when she entered the church the next Sunday morning was to be noticed by Reverend Cairn. Unfortunately Maggie found herself walking directly behind him, watching the polished backs of his black shoes as he headed through the sanctuary to the pulpit. They were halfway up the aisle when he abruptly stopped and turned around to face her. Startled, she held her breath, expecting him to scowl, but when he saw her his face lit up with a big smile. He thrust out his arms for a hug, and exclaimed, "There you are! Good morning!" Relieved, she let go of her breath, and allowed herself to sink into his hug.

Reverend Cairn preached that morning about temptation. Wouldn't a minister say to not trust your impulses? To hold to rules and guidelines developed by loftier minds? But this minister's concern was about being yourself. He said God created us as we are, and wants us to be all we can be. Temptation, as he saw it, is anything that draws you away from letting your truth and talents shine forth in the world. Temptation is whatever holds you back. Temptation gets you to try to please someone else or avoid judgment or to settle for the safe choice. Temptation closes you down.

Damn, Maggie exclaimed to herself. Last Sunday I stopped myself from saying, "I think you are why I came here." I dove for cover and said something more safe and acceptable instead, and now he's up there talking about it in his sermon.

❧

For as long as she could remember, Maggie had wanted to find that deep, sacred core of herself where she could be conscious of the divine and feel truly alive. Her parents called such yearnings ignorant and foolish. One exciting benefit of marrying Dan had been that it opened up the possibilities of Jewish faith. If all religions really did end up in the same place, maybe any religion would get her there, and it didn't matter which one. Maggie found some of what she was looking for at the local Reform congregation, and some acceptance for valuing it, but as she got used to that much, she wanted more.

The best she ever encountered was outside of Judaism. Readings and a few tentative experiences of ancient and indigenous spirituality enthralled her. Standing stones, mounds and earthworks, sacred sites and sacred mountains, prehistoric carvings and paintings, spirals and labyrinths, images of the fertile feminine, underground holy places, and celestially-aligned architecture, anything that found spirit and meaning in natural rhythms and patterns and experiences, and saw holiness in all that is, spoke to something deep within her. And now she felt all that calling her to these mountains.

"See which stone catches your attention," said the tall redhead, dramatic in a black turtleneck sweater and long, colorful skirt. Tory's dark eyes sparked with mischief. She was clearly eager to lead the gathered women on an adventure. She had laid out a circle of stones to begin this "Talking Stones" workshop held on a Saturday in the lower level of the church. "Let your stone find you," Tory added.

Maggie made herself keep looking and not rush to settle on that first one that caught her eye. That one, a rounded gray stone covered with light-catching gold flecks, was flashy and bold. It was too much, wasn't it? How about something more reserved? How about that green one? But its shape wasn't at all appealing, too hard-edged. She loved the smooth, sensuous shapes of river stones.

"Oh, yes, go take it when you know which one it is," Tory replied when someone asked. Two people immediately seized theirs, then three more, so Maggie grabbed the sparkly one before someone else could take it. Then she marveled at herself. She got to have this exciting stone, the pretty, sensuous one that stood out from all the others.

She held it in her hands and watched the others choose. One woman picked up each remaining stone, carefully feeling for just the right one. Rachel would do that, thought Maggie. Her daughter was thorough like that. This was why Rachel was still, at almost twenty-seven years old, a graduate student, making sure she knew everything she could possibly need to know about low-income residential architecture.

Another woman waited while every other person found a stone before she picked from what was left. Maggie had seen this woman put herself last before, making do with what no one else wanted. Lydia, Maggie's best friend up north, would do that, insisting "the stone that's meant to be mine will still be there."

Would it? Or was that an excuse for being passive? For most of Maggie's life she had hesitated to claim anything for herself, and she was glad to finally begin to make a choice and go for it. Look how I took this stone right away, she thought. Good for me!

"Who would like to talk about your stone?" asked Tory.

When it came to her turn Maggie said, "I've been looking at this stone while listening to the others speak about theirs. I see that there's more to it than the gold flecks that first caught my attention. It is made up of several different types of rock all stirred together. This stone's formation has a complex history. There's a lot more to this stone than first meets the eye, and the same is true about me." Maggie glanced at Tory and saw her wide smile.

"It's a river stone," she continued, "worn to an almost nice, rounded shape, but it doesn't quite do round, it's uneven. And despite all the wear, it has a very course texture. This stone holds onto its individuality. It keeps its shape and texture rather than give it up to what is going on around it. I'm starting to do that a lot now, maintaining my independence, not cooperating with other people's expectations. I don't want to be boxed in."

Later Maggie wrote in her journal, "*I sure do react to any hint of being boxed in. I don't even like to sit with someone, breaking loose as fast as I can to avoid being limited. After all those years of following along, deferring to others, and cooperating, now I want to find my own way with things, and that feels very good. Am I really going to be this fiercely independent? I think I like that."*

❧

Teresa Jasper invited Maggie to attend a gathering at the Montford Center. "You haven't met my friend Stephen, yet," she said. "His work is based on sacred geometry and it's very exciting. He's going to have us do something for the Center involving crystal grids, and I'd like you to be a part of it."

Grids? Maggie often found herself working with intricate, multidimensional patterns in the bioelectric energy fields that permeate and expand out from everyone and everything that exists in this physical world. She called some of these patterns grids because they seem to stabilize and hold things in place. She had wondered if sacred geometry might explain some of what she was discovering. Perhaps this man Stephen would answer some of her questions.

On the day of the gathering, Maggie had an early session with a client first. She helped Jon release a deep-set blockage in his right shoulder, held there since a childhood trauma. By the end of the session, before he even got off the treatment table, the numbing he had experienced in his hand for the last several years was already gone.

"I can't believe it!" he said. "I have tried every medical intervention short of surgery, and every alternative bodyworker and healer I could find, and nothing helped. Now in one session you've fixed it. I don't know what you did, Maggie Blume, but this is terrific!"

"I'm glad I could help, but what I do is only effective if you are ready for healing, so thank yourself, too. I reach deep into the patterns underlying what is, releasing and repairing whatever is available to be healed there. Your allowing it is the key, so it's really up to you. Today you are ready for your arm and hand to be more active and involved in your life. That's why you came to me, and that's why we could do this work now.

"Jon, this is about more than your hand's numbness. The fact that it is your right hand and shoulder tells me that it's about your taking action in the world and being effective. I think after this you are going to find yourself making things happen. Be open to that. Allow it and explore it. And trust it. You're ready for it."

Jon stared at her and said, "My friend Ted just lectured me about that yesterday. He said I don't follow through on what I think and what I want. He encouraged me to fulfill more of my potential. Now you're saying the same thing, and you just met me today. How can you know that?"

"Your arm and your energetic field tell me that." As she spoke Maggie cleared his field of old expectations and fears related to this so that he could go forward more easily. "Here is your homework," she said. "Look for two opportunities this week to reach out and make something happen. I'd like you to come back next week to take care of any residual elements that may come up. You can tell me then if you have noticed differences."

"Maggie, how did you get so good at this?"

"Three things: willingness, experience, and commitment. I'm willing to do whatever I'm guided to do. I've had good training and a lot of experience. And I do about an hour of energetic and meditative self-care every morning."

"Every morning?"

"I hardly ever miss a day. If you'd like, when you come next week I'll show you an easy energy balancing sequence that you can do yourself in as little as five minutes. It would be very good for you to do it regularly."

"Great. I'll look forward to it. Maggie, how did you learn all this?"

"My first steps were with classes and teachers, and I've learned a lot on my own since then. When we are willing to know more than we think we know, we can learn and do much more than we ever imagined."

"Well, I'm impressed with you, and with this work you do. My hand feels great! Thank you very much!"

After Jon left and Maggie cleared the energy of the room, then she lay on the table herself for a few minutes and thought about what she had told him. She had developed a series of daily practices to clear, balance, and expand her energetic systems. Over time this raised her field's vibration rate and broadened her consciousness, increasing perception and intuitive awareness and the depth of her reach. The benefits accumulated and multiplied over time. She had, indeed, come a long way.

Maggie didn't realize how similar all of this was to what shamans practice. She didn't know that now she operated in the same deep realms where shamans do, used some of the same sources, saw the same kinds of patterns and possibilities, and moved in similar ways, doing equivalent work.

If she had trained as a shaman, with that label, if she had been handed language and techniques to define what she now experienced, and validation for what she did, if she had lived with people who were convinced of the reality of such things, she would have more easily accepted and believed what she was discovering. But in a society of Newtonian pragmatists, where physical and scientific concreteness reigned, and surrounded by skeptics and sarcasm, it was hard to allow poetry, let alone mystery and miracle.

So Maggie lived in two separate worlds, the ordinary and the extraordinary, unable to reconcile her own experiences of unexplainable healing and stunning transformation, of knowledge and understanding far beyond the accepted, of experiences usually dismissed as fantasy or chance or delusion. To do the sacred work of healing, Maggie stepped into another, mystical way of being, and yet most of the time she lived an ordinary, simple existence with limited perception and cautious judgment. This dichotomy bound her experience of life, and kept her from seeing it as all true, and all one amazing, mysterious, abundant, and exuberant whole.

Maggie glanced at the clock. It was time for the gathering. She slipped off her work jacket and went out front to join the group and meet Stephen.

His appearance caught her off guard. He looked more country club than crystals. Stephen was tall and distinguished looking, sophisticatedly casual in an attractive sweater, slacks, and soft leather shoes. As he spoke he became more casual. He pushed his thick, white hair away from his forehead, and hid his height in the seat of the chair. A child-like eagerness slipped out from behind his opaque, formal-gray eyes.

Stephen had walked away from a successful high-level, high-living business world to devote himself to installing geometric configurations of quartz crystals at sacred sites and powerful places throughout the region. He explained that the well-known electromagnetic conductivity of quartz crystals intensifies dramatically when laid out in these ancient, timeless designs. It helps people to incorporate more of their soul's potential and to heal.

He hadn't mentioned sacred geometry, so Maggie asked about it. Stephen smiled and said, "I can see why you ask that. I've asked it myself. These grid designs and their functions come to me through guidance with the help of several psychic friends. I've never been told anything specifically about sacred geometry, but I wouldn't be surprised if there is a correlation."

Very much like her own situation, she thought. How interesting.

The group moved outside to install a golden mean spiral pattern of crystals in the front yard of the Center. Maggie noticed that Teresa positioned herself next to Stephen and was shamelessly flirting with him, but then forgot about it as Stephen began the ritual.

"Each crystal in the spiral represents a planet in our solar system," Stephen explained, "starting with the sun at the center. Each of these crystals has been charged in the master grid on the mountain near my home, so they carry that energy. This new grid will connect vibrationally to that grid and to all the other established grids in the area." He handed out small quartz crystals, one by one, in order around the circle.

Maggie felt a surge sweep into her as he laid a crystal in her hand. She looked at the name attached to it and said, "Tiamat?" She knew of a Tiamat from Babylonian mythology, a version of the Great Mother Goddess who was said to have created all that exists from her own body's substance. But what was this planet Tiamat?

Stephen smiled and nodded at her question, then explained to everyone, "I include three extra planets: Vulcan, Tiamat and TransPluto, plus the sun, so there are thirteen positions on the spiral. Vulcan is so close to the sun that we don't see it. TransPluto is so far out at the edge of the solar system that although scientists find evidence it is there, no one has seen it, either." Stephen turned to Maggie and continued, "Tiamat is believed to have been a planet beyond Mars. It was destroyed long ago with such violence that its fragments now form the asteroid belt."

Maggie closed her hands around the crystal, wondering how this planet Tiamat connected with the Goddess mythology. She was glad that the setting in place of the Tiamat crystal had fallen to her.

Once all the crystals were buried Stephen said, "Now let's activate and expand this grid to let it become an influence of healing and stability at this place and out into the community." As Stephen led them through the activation process, Maggie felt the grid take on a powerful energetic presence, and she actually stumbled back from the edge, pushed by its expansion as if by a strong wind.

"Now we're going to energetically connect this new grid to the big grids at major sites for many miles around here," said Stephen. He called out the name of each site: Mount Mitchell, Roan Mountain, Grandfather Mountain, Shining Rock, over a dozen sites in all. As he named each one, Maggie felt a surge and a massive locking in of connection, as if a huge switch in a regional electrical network had been thrown on and a powerful flow of current established.

At the end Stephen asked the group, "Did any of you experience any sensations or get any impressions as we did this?" Two participants told about feeling a lot of energy. When no one else spoke, Maggie described being pushed back as the grid was expanded. Stephen encouraged her to share as much as she could recall, so she spoke about feeling the locking in of the connections and a sense of completion at the end.

When it was over, Stephen walked back into the building alongside Maggie. "Thank you for your feedback," he said. "I don't sense much myself, so I depend on others to tell me what they experience. I really appreciate your comments. I'm always glad to find someone who can do that for me."

"It's wonderful for me that you trust my impressions. Too many people in my life have doubted anything they couldn't sense themselves, and even humiliated me for it."

"An ex?"

"How did you know?"

"Personal experience."

"Actually, it is an entire ex-world: husband, daughter, family, friends, community. They all think I've gone insane."

Steven nodded. "I've seen that many times."

Maggie smiled at him. "I'm finding good support here in Western North Carolina, including my clients, these mountains, and now you. This is a good place for me."

"Me, too. I love it here."

Back inside, Stephen had displayed a table full of small grids for sale, quartz crystals glued to cardboard in simplified versions of the patterns at the large installations. When Maggie picked up a triangle formation, Stephen came over and explained, "This grid connects you with all the healers of the universe."

Maggie smiled and nodded. "No wonder it feels so familiar. I am already aware of a vast system of healers throughout time and space. Thanks for explaining that." She touched another grid, then asked," Stephen, how do these small grids work? What do people do with them?"

"I'm hoping you will tell me. I've gotten a variety of feedback, but I'm not sure."

Maggie tried holding samples of each of the grid designs to see how they affected her. She kept coming back to one that challenged and intrigued her more than any of the others. It was a six-pointed star, like the Jewish "Star of David," with two interlocking triangles, one pointing up to God and the other down to earth.

"This grid is called 'Spirit into Form,'" said Stephen. "Its pattern helps a person connect with their higher self and soul energies."

"It's powerful," she said, holding it in both hands in front of her. "I think there's more to it than what you're saying. This is the one I want to take with me."

Stephen smiled and said, "Please be sure to let me know what you find out about it. Meanwhile, let me tell you that in the 'Tree of Life' grid, which is a complex grid made up of all the other grid patterns set into a Kabalistic 'Tree of Life' design, this 'Spirit into Form' pattern lies at the center, in the heart chakra position."

Maggie took another look at the grid, then looked back at Stephen. "Good," she said. "I've got plenty of heart trouble to heal. Maybe it will help."

Stephen stepped closer, gently touched her arm, then added, "There's more. You'll like this, Maggie. Each position on the 'Tree of Life' also represents a planet. The center point, at the heart, where the 'Spirit into Form' pattern lies, is Tiamat."

They both grinned.

"Now I definitely have to find out more about Tiamat," she said.

❧

Ancient stories told that the Great Mother Goddess Tiamat was in her form as a dragon or cosmic serpent when the Sun God Marduk killed her in order to take over as supreme deity. This story was repeated down through the ages in the many myths of gods and saints and heroes killing dragons and serpents and snakes. Each story recreated the triumph of patriarchal rule over the sacred feminine, and the suppression of the Great Mother religions.

The creation story of the *Old Testament* repeated this story in "Genesis," translating Tiamat, known as Mother of the Deep, into *tehom*, meaning the abyss, darkness, chaos. The God of the Jews and Christians displaced the darkness and, like Marduk, declared himself the one God over all other gods.

In her reading Maggie discovered that Archangel Michael was revered by the church as the chief dragon-slayer, leader of the angels who went to war with the dragon. He led the destruction of the Goddess religions. Archangel Michael, along with Marduk and all the other patriarchal heroes, murdered Tiamat and every other form of the sacred feminine, conquering and destroying all they stood for.

Ancient Goddess worship spoke to profound yearnings within Maggie, deeper than anything she found in current religions. How could she compromise this? Was it a mistake to go to anything called a church? Was this information about Archangel Michael a warning to be careful of a minister named Michael? Was it even possible to be a Christian minister and not be a dragon-slayer? The God of the *Old Testament* ordered the massacre of whole peoples who followed the old religions. Maggie knew very little about the *New Testament*. How did Jesus fit into all this?

She decided to be much more cautious about this church she'd been going to. There was a whole new world out there to get involved with. She turned her attention to building her healing practice, became a regular at a weekly downtown drumming circle, and joined Stephen whenever he did an installation or group experience. She signed up for a course on regional geology at UNC Asheville, and made new friends through class activities and field trips. She began to find community outside of the church.

Awakenings

She wakes with sun in her eyes and sounds of running water.
She wakes with stars and dark distance and silence.
She wakes within waves of cascading memories,
rhythmic patterns of disappearing past.
She wakes within stillness grown to stone's resistance,
deeper than eternity,
isolation, impenetrable, impossible.
She wakes within unfinished change,
both too early and too late,
between, where she does not belong,
wondering where she is until she falls back to sleep and dreams
she wakes with sun in her eyes and sounds of running water

in the next room. Fountain.
Golden wall and heater hum and creaky floor.
Mountain view and morning.
Reaching ivy tendril over kitchen sink
touching memory of mystery and magic
and seven bags of irises,
of drum and flute and bonfire,
of rooting deep into land and love planted into soul's realm.

Open eyes, seeing wide and far in dark and light,
she comes awake within life's embrace,
and she remembers it all.

Chapter Two: Wondering

"Maggie, I need your help to get me past this," said Lydia on the phone.

The two of them used to spend every Wednesday together, learning and practicing and reviewing energetic healing techniques, doing treatments on each other, and exploring ideas about the work. Now they had to settle for telephone and internet conversations, and exchanging remote healing sessions. Maggie missed seeing Lydia's expressive, often mischievous face, where every nuance of feeling showed up. Now she had to guess Lydia's expression from her voice and the words she used. Today Lydia was obviously distraught and intense. No mischief now, no sparkling blue eyes or lively golden curls.

"I've realized something," Lydia explained. "Whenever anything starts to seem important, I run away. And I know why. Because if I stayed and learned anything, I would have to do something about it."

"You never bring me the easy ones, do you, Lydia?" Maggie took a deep breath and pulled her focus into her own center before she spoke again. "So, if you did stay and face things, what would be so bad?"

Lydia poured out her answer in a flood. "The effects go deep, fast. I'm afraid I'll find out there's nothing worthwhile in me, and I'm also afraid of the opposite, that I am really something and I have tremendous responsibilities that I don't live up to, and that I've been destroying a thing of beauty and wasted fifty years." Lydia went silent, barely breathing.

"Is that all?"

"Don't joke. I'm serious."

"I'm not joking. Is that the end of it? Are you at the bottom?"

"Yes."

"Okay." Maggie let herself slip into that deep consciousness in which she connects with guidance, and she spoke from there. "Listen to me, Lydia. You are a beautiful, glorious, sacred being, who has chosen to come here to this life to do exactly what you are doing today and yesterday and tomorrow.

All the pain and joy and mystery you experience serve purposes beyond what you can see and realize. Everything truly is what it is meant to be. Judging it, or judging ourselves, keeps us from moving on through."

"Wow, Maggie, that was good! You should write that down."

"Don't get in your head, Lydia. Feel it."

Lydia took some deep breaths, then asked, "Are you working on me? I'm feeling better."

"I'm pulling the pain and doubt out of your field as soon as you bring it up and are willing to release it. We're getting down to some of the old beliefs that cause it, too. You're doing great, Lydia. Now don't close as it eases. Keep allowing and releasing."

"I'm trying."

"When you try, you tighten up. Let go, instead. Relax your grip on what's happening. Just let it happen. Let go of knowing, of expecting, of figuring this out."

After a few minutes Lydia said, "There is still the fear that I'm not worth your time and effort to do this. That I'm a jerk or I'm just nothing, empty. Like I dig for treasure and the box is empty and everyone is laughing at me."

"Lydia, do you hear how extreme these statements are? Such condemning words of worthlessness come from outside of truth. Can you tell that they're not yours?"

"It does feel like they are shoved into me or plastered onto me, and I've grown around them over time so that now I hold onto them."

"You don't have to keep them. It doesn't matter how they got there, or who said what. Trying to identify all that will just keep you tangled in them. The only question is, do you want to keep them?"

"No," she declared. "Let's do it. Clear them out."

Maggie worked silently for a while. Although they were hundreds of miles apart, connected only by the telephone, Maggie felt Lydia's energy field as if she were right there. Drawing her hands through the field, Maggie gathered and removed any density or heaviness or inconsistency she found, lifting out anything that did not belong there. When the field felt smooth and clear she said, "You're doing great, Lydia. You've released a lot more. How do you feel?"

"I feel peaceful. I feel a lot more hopeful. I'm content to just be in this moment."

"You did very good work today. Now, be really nice to yourself for the rest of the day."

"I like that idea," said Lydia.

A couple of days later, while watching a romantic movie alone at home Maggie felt her own heart break open. "My heart hurts!" she exclaimed out loud.

"Of course it does," said Nu, Maggie's closest spirit guide.

When working with clients, Maggie always asked for guidance to help her know what was going on and what to do. She made sure she was very receptive then, and it worked well. Guidance and messages more directly about herself and her own life came through as she meditated or wrote in her journal. Being deeply relaxed and in a somewhat altered state made that possible. Only on rare occasions, such as on that Sunday when she was so strongly told to speak with Michael about his doubts, did guidance sometimes make it through to her conscious mind right out in the middle of life's happenings.

For Maggie, guidance usually came as an intuitive knowing, a direct, sudden sense of understanding something. Most guidance she received was not consciously attached to a specific spiritual guide, but just an idea out of nowhere planted in her mind. The one time she usually did get an impression of an individual guide was when Nu spoke to her as she wrote in her journal.

Although she didn't "see" Nu, an image had grown in her mind as a result of her impressions. She pictured a tall, numinous, hence the name Nu, not-quite-human creature whose very essence was kindness, wisdom, and knowledge.

"Of course my heart hurts?" she asked Nu.

"There's the whole marriage and divorce history, that's obvious," Nu explained. "And then there is Alex. You opened your heart to Alex and allowed yourself to love, and now you're finally allowing the painful results. Of course it hurts."

"I never should have gotten involved with Alex. I barely knew him. He was exciting, and I had just left Dan. It was such a bad mistake. Well, it won't happen again. This hurts too much. I'll never fall in love again. It's not worth it."

"Okay, sure," said Nu, "...except you will."

"No," she groaned. "Please don't tell me that."

As spring came into bloom Maggie drove the mountain roads and walked the foot trails, letting the mountains absorb her heartache. On the Sunday when she eventually went back to the church, Reverend Cairn spoke about letting go of old relationships, healing your heart, and opening to new love. How could he have known?

"Hi, Maggie? This is Michael Cairn, from church. Evelyn said you had offered to step in for her this week to help with arrangements for the discussion group tonight."

This was a surprise. Evelyn had asked her to be available, but assured Maggie that he usually took care of everything himself, so he probably would not call.

"What can I do for you, Reverend Cairn?" she asked. Maggie doubted he knew her name, so she wondered if he had any idea who he was talking to.

"First, please call me Michael. Everybody does."

"Okay…Michael," she said, tentatively.

"I was thinking a bowl of oranges would be good for the centerpiece tonight.

Maggie laughed. "I just bought a big bag of oranges a couple of hours ago, and wondered how I was going to use them all."

"Great! Bring them! Say, since we're on such a roll, you don't happen to have castanets, do you? We might get a Spanish theme going."

"No castanets," she said, "but I might be able to come up with an old Tijuana Brass album."

They both laughed and fell into easy, comfortable conversation, generously sprinkled with more shared laughter. Michael ended up going over his whole plan for the evening and they were on the phone for twenty minutes.

As Maggie said good-bye, a sudden, sharp-edged sadness overcame her. She didn't want to disconnect; she didn't want to let go of him. It seemed like it could be forever, and that felt devastating. Then a voice on the radio sang, "I forgot to tell you I love you," and a strong wave of loss and grief startled her. What was going on?

That evening Maggie watched Michael when she got to the church, and yes, he was surprised to discover that she was the one carrying a bag of oranges. He thanked her with a big smile and for the rest of the evening he used her name whenever he got the chance.

Another strong reaction jarred Maggie after next Sunday's service when she overheard Michael say, "I'll be out of the state all next week." Her body lurched as if she'd been punched in the stomach. She felt her energy reach for him, desperate to know he was still near. It was as devastating as if the mountains had suddenly disappeared.

Michael abruptly stopped talking. He stepped to where he could see her and looked straight at her. She couldn't do anything but stare back at him. Had he felt that, too? He went back to finish what he had been saying, then turned again to Maggie and came toward her, past others who were waiting, and he reached to hug her. She sank into the hug and into the next moment, letting everything else fall away.

On another Sunday, as she thanked him for the message in his sermon, she sensed many people coming at him, each wanting something from him. Without thinking, she laid her hand on his arm and kept it there while they talked, unconsciously providing him with energetic support and balance.

Later she told Lydia, "I don't even try to connect with him, it just happens. It's like I've known him forever and there are no barriers between us."

"There is a joy in how you speak about connecting with Michael," said Lydia. "It's very special. Are you falling in love with him?"

"No! Are you serious? I'm not ever risking love again. It always leads to anger and pain. I'm done with that. And I sure don't want to love Michael Cairn! A Christian? A minister! Good grief, no. And I definitely do not want to be involved with another man who seeks the spotlight. I've tried that twice and it doesn't work."

"Well, you pick them," said Lydia.

"Okay, yes, I'm attracted to men who are good at what they do, who stand out in their field, who are impressive."

"How's that working for you?"

"I think the problem is that being leaders isolates them, no matter how compassionate they are. And then people gather around them who want to use them and draw from them, so of course they become wary."

"And isolate themselves more."

"Yes, they build walls around themselves and retreat behind them."

"This certainly describes Alex," said Lydia. "Your husband Dan, also?"

"Yes, it sure does. And maybe it's Michael, too, at least to some extent. He definitely protects himself. Am I playing out the same pattern again?"

"That's a worrisome thought."

"Another commonality is that they all like that I see the real person behind the professional persona, not just the star. I see who they really are."

"It must be both a relief and frightening to be seen so clearly."

"I hadn't thought about it that way."

"They do seem to delight in your perceptive questions and observations. Probably because they get to feel so smart."

"You sure sound cynical, Lydia."

"Just saying what I see."

"They do like having me around, don't they?"

"Most people do. Your energy is supportive, empowering, and stabilizing."

"I like the star's liking me. I like feeling special."

"But it's a distorted kind of special, isn't it?"

"Is it? Maybe the challenge of their isolation attracts me. I want to be that special one who manages to break through when others can't, who gets them to open up and let me into their inner circle."

"It's not so great in there, is it, Maggie? That's where all the monsters hide."

"True," Maggie sighed. "With Alex the inner circle was where he kept all his fears and insecurities and frustrations, and he let them run rampant there. It was a nightmare in there."

"I saw some of that. You sure got a big dose of it when Alex turned on you at the end."

"Dan's inner circle was a place for crashing, a place where he didn't want to put any effort into anything, a place to rest up to get ready to go back out into the world again."

"A different kind of nightmare."

"He resented my asking anything of him in his downtime, and got angry if I did anything but agree and cooperate and fall into line. I learned to be numb and invisible."

"Serious stuff. So, does Michael live a separate, inner circle life?"

"I don't know, Lydia. Do you think every star does this? And is the inner circle always so screwed up?"

"You better find out, kiddo."

"I cannot, will not, must not get involved again with a person whose way of being intimate is to close us into a dark place where it is us against the world. If I'm ever with a star again I have to be very careful that the person is healthy and happy in their private world. Otherwise, being attracted to stars is an absolute setup for disaster, and no way to find a person to be happy with."

"Maybe you should be looking for a person who has learned a lot but doesn't feel compelled to get up at a podium about it. Of course, then where is the excitement?"

"Do I want the drama and intensity? Is that what this is about? Can I be happy with a simple, good, balanced relationship?"

"I don't know, Maggie. Can you?"

Maggie forgot to change her clocks for the beginning of daylight savings time, so she missed the early service. Just before Michael started the second service he saw her, grinned, and shook his head.

In all the time that Maggie had watched Michael during services and discussion groups, she had never looked at him as someone she might be attracted to. Today as he read from the scriptures she found herself wondering about the possibility. All of a sudden Michael turned and looked over at her with a startled expression on his face. Oh, no! Did he know? Horrified, she immediately dropped it. Ten minutes later she tried it again, very gently this time, like tiptoeing, and right away he looked at her again. He must have felt it. She gave it up and hoped he didn't really know what she was doing.

Thank goodness he seemed okay with her when she went to hug him at the end. He smiled a bright smile and said, "I see you made it here."

Maggie laughed. She'd forgotten all about being late. "I put off changing my clocks last night and then forgot," she said, still laughing. "I think I sort of believe I have to do it right at 2 a.m., or at least wait till the last possible minute before bed. How silly!"

Michael laughed with her and they hugged a big, tight, long hug. It was not a careful hug, not one of those bend forward and don't-touch-too-much hugs people do. It was a real hug. And it felt good.

Emboldened by the relaxed mood between them, Maggie said, "Michael, I need help with this Jesus stuff." He nodded, his face turning earnest. She went on to explain how little exposure she had had to anything Christian, and that she'd been left with blocks against it.

"Oh, yes, I know what you mean," he said. "We all grew up with plenty of confusing influences. For myself, I have to peel away a lot to get to Jesus."

"Is there a book I can read?" she asked.

"Let's talk about it. Call me at the office and we'll set up a time to talk."

"Oh, you do that?" she asked, surprised. She hadn't considered that.

He nodded and smiled. "Call me."

Maggie and Michael played phone tag through the week. Meanwhile Stephen came looking for Maggie at the Montford Center and asked, "Tell me what you have noticed since you took that small grid home."

"There is so much going on for me, Stephen, it's hard to say what causes what."

"Just start talking about what's happening. You'll say the right thing."

Maggie could see he really wanted answers, so she grabbed whatever she could think of to say. "It does seem easier now for me to stay balanced and keep moving forward. Maybe the grid stabilizes things."

"How so?" he asked. "Can you elaborate on that?"

"I've long been aware of a flowing path, like a river current, and sometimes I'm hung up on something, then get free and back into the flow. I think it's easier to get going again now."

"That's what I believe the grids do. Thanks, Maggie. I appreciate the validation."

Now she had more to say. "The amazing thing is that all this with your grids feels so familiar to me. The energy patterns of your grids must relate to the energetic patterns I work in, and to the energy in these mountains. And it feels like my own personal energy patterns are directly aligned with all that, too."

Stephen nodded, and Maggie stopped for a moment to think.

"These patterns I work in are the basis for the designs and processes and pathways for everything that exists and everything that happens." She looked at Stephen to see how he reacted to that, but he just looked back at her, waiting for more.

"The individual patterns in my own energy make it possible for me to access those deeper patterns." Taking a breath to steady herself, she added, "Stephen, I think I'm somehow, purposely designed for this."

Maggie sat there for a moment in the silence, wondering what that meant. Stephen watched and waited.

"Sometimes I work extremely deep into the layers," she said. "The layers of patterns go infinitely far into the depths of what is. I have even reached to infinity to get under an intrusion to lift it out." She stopped and looked at him again, trying to imagine what he was thinking of all this. He didn't even blink.

"Okay, I can't tell what you're thinking, Stephen, but it is such a relief to admit and say all this that I'm just going to be bold and say the rest of it."

A bit of a smile snuck around the edges of his mouth.

"I get an impression that there is some place where all this comes together. It feels very far away, and I don't know if that distance is in dimension or time or space or some other variable. Do you know about this?"

He slightly shook his head.

"The weirdest part is that it feels quite familiar and comfortable to me. I think the patterns and the energy in these mountains and in me all, somehow, have roots there. Does this sound crazy? I don't want to be weird. I want to be grounded and practical and cautious. Stephen, I don't know what to do with this."

Now he shifted in his seat. "Just let it be there, Maggie," he said. "See what comes of it. That's what I find works for me. I never know what's coming, and I don't try to. I just let things play out."

"You and I come at this deep patterning differently, Stephen, but we're working with the same basic elements, so we understand each other. I can't believe I found you. What are the chances of that?"

"Oh, pretty good, I'd say," said Stephen, laughing.

"Congratulations on your award, honey," Maggie said into the phone. "I'm very proud of you."

"Yeah, Mom? Then why aren't you here for dinner with us to celebrate?" asked Rachel.

"I just can't get away, not even for a few days. I've got clients and classes scheduled." In her daughter's silence they both heard the truth that Maggie could have been there if she wanted to. Maggie tried to move on. "So, tell me, what are you doing this evening?"

"Dinner with Dad, then Joanie and I are going out later. We'll find some music and have some fun."

"There's great music here in Asheville, Rachel. The whole downtown turns to music after dark. You'll love it. Every night of the week there's just about any kind of music you could want."

"It's a little far to drive tonight, Mom."

"I meant maybe sometime soon you'll come check it out."

"I doubt it. I've got a really busy term ahead of me. They're working us hard."

"Well, keep it in mind, that's all," Maggie sighed.

"Gotta go. Dad's waiting for me. Do you want to say hi?"

"That's okay, hon, say hi for me. I've got to go, too."

"Sure. Well, bye then," and she was gone.

"Wait…I love you," Maggie whispered into the silent phone.

❧

"How about if I remove old relationship cords from you that may be in the way for your opening to new ways of relationship?" asked Lydia.

"I guess it's pretty obvious I need that, huh? Okay, see what you can do. Thanks."

At the end of the treatment, after discussing what had happened, Lydia paused, then added, "Do you know there's a figure—I think it's a woman—standing back in the shadows watching you?"

"She's still there? Someone else told me about her when I first started doing energy work. I forgot about her. Why is she there?"

"All I can tell is that you'll find out when the time is right."

"Now I'm curious, but I don't sense more, either. So, let's trade places now and do your treatment. What can I help you with?"

"I'm still running away from facing things."

Maggie tuned into Lydia's energy field like tuning a radio dial to establish clear reception. "It's about trust, Lydia, real trust," she said. "It's about opening clear down into the deepest levels of who you are, without knowing what will happen. What a scary thing! But what the hell, Lydia, you tell me that your self-destructive choices are already putting your health and survival at risk, anyway. You might as well take a chance and really go for it."

Lydia laughed, and the sound reminded Maggie that when Lydia laughs her whole body laughs. Maggie smiled, picturing Lydia's wide grin and loose blond curls bouncing in syncopation with her shoulders and belly.

Suddenly Maggie turned serious. "I'm getting a strong message now, Lydia," she said, "and it's for both of us. You and I are supposed to be clear channels of energy and healing and spiritual connection. No more of this doubt and hesitation. We're supposed to know it and live it and be it, like holy people on the mountain do. We think it takes some sort of effort or learning to get there, but that's all distraction. We're already there."

"Holy people on the mountain?" exclaimed Lydia. "No cookies or chocolate or sexual fantasies? EEEEK! That sure frees up a lot of time for prayer and piety!"

"Take it easy," Maggie laughed, "not literally like them. The point is to fully live what we know and who we can be, clear and committed and effective. Hey, maybe we'll get lucky and find out that cookies and chocolate and sexual fantasies are an essential part."

"You wanna bet?"

"We both love experiencing strong energy, and that's exactly what this is. It's about being who we really are, going for it, full out. It's about letting ourselves be powerful, Lydia, and not be scared by the power."

"I'm already scared just listening to this."

"It's not our power, Lydia, and the effects are not ours, either. We are the means, the access, the bridge between source energy and this world. We are servants. There is profound humility in this powerfulness. When we allow ourselves to be strong and capable and effective, then we fulfill our spiritual purpose, we do our work, we serve. It's all about serving. This is exactly what we have been working so hard to get to."

"I'm thinking this may be for you, Maggie, but not for me. I'm not of your caliber, never have been and never will be."

"Oh, stop it, Lydia! That's ridiculous. Besides, you wouldn't be hearing this if it weren't for you, too. We are just different, you and me. You need to understand things in your head, but information comes very abstractly to you, in your body and in your energy field, in sensations and impressions. I am more experiential and conceptual, more right-brained. I need to feel it and know it deep in my being. Instead I get all this head stuff in words and sentences and explanations."

"Words and sentences and explanations would be a big help, Maggie. Just getting a feeling doesn't take a person very far."

"But for me it does! Words or messages don't convince me. I need something deeper. I need belly-knowing or cellular-knowing or something else very deep in. You get these deep impressions I'm talking about, and that doesn't do it for you. You need to get it in your mind. You need to hold it in front of you, look at it, and understand it in your mind. Then you have it. And yet I am the one who explains everything. What is this?"

"Beats me."

"You want what I get and I want what you get. Somehow we're together to make this work. Maybe it is to learn from each other until we each trust ourselves enough to learn in our own way."

Lydia laughed.

"You may not trust your impressions, Lydia, but through them you are always validating me."

"That's great, Maggie, but I have nothing for you to validate."

"Not true! I validate you all the time with all this explaining I do. You're always saying 'Oh!' because I just explained the abstract sense you have of something."

"Maggie, I feel like I'm pulling garbage out of a black plastic bag looking for a treasure, without even knowing what the treasure looks like. I'm getting quite smelly and messy in the process. And discouraged."

"I don't think it's in the garbage bag, Lydia. Get out of the garbage."

They both laughed at that.

"Enough talk," said Maggie. "Let's get you on the treatment table and see what I can work on today."

❧

On Palm Sunday Michael read the story of Jesus' final days. He talked about the humiliation and physical abuse, the taunting and criticism and cruelty. And he talked about Jesus being so demoralized that he cried out to God, "I don't want to do this!"

As Michael spoke, Maggie felt Jesus' agony as if she were there and it was happening to her. It was excruciatingly physical; her body screamed from the pain. It was devastating, beyond any emotional pain and anguish she could imagine. And she had never known such spiritual despair. The most disturbing part was that somehow she recognized it all. She knew it; she remembered it as if she held it within her own experience. When Maggie told all this to Michael afterward, he nodded vigorously.

"Yes, yes, I know what you mean," he said. "I feel that, too."

"And then," she continued, "when you spoke of Jesus' faith at the end, and you had us repeat his words, 'Into your hands I commend my spirit,' I felt that just as intensely. I felt it deep in my body, in my belly, in my cells. This is the deepest, surest faith I have ever experienced."

"Yes," he said, his eyes shining into hers. "And this is a very good time to get in touch with that. Maggie, let's go look at my calendar right now and find a time to get together to have that talk about Jesus. Maybe we can do it this week." Maggie followed him upstairs to his cubbyhole office under the church's eaves. One square window between bookcases looked out into the trees behind the church.

"How about lunch this Friday?" he asked.

"Are you sure you want to do this on Good Friday?"

"I don't know why not."

Maggie smiled. "That's also Friday the thirteenth, and lots of good things have begun for me on a Friday the thirteenth."

"Sounds good to me," he said. "Let's do it."

That Tuesday on an impulse Maggie pulled a book about love down from a shelf and started reading where she had left off nearly a year before. Turning the page, she came to a startling passage about the word *behold*. It said Mary Magdalene was the first to behold the resurrected Jesus on Easter morning because through their deeply sacred love she, more than anyone else, had always clearly seen his radiant self. The author explained that holding another's true beauty, even if they do not see it themselves, keeping it safe, being trusted with it, is how we come into our own fullness of being.

Maggie read the passage again.

"I hardly believe what I'm reading," she wrote in her journal. *"Holding another's beauty when they don't know how beautiful they are? This is what I said to Michael that first time we spoke. I told him I hold his beauty, even when he doubts it, and he can trust me and count on me to do that. Now I find it in this book, and the author relates it to a deep, sacred love between Jesus and Mary Magdalene."*

Maggie stared out the window to the mountains, wondering what she had come into here.

"I got to that dark night of the soul when my wife died ten years ago," said Michael, slouched on the edge of his seat, collapsed into the oversized gray sweater he wore. This was the next evening, Wednesday, and the discussion group was just getting started. "Our two sons were both in college, headed out on their own, I was in a job that wasn't working for me, and then my best friend, my life partner was gone. I was devastated. I couldn't see any reason to go on, to make any effort, to even take that next breath. I couldn't find any shred of faith. I cried out, 'I can't do this!'"

Suddenly Maggie saw him with family and big Sunday dinners and car trips and squabbles and history. She was overwhelmed by the reality of him.

"The story of Jesus' last days is all about faith, about trust, and about letting go," Michael said. "What are some of the ways that you let go?" he asked the group.

People called out things like take a walk, listen to music, and play with a child, and Michael wrote them on the board. Maggie listened, then said, "Give up."

"Good one," he said, nodding his head. He wrote it on the board and spoke about it before asking for more ideas. Then continuing on, he said, "No matter how good we get at letting go and going with the flow, we inevitably lose our way and again feel lost in the struggle. We have to reinvent how to get out of it, as if we never knew. We loop around and around this circle, continually losing our way and reinventing how to find it." Heads nodded all across the room.

"But then life is hopeless," Maggie protested. "Why bother?"

"Say more," Michael urged.

"What's the point of staying in that same, endless cycling? I want get some place. I want to find answers."

"So what do you do to stay in the flow?" he asked.

"I see it as more of a spiral, circling but coming to a new perspective because I have learned and I have opened to change."

Michael wrote "open to change" on the board, then turned back to the group and asked, "What are some other ways we can stay in that letting go mode?"

No one spoke for a while, so Maggie said, "I have a sign in the middle of my apartment where I see it all the time. It says, 'Remember who you really are.'" She had made that sign a very long time ago to remind herself, when she was at home in the heaviness with her husband Dan, that she was still the bright, lively person and capable healer other people knew and appreciated. The message eventually came to mean much more. "It brings me to my center," she told the group, "to my core self, to who I am meant to be. It brings me to meaningfulness and spiritual connection and to being on my path. That sign has become a touchstone to bring me back to who I really am."

Michael listened intently, then wrote it on the board, "Remember who you really are," and spoke about knowing what matters and letting go of what doesn't.

Maggie wanted him to impress her, and he did. The way he handled the group was masterful, sometimes holding himself back so they could be where they were, sometimes running a bit with the exciting comments, and finally gathering it all up and balancing it so everyone felt validated and empowered. But all this was the facilitator, not the man, and she couldn't tell what he knew and where he stood himself. How open was he? How far could he see?

She watched the discussion for a while, listening to other people's questions and comments before she spoke again.

"I have a question," Maggie said, "and I really, seriously, want an answer."

"Let's hear it," he said. "We'll do our best."

"Why do we lose our faith and do this cycling? What purpose could that serve? And how can we resolve that, so then we can stay in the knowing and faith?"

Michael turned to the group and asked, "What are some ideas on this?" They talked about learning from challenge, and about needing a kick in the butt to get them moving. Then they returned to resignation and the inevitability of cycling, and Michael followed them. Maggie tried to draw them back to her question again, but then she sighed. There wasn't going to be an answer this way.

Later, far from the question, when Michael was pulling everything to a close, he spoke about how to deal with feeling lost, and he said something about "living as if."

Maggie burst out, "That's it! That's the answer to my question. Live as if."

Michael stopped, looking confused. "Live as if?"

"Would you explain that, please?" a woman asked. "How does that answer your question?"

Maggie panicked for a moment. Her reaction had been impulsive, and she wasn't at all sure what she meant. She'd just had a vague, but powerful feeling about it, and didn't know that she could explain. She took a deep breath, and began, blindly feeling the way.

"We're talking about losing God and losing faith, and about having to reinvent how to get to them. Take a step back from it and see what's really going on. God is always here. Faith is always real. We don't need to pretend they are so that they will come back. They never left. My losing knowing doesn't make them go away. No matter what happens, no matter how messed up I get, God is here and faith is real. There's never any question of that. The question is do I know it. What I need is to allow myself to know that. The 'living as if' is not living as if God is here and faith is real. They are. The 'living as if' is living as if I know."

"That's different?" asked the woman.

"Oh, yes! If God and faith are still right here and I just, for whatever reason, feel unable to reach them, that's very different from actually losing them. As long as God is here and faith is real, even though I feel lost, and even though I may not believe it right now, all I have to do is reach out and I'll touch them. That's all I ever have to do. So, if I go ahead and live as if I can reach them, and I do reach out, no matter how much I doubt it, I will touch them. It will work."

Maggie took a breath and didn't know what else to say. "Does that explain it?" she asked.

The woman nodded. Maggie turned to look at Michael and he was staring at her. Someone else said something and it was late, so Michael went back to finishing up.

As people were leaving Maggie went to Michael and said, "Thank you for this evening, and thank you for the answer to my question."

"I'm not sure I did that. I'm not sure what happened there."

"It worked, whatever it was," she said.

"It sure did," he replied.

The next evening Lydia told Maggie on the phone, "He probably won't get any sleep tonight, knowing he will have you one-on-one tomorrow, with no one to pass your questions off to."

"Do you really think he is impressed with how I think?"

"Only frightened, fear-ridden people, who don't like being challenged or don't like to think, are not impressed with what you say."

"Can you say that again without the multiple negatives?"

"Anyone who has it even minimally together is impressed. Better?"

"Thanks."

"Maggie, you have a way of seeing things from different angles, and you are willing to express it in a non-threatening, 'hmm, look at this' way. You invite people to think outside of the box, to glimpse new concepts and even whole new paradigms. I bet he was glad you asked your questions."

"I don't try to challenge, Lydia, I just ask what I want to know."

"I know that. Your questions are part of expressing your truth. You're not trying to attract attention. They are from the heart of you, so they are wonderful."

"Tomorrow is going to be good," said Maggie. "We'll get to know each other, and he'll help me understand Jesus. Tomorrow we'll become friends. And I'll finally find out what color his eyes are. I forget to notice or when I think about it I can't tell because they scrunch up when he smiles."

Chapter Three: Ivy and Iris

"So, Maggie, tell me what's happening," Michael asked when they had settled at a low table in the back room of the Jerusalem Garden Cafe.

"I have a hard time getting to Jesus." She explained that her atheist upbringing and Jewish married life had always required her to be completely closed to anything Christian. "Going into energy work introduced me to Jesus in a limited way, but I'm still caught off guard every time you mention him. I instinctively cringe, as if it's not allowed and you shouldn't do it."

He looked startled so she quickly added, "Your explanations are helpful. I even got comfortable with communion one Sunday when you explained it without mentioning body and blood. The trouble is that doesn't last. Every time I start to get anywhere about Jesus, I hit a wall."

Michael nodded and said, "It helps me to clear away the religious trappings, and look at Jesus as a person." He spoke about Jesus trying every way he could to get God's message through to people. "Jesus gave us all he had to give. And at the end, he gave all the rest, all he was. He gave himself, his life, he gave his body and his blood, literally and symbolically, so that we would hear his message. That's where communion comes in."

"I sort of get that sometimes, but not so that I can keep hold of it."

"I don't think a person can ever really, fully understand Jesus."

"Because you don't get definite answers?"

"Right, and if you do get a grasp on Jesus, you just lose it again."

"Because everything about him seems to be parable and allusion."

"Yes! He is such an enigma," Michael declared.

"So, this is the kind of thing where once you get it figured out and understood, once you set that last piece into place, that completion itself propels you through to a new level, with new questions, and you have to start all over."

"Yes!" Michael exclaimed. "Where once again you know nothing and you're starting from scratch."

They grinned at each other and laughed. And they saw that they both relished that challenge to move to a new level and begin again.

As they spoke people passed by and some sat at nearby tables. The waiter took their orders and brought glasses of water. Maggie realized she was sitting in a public place openly talking about Jesus. Had she become one of those people? She looked at Michael, felt his earnestness and caring about the topic, and settled herself back into it.

"There's a story that I relate to Jesus' being an enigma," Michael said. "But it's a bit bawdy." He took off his glasses and peered at Maggie quizzically from under lowered brows. "Are you okay with that?" he asked. Maggie had no idea where he was headed, but how bad could it be? She shrugged and nodded.

Michael told the story of a woman searching for a guru she had heard was the wisest on earth. She found him living in a cave up a steep mountain. As she approached from below, he came out on a high ledge, naked. He looked down and saw her, and to her dismay, he took hold of his penis and shook it at her. As Michael related this he raised his hand from the table and made the gesture in the air right out between them.

Maggie watched him, amazed, realizing that this man had decided, through whatever level of consciousness, after all this good conversation, to talk to her about penises. And he made it very personal and real with that gesture. Did he know that his maleness was a challenge for her? He had put the question right out on the table between them—how are you with my having a penis?—and made it impossible for her to ignore it. She maintained eye contact, staying right with him even as she marveled at the whole thing.

He explained that the guru's point was, "Don't take me too seriously. I'm just a man, shaking my penis at you." And there right next to that was Michael's silent declaration, "No big deal, I'm a man, I've got a penis. We all do."

Michael kept going and Maggie had to scramble to catch up with him. He spoke about awkward humor Jesus had used, and about judgmental and hurtful things he sometimes said, which were all hard to incorporate into a holy image. Michael lowered his voice and leaned toward her. "I think," he said softly so Maggie came nearer and only she could hear. "I think that sometimes Jesus is shaking his penis at us."

Their faces stayed right there, close together, and they looked at each other, eyes wide open and steady, waiting to see who would breathe first.

Maggie couldn't help but smile, and then she leaned back and laughed, even more at Michael's delight than at the image she saw. There they were, the three of them, the guru, Michael, and Jesus, all lined up, naked, shaking their penises at her, declaring that penises exist even in the most spiritual of men and they are not something to make a big deal over.

Maggie looked at Michael and laughed again. Finally, still grinning, she said, "I'm not sure how to fit that into communion."

Michael didn't miss a beat. He was really into this. "Maybe we can fit it in with the bodily reality of Jesus as a man. And then with the body and blood."

"Now, see? You said 'body and blood' and I felt myself jump back."

"Are you trying to get this intellectually?" he asked. "We western-minded people tend to be so concrete, so left-brained, and that gets in the way."

"I don't think so," she answered. "I'm having a gut-level reaction."

"What was going on right when you needed to jump back?"

"It was the cannibal thing. I just don't get eating his body and blood."

"I think the idea is that you take Jesus into you so that you experience Jesus in you. Though it's always true that the Christ is in you, people seem to need some help being aware of it."

"I can understand wanting to take the bright, beautiful, clear Christ energy into you to experience it," said Maggie. "I'm fine with Christ energy, but why do it so graphically as body and blood?"

Michael leaned into the table and said, "Bear with me while I dig back into my seminary studies." He then spoke about indigenous traditions in which people ate whatever animal had the qualities they wanted to have. "If you want to be fierce, you eat of a bear. If you want to have sharp vision, you eat of an eagle."

"Oh! Yes!" Maggie responded eagerly. "Now I can understand this in terms of energy. I do this same thing in my healing work. I reach for the healthy, whole energy pattern and bring it into the client's field. I offer it to them, and if they are ready, they take it on, they become it."

"As if you're offering them the bear's energy?" he asked.

"Exactly." Seeing him nod, she continued. "When we reenact this ancient, physical ritual through communion, it must touch visceral memories in us, familiar and recognized at very deep levels. I bet we tap into old, sacred expectations and they still work."

"Takes us right back to the circle around the fire in the cave?"

"Yes. So, I bring the Christ energy pattern into myself by ingesting Jesus' flesh and blood as represented by the bread and wine, allowing his cellular material to come into my own cells and then I become him. It's energetic, but what I'm seeing now about communion is that it's also very physical. As we experience it in our bodies it becomes very real. This is quite profound. I'm impressed. I get it now. Thank you!"

"That did it?"

"Yes, now I understand how it works and I know how to approach it."

"Fascinating," he said, shaking his head.

Their food came and they kept talking. They often got going on something, following a strand of thought, taking turns with it until they'd gone several steps beyond where they both expected it to stop, beyond where they'd gotten used to most people leaving things, and there they'd be, out there together, looking into each other's eyes, marveling. That's when Maggie knew this was really good.

She asked how he had become a minister. He grew up the son of a minister, so he decided to be one, too. He quit part way through seminary, but after a few months of selling appliances for his uncle he went back and finished.

"Why did you finish?" she asked.

He shrugged and looked pretty lost. "Because I was supposed to, I guess."

"It did get you to here," she gently offered.

Relief flooded his face and he brightened. He set off speaking about how that piece of paper had served him well. He mentioned a few occasions when he had used it to have some influence while taking controversial stands. Maggie could have said something encouraging about being true to your path and purpose, but no words came. She just looked in his eyes and held the space for his feelings and thoughts.

His eyes were hazel. She'd never really understood hazel until she watched Michael's eyes change colors that day. At first they looked gray, but then she caught a flash of green, and there was definitely blue, too. The changes were startling, and delightful.

"Tell me your story," he said.

"You mean spiritual or history or what? I have a lot of story."

"You've lived your life," he said, nodding.

"Yes, I guess I have."

"You choose. Tell me whatever you want to tell me."

She told him that when she was very young her father had been a Presbyterian minister.

Michael's eyes widened, "Where did he go to seminary?"

"McCormick in Chicago."

They decided there was little chance their fathers had ever met. Still, Michael was intrigued, and he asked questions about her father's experience. Maggie didn't know a lot. By the time she was in grade school her father had quit the ministry and declared himself an atheist. Michael nodded and said he knew of other young ministers who had done similar turnabouts.

Then Maggie talked about her own studies to become a healer, and about discovering that Mary was one of her guides.

Michael sat forward and interrupted, "Which Mary?"

"Which Mary?" Maggie was confused. Was there more than one?

"There are as many as five Marys in The Bible."

"Mary the mother," she said, stumbling, still thrown by the intensity of his question. "Jesus' mother, Mother Mary."

"Oh, okay," he said, sighing back into his seat.

"Why?" she asked, seeing his disappointment, and almost remembering the book passage about Mary Magdalene and Jesus.

"I just wondered," he replied, shrugging it off. "Go on. What were you saying?"

"When I work I always ask my spiritual guides and the client's guides to support the healing session. Mary—Mother Mary—started to come regularly. Often she just stood there holding the space for whatever work I was doing. Sometimes she laid her hands on the client or on me. It was wonderful."

"It sounds wonderful."

"The down side was that I couldn't talk about it with my husband or family or any of my Jewish friends because Mary is Christian. They would have been very upset. So I began to live in two separate worlds."

Michael's smile turned to concern.

"Sometimes," she said, "I teamed up with other healers who invoked the Christ energy and the effects were awesome, so eventually I tried it myself. I was surprised it worked."

"You were surprised?"

"Because I wasn't Christian. But I guess all you have to do is ask, no matter who you are." Maggie paused, looking over at Michael and he nodded, confirming. "I'm still hesitant to use it, though. I feel I'm asking for something I'm not supposed to have access to."

"Maggie, I'm really sorry you feel that way. It's not true. You know that, don't you?"

"I'm getting more used to asking now, but I still only ask when I need really powerful help," she said. "It's a great back up. So far it has handled anything that has come up, and I've dealt with some pretty heavy-duty situations. The Christ energy is incredible. It's brilliantly clear and bright, and more powerful than we can imagine."

Michael smiled and nodded again.

"One time Mother Mary stood behind me and Jesus stood behind my partner, and the work we did together was amazingly powerful."

"I bet it was!" said Michael.

They grinned at each other, and Maggie realized what a relief it was for her that he felt comfortable with talk about her work and guides and energy. She couldn't talk this freely with many people.

"Maggie, how did you come to our town?" he asked.

"I'm getting divorced," she said. Michael drew back and it felt like the sun went behind a cloud. The brightness around them faded, and her words sat heavy between them. She paused, not knowing what to do, then decided to continue. "I came here for a new start in a new place," she said. "Next Tuesday I'm going back to finish moving out of the house."

"Will that be hard to do?" he asked from far away.

"Dan gets angry, and that makes it hard. But I'll be okay. I'll manage."

"How long have you been married?" he asked.

She noticed that he didn't ask how long *were* you married, but kept it clear that she is still married. This answer wouldn't help ease things. She took a breath first, then said, "Twenty-eight years."

He stared at her, silenced.

"I know, pretty amazing." Maggie pushed through the discomfort, wanting to get all this said and over with. She explained that the relationship had changed right after they married, and that she should have left right away, but she stayed. Then she remembered what Michael had said earlier, and looking him straight in the eyes she said, "I stayed because I was supposed to." A flash of recognition passed between them.

"Then later I stayed because of my daughter, Rachel. She'll be twenty-six next month. She's just finishing a post-doctoral architecture program in low-cost, energy-efficient housing design."

"You're not old enough to have a daughter that age," he declared, "or to be married that long."

"But I am," she laughed. "Rachel is very real."

"Any grandkids?" he asked.

"No, Rachel hasn't married. Do you have grandkids?"

"Three," he said, "two in L.A. and one in Memphis. All too far away." Michael sighed, then looked at Maggie, collapsed to the back of his chair, shook his head, and exclaimed, "Twenty-eight years!"

They cleared the air by talking about the church, its board of directors, and the building. Then he told her about the Saturday Easter egg hunt the next morning at the church.

"You ought to come," he said. "We have a lot of fun. As a matter of fact, I have to go pick up eggs next."

As they got up from the table they hugged and he said, "I hope it goes well for you Tuesday."

"Thank you, Michael," she said, surprised he remembered which day it would be. "I appreciate that. I'll be okay." Then she sighed and added, "I do what I have to do to get through things." Now she was the one who was far away.

Michael looked at her, really looked at her, and then he nodded. For just a moment it occurred to her that she could be the one who disappeared from here, not him. She wondered where that idea came from, then she shook it off.

"I really enjoyed this," she said when they got out to the street.

"Same here," he replied with a smile, pressing her arm. They hugged again, then headed off in different directions.

As Maggie turned to leave, a vague sense of movement beyond her right shoulder drew her attention. When she looked and saw no one there, a clear thought of that spirit, the mysterious woman Lydia saw hovering around the edges, came into her mind. Was it her? Was she watching them? Did she want something? The moment melted into shadow leaving Maggie puzzling. What was it Lydia had said? When the time is right? Shrugging, she let it go.

Maggie had never paid much attention to the grounds around the church. Now she saw that someone had lovingly landscaped from front to back. Plantings glowed in the morning sun, lush with early flowers and fresh spring growth. Kids scrambled everywhere, looking for goodies. Maggie wandered, taking the opportunity to examine flowerbeds and trees and shrubs. She resisted pointing out well-hidden treasures, leaving them for the kids to discover. After the baskets and bags were filled with colored eggs and candy, people lingered to talk.

"What a wonderful place this is," Maggie exclaimed to Michael.

"Yes, it is," he replied, smiling. "We're lucky to have it. Do you know this church has been here for almost 75 years? All the stained glass is original and the woodwork is hand carved."

"It's beautiful. And so well maintained."

"It was closed for a while, but people got together to reopen it a few years ago and here we are."

"Michael, I have some wonderful old irises at the house up north." She paused, amazed again at her boldness, searching his face for any sign of hesitation.

"Irises are my favorite spring flower," he replied.

"Mine, too. I was going to have to leave them, but I would love to bring them here. Can we plant them in the churchyard?"

"Sure," he said with a big grin. "I'm sure we can find a spot for them."

"Oh, good! I like that."

Back at her apartment Maggie wrote in her journal, "*Michael and I have one amazing connection after another. Am I exaggerating things? Nu, give me a sign.*"

"What would you like that to be?" asked Nu.

"Okay, how about this? If he puts his hand on my right arm, just above the elbow, this spot right here, and keeps it here, and then he moves it to rest on the back of my right shoulder, right here, and keeps it here, then I'll know. I'm not asking that this happen, just saying that if it does, then I'll know."

"You'll know what?" asked Nu. "Let's get this clear."

"I'll know we really are connecting on many levels, and there is something truly amazing going on here."

"And you'll believe that it's real for Michael, too?"

"Okay, yes," said Maggie, "then I will believe it's real for Michael, too."

Maggie woke early the next morning, Easter morning. There was plenty of time before the sunrise service, so she lay there and thought about Easter. This was the day the tomb was empty and Mary Magdalene saw Jesus on the road, the day she *beheld* him again.

So, what did she think, she wondered, did Jesus actually rise from the tomb? At first her mind resisted. It was myth, fairy tale, metaphor. It was a way the church caught everyone's attention: suspend ordinariness, tell a fantastical story, engage our mystical yearnings, mesmerize us. Except, suddenly Maggie realized that she knew, somehow, that he did. She knew with that deep part of her that shares Jesus' anguish. She knew with that expansive part of her that understands more than meets the eye. And she knew with that healer part of her that is so aware of the alchemy where physics and spirit overlap.

About fifty people gathered for the sunrise service in the chilly predawn behind the church. The sky had barely begun to brighten, just enough to see that the sun would come up behind a veil of clouds that might offer much needed rain.

Michael came all the way across to hug Maggie before beginning. She didn't even realize what happened next until later when she was writing in her journal. All she knew at the time was that it felt wonderful. As they separated from their hug, with his eyes never leaving hers, Michael kept his hand on the back of her right shoulder while he said, "Happy Easter, Maggie." Then he moved his hand up onto her shoulder and down her arm to just above her elbow, and held it there. Only after Maggie said, "Happy Easter, Michael," did he then slide his hand the rest of the way down her arm and clasp her hand before they separated.

"Nu, did you see that? He did it!" she wrote in her journal that afternoon.

"Yes, he did," said Nu.

"And he did it the very first chance he got. He held exactly the right spots, just the way I imagined it. What does it mean that it was reversed?"

"Maybe that things won't happen in the order or in the pattern of timing that you expect."

"But it still counts, right?"

"It's real, Maggie."

"All the connections between us, the coincidences, the familiarity?"

"Yes, it's all real," said Nu.

Michael spoke a little bit at the Sunrise Service, then more at the regular church services, about the first Easter, about the women coming to the empty tomb, about the guards and disciples, and about everyone's fear and disbelief.

"If we have a hard time accepting the idea of resurrection, imagine how it was for them. Just when you think you've got things figured out and under control, suddenly there's resurrection, there's new life and change. It's scary." As he said this he looked at Maggie and she remembered their conversation at lunch two days earlier.

Michael followed Easter to its roots in ancient celebrations of spring. He spoke of new life coming into and through all creation. "Jesus showed us that nothing, not even death, can stop new life. The resurrection means new life for all of us. Christ is risen in what we do and how we live, in how we love, in how we open ourselves. Roll away the stone that blocks the light in your life. Let the holy come out of the tomb and flow through you. Let the resurrection create new life and new love in you." And he looked at Maggie again.

Maggie stayed for the late service, too, then she waited for another hug at the end of this long morning. Michael took one look at her and said, "Too much?" She smiled a tired smile and nodded, relieved to not have to try to figure out anything to say. He hugged her and said, "Go get some rest." They both nodded.

Later Maggie wrote in her journal, "*Michael, there are things you should know about me while you can still get out.*" She could feel him as if he were right there, absolutely present and real. It felt like he took hold of her hands.

"Then now would be a good time to tell me," she heard him say.

She stopped and turned away. "Nu, I don't want to be imagining like this," she said. "I want to stay in what's real."

"This is not imagination," said Nu.

"It's not? How can you say that?"

"This is real."

"Then what is it? Some sort of alternate reality?"

"It's all one reality. In your work you deal with different aspects of the whole of reality. It's that."

"His saying that just now was real?"

"It's real, Maggie."

"Is it another level of consciousness? Are he and I operating at other levels of consciousness?"

"Of course you are. You know that."

"I mean at the same time as the ordinary one."

"Why not?"

"And I'm aware of it?"

"Maggie, just let it be whatever it is."

"Is Michael experiencing this other level, too?"

"Of course," said Nu.

"I mean consciously."

"Oh, we never know exactly what another person notices or misses. But he is definitely affected by it."

"So he does feel it when I react to something or when I think of something?"

"Certainly. You two are very attuned."

Maggie went back to this other level of consciousness with Michael and she told him everything she could think of that might turn him away from her. Michael listened, and he stayed.

The next morning Maggie picked up that same book again and opened it randomly. This time it sternly warned her that loving is the most courageous and vulnerable thing a person ever does, then challenged her to choose between risking everything or settling for a sad and empty old age. Maggie took a deep breath and then carefully put the book back on the shelf.

❧

The trip north was a lot more difficult than Maggie expected. She wanted to feel like a stranger there, but she kept recognizing things and remembering the stories attached to them. It all began to feel like hers again, pulling her in, trying to be her life. Dan was familiar and predictable, and their shared history created intimacy and understanding. It would be very easy to collapse back into being here, to just sigh and give in.

Now Maggie realized that the idea that came last Friday as she said goodbye to Michael, that she might disappear from Asheville, was his. He must have suspected how easy it would be, once back here, to give up on the new and settle for the old, how easily she could vanish and never show up at the church again. Maggie took a deep breath. She had made it out of here once; she would have to make it out again.

Fortunately Dan found reasons to be gone from the house most of the time Maggie was there. The cat was her only companion as she sorted through the remnants of her life and marriage. She had never felt so alone. Hour upon hour, day after day, she dug through cupboards, closets, shelves, and drawers, emptying them, salvaging only what she knew she would miss, leaving only what Dan might want, bagging and piling the rest to be disposed of.

On a break she called Lydia. "I now realize that back in Asheville I always know Michael is somehow close by. I feel his other level presence even when I don't notice it. But here at this house I can hardly even think of him, never mind connect with him energetically. I can't feel him at any level. It's like he won't come here."

"I'm not surprised," said Lydia. "At some level he knows you have to do this yourself. He's honoring that."

"You really get this other levels of consciousness thing, don't you. You believe we're in touch that way."

"Sure," said Lydia.

"I'm not making this up?"

"You don't make stuff up, Maggie. And you operate at other levels all the time in your work. Why do you doubt this?"

"Tonight I left the house to go out for dinner by myself, and when I finally relaxed, which was not easy, I put out my hand and I felt Michael take it. I felt it, Lydia, physically. If I closed my eyes I'd swear he was there. How is that possible?"

"It's not that strange when you consider that when I work on you from here you've said you feel my hands touching you. Maybe all it takes is willingness."

"You're awfully calm about this. He sat across from me all through dinner, Lydia, some form or essence of him anyway, just being there with me. I wanted to cry."

"Yeah, I bet."

"Do you think he was there, Lydia?"

"It sure feels like it, Maggie."

After several very full days of sorting through the past and a miserable dinner with Dan peppered with disagreement and accusations, the heaviness of their relationship and the house began to reclaim Maggie. She sank into the old, familiar quagmire and soon wondered if life away from there even existed. Outdoors, sitting on the big rock next to one of the massive oaks that ringed the house, she remembered how that long, curved driveway through the woods with no view of the road beyond had always made the way out seem impossibly far. It was starting to feel like that again.

The next morning Dan left for a conference and he wouldn't be back for a week. Maggie threw herself even more diligently into the work of clearing out the house, hardly knowing why any more, just that she had to keep working at it and get it done. Would there even be life afterward? Not if she didn't finish before he returned. She didn't stop to go out for dinner any more, she hardly ate, just took short breaks outdoors to get out of the house for a few minutes at a time. Through the trees and land and sky she tried to imagine far-off mountains she barely remembered. Had she ever really been there?

"Michael, will you please somehow come get me and take me to church with you tomorrow?" Maggie pleaded toward the south on Saturday afternoon, like sending a message out to sea in a bottle. She could not hear or feel or know if he answered or if he even heard.

The next morning she got up early again, worked on emptying her old desk, and lost track of time. Suddenly something changed so definitely that she looked around the room, wondering what was happening. Then she knew. Michael had entered the sanctuary at the church. A glance at the clock confirmed that it was time. Maggie felt him working his way through the room toward the pulpit, greeting people along the way. She let herself open and go deep, and for the next hour she was there. She heard him speak about allowing your heart to shatter into a million pieces and then re-form as new. He spoke about being open to love and open to ecstasy, in whatever form God sends them. "It can happen on a mountaintop, or watching a sunset, or right here at church," he said.

"I want to go home!" Maggie cried to the cat. He just looked at her and shrugged, but it felt so good to say it. This place was not home. Her new life was home, and saying that felt good. She got busy emptying shelves and cupboards in the back room, sorting and stacking and filling trash bags, determined to somehow finish this huge job. When she opened the double doors of the closet and saw it was stuffed full, she burst into tears and sank to the floor between piles.

"I want to go home!" she sobbed, rocking and moaning in the midst of all that chaos. When the crying eased, she escaped to outdoors.

"I want to go home!" she keened to the trees and sky. And she kept saying it, right out loud whenever she felt like it from then on. "I want to go home."

One morning she walked the land, following deer trails and intuition through forest and meadows. Things had changed. A favorite arching tree had collapsed, new animal dens were dug and old ones abandoned, a neighbor's tree clearing had made another house visible through the woods, and a new house surprised her at the edge of the meadow by the road. Most of it was still familiar, the lay of the land, the trees and grasses, wild black raspberry patches, and bird songs, familiar like many things had been since she arrived. But now it was a stale familiarity, fading, giving way.

She discovered a gorgeous display of deep purple wildflowers, brilliant in the sunshine, a sea of beauty here in this terrain of abandonment. From the midst of them she asked God to bless and heal the house and land so it could be a good place for those who live here. She saw Dan with a happy life, no longer needing to harden or blame, and she was grateful.

"But this is not my place," she said. "I want to go home."

"I'm done!" Maggie wrote in her journal after eight long days of hard work. *"I've emptied shelves and closets and cupboards and drawers, garage and basement and barn, cleared it all out, leaving only what Dan might want. The irises are dug, bagged, and in the trunk. The car is packed and ready. In the morning I'm going home!"*

Just before dark she sat on the big rock and watched a single Canadian goose fly over, honking all the way. A bat zipped in and out over the garden, the first star appeared, and a silver-blue glow surrounded the trees against a darkening sky. "Dear God," she prayed, "please take care of this place and the people and animals here. And please take care of me, too. I'm going home!"

She left at the first hint of dawn the next morning, and by early afternoon, still two hundred miles from them, she began to feel the mountains. They were like a beacon shining out from home, calling her back. She drove into the mountains four hours later, following the road's windings through National Forests and skirting the edge of the Great Smoky Mountains National Park. Every turning held another stunning array of nature's grace and beauty. The rocks and trees sparkled in late afternoon sunlight and glowed in the shadows. She had entered another realm. Everything turned mystical, an enchanted place where reality lost its familiar substance, transformed into shimmer and delight. It took her by surprise, again and again. Had she come here on an ordinary road? Or on some magic highway that passed into another world?

She had been shaking ever since she reentered the mountains. Was she that out of touch with this energy? Her knees buckled when she got out of the car at the rest stop in the Pigeon River Gorge between Tennessee and North Carolina. She made herself walk up and down the parking area until it was easy.

Taking to the road again, she recognized the familiar play of light on stone outcroppings, the mix of hardwoods and evergreens, the plunging mountain terrain, the growing shadows of day's end. This was her place and it was real. If it had seemed to fade from existence while she was gone, it had now come back into being. She knew the landmarks, the roads, the turns, and the last of the way until she parked the car in her space. Her key worked in the door lock, the hall and rooms were the same, it was all real. Her belongings waited here, her life waited here. This new world resumed again, and the other, old one faded into transparency. It was very good to be home.

"Can you drum?" asked the flute player. "My drummer is not showing."

Maggie had arrived early for the May Day bonfire to place her bags of iris plants around the firepit behind the church. As she took up the African djembe she realized that she was becoming a part of this church community, speaking up at discussions and now drumming for this gathering. No more hiding tentatively at the edge. She had left the old life and entered a new life here.

"Maggie!" exclaimed Michael as he dumped an armload of logs by the fire. "You're back," he said with a warm smile and he headed toward her for a hug. "It's good to see you."

Nearly a hundred people came to encircle the bonfire as Maggie fit her drumming in and around the melody of the flute. She didn't know many of them, but they smiled and nodded to her anyway, welcoming her in. A few people cut ivy vines and wrapped strands into simple head wreaths. Someone placed one on Maggie's head from behind as she drummed. The sun dropped low as everyone joined hands around the fire. Michael spoke of fertility and fairies and magic and expecting the unexpected. They sang and prayed and danced and the bold ones jumped the fire. It was quite dark when Michael brought an end to the celebration.

"Maggie has brought these irises from her old life," he said, "to plant them here in her new one, a new beginning, for them and for herself. We haven't figured out just how we're going to do this, and I just got an idea which I have not checked out with Maggie." He turned to face her, "Do you think…" he began to ask, gesturing around the group.

"Oh, yes!" she exclaimed, realizing what he meant. "I love it! Yes! Please!"

"Good!" he said with a big smile. "Let's all plant Maggie's irises in our yards, throughout our church community, spread throughout the city and out into the mountains. Whoever would like some, help divide them up."

Maggie watched as others opened the bags and made sure everyone got a plant. Michael took a good clump to plant there at the church. She could have helped, but she knew this was a time for her to be still and quiet, to fully experience what was happening. Just as her favorite flowers were being planted into this community and these mountains, she was, also. She felt herself growing roots into the earth here, finding her place, coming home.

"Michael! That was inspired!" she declared after most of the crowd had left.

"Yes," he grinned, "sometimes I do get inspired. I'm glad it was okay with you. I really put you on the spot."

"It was perfect. I love knowing the irises are growing and blooming in everybody's yards. I feel so taken in, so accepted, so here. What a wonderful evening this has been. Thank you."

He reached for a hug. "Yes, it was a wonderful evening. Thank you, Maggie." They shared another smile and clasped hands, then he turned to someone else waiting to talk with him, and Maggie headed home.

Be Here

Life looks in my face and asks,
what could go so wrong
if you let loose to be all you can be?
A little-old-proper-southern-lady neighbor
scowls at my indifference to expectations.
I rise up into the air,
buoyant on freedom and joy.
She bursts out her front door, fly swatter flailing,
determined to bring me down.
I laugh,
moving so far, so fast
that her indignation is irrelevant.

Love looks in my face and asks,
who do you want to be?
I want to know I'm alive, I say,
spread my wings and fly when I might fall,
ride a stream of glory into the mystery,
melt into moments of grace,
hold beauty,
know love,
be God's peace,
be God's peace,
be God's peace.

God looks in my face and asks,
where are you?
I'm coming, I say.
I'm turning the day,
I'm rising the moon,
I'm laughter and birthing and bubbles and song.
I'm over there, no, there, no, there.
I'm coming, I say.

Paint and pen and healing hands and lines on the page,
waking at 5 a.m. to write a poem,
following a pain to its source,
reaching for explanation in the midst of chaos.
Try color, try music, try words, try talk.
Where am I?
I'm coming, I say.
Where are you, God? I ask.
I am everywhere, God says.
Then I am here, I say.

You look in my face and ask,
what are you doing?
Trying to fix this, I say.
Please stop, you say.
A crow flies away, cawing,
a blaze of sunshine fires the day,
clear-toned harmony swells the bounds of consciousness,
grace claims all.
I'm here, I say.
Welcome to yourself, you say,
welcome to love,
welcome to life.

I look in my face in the mirror,
alone just before the dawn,
softened eyes peer back, open, seeing.
Wisdom emerges, steady, holding me
within the flowing currents of change.
I say be,
I say love life,
God's peace is everywhere in me,
I am here.

Chapter Four: Be Here

Sometimes, when the breeze was just right, Maggie could hear the wolves howling from the Nature Center. She had visited them several times in the fall, sat with them, and asked the big, gray male if he had any message for her. He always gave the same answer, and now, in the spring, the wolves' calling reminded her, "Don't volunteer to be penned in."

Two days later a psychic saw in Maggie a yearning to settle down and warned her that it would trap her. The psychic said Maggie is one who needs to be free, to keep moving, and that she would give up too much if she tried to stay in one place. "Don't make any commitments, don't sign any contracts."

Maggie listened to the wolves howl, then got out her journal to write. *"I think this psychic grabbed the easy explanation for what she saw in me. Yes, I need to be free, but staying in physical motion does not ensure freedom. Moving on limits connection and depth so that I barely touch people and place, so that I have no real presence, so that I do not engage with life.*

"I think being penned in is a matter of attitude and perspective, not place. It is caused by accepting limitations. I need to be expansive and inventive and fully present wherever I am and whatever I do. I can go anywhere or everywhere or nowhere and be either penned or be free. My challenge is to stay in these mountains, which are so good for me, grow roots and make commitments, and also be open and lively and expressive and free.

"Both the message of the wolf and the one the psychic side-stepped are really the same as that well-known message of the Hopi elders. Don't cling to the banks of the river. Don't resist the flow of life. Be open to what is and to what comes, be fully present in what is happening right now, right here."

"We have a guest tonight," Michael told the Wednesday evening discussion group. "For any of you who don't know him, let me introduce my friend and mentor, Simon Stiles. Simon keeps my mind full of questions and my eyes and heart open. He's a singer-songwriter and piano player extraordinaire. He travels around the country performing with his band, Prodigal Tracks. He's also the minister at an innovative and dynamic church downtown, where you never know what will happen next. Simon, did I hear that a live donkey walked through your sanctuary on Palm Sunday?"

"We had a shovel brigade ready," said a man in the back, laughing.

Michael laughed too. "See what I mean? I have to admit that if I didn't need to be here every Sunday, I'd be at Simon's church. So, what we do is share an exchange twice a year, and tonight he'll be leading our discussion. Let's welcome Simon Stiles."

The man looked more like an aging surfer than a minister in his brightly flowered shirt, sandals, and ponytail. Maggie scowled as he walked to the front, sorry she'd come. But his face was open, with sparkling eyes and a wide smile, and Michael clearly admired him, so okay, she would give this a chance.

"Life is an adventure," Simon declared, "or it is nothing at all. Helen Keller said that. We go through life skimming along the surface, content to deal with one minute after another, just doing our thing. Helen Keller couldn't do that. She didn't have any easy, get-by, skim-along track. She had to dig into life just to get a glass of water, just to say hello. I figure she knew what she was talking about when she said, 'Life is an adventure, or it's nothing at all.'

"She didn't say this when she was young, when she was learning how to get along in the world. She said it way later, when she had all that figured out. She said it when she was making choices like all the rest of us make. Do the usual, or take a new path? Keep to the rut, or take a chance? Stay where we are, or go for it?

"Mantra time! Say it with me, 'Life is an adventure, or it's nothing at all.' Again, 'Life is an adventure, or it's nothing at all.' Again! 'Life is an adventure, or it's nothing at all.' Stand up! Let's get moving! Mill around, find someone, and say it to them. Then find someone else. Tell five people, 'Life is an adventure, or it's nothing at all.'"

"This was great!" Maggie said to Michael at the end. "I'm really impressed. I see why you like him so much. Thanks for bringing him here."

"You're welcome," said Michael. Then his face fell. "You're not going to start going to his church instead now, are you?"

"No," she said, laughing. "I'm where I want to be."

Michael smiled. "Good, we need you here."

"Lydia, remember when Michael asked me, 'Which Mary?' and it felt so intense?" Maggie asked several days later.

"Sure," said Lydia.

"You know that young, female spirit guide you saw near me before Easter? The one who stays in the background?"

"Yeah, and keeps her face in shadows."

"She's more active now. I wouldn't say she has come forward, but I think she is influencing me in ways that go deeper than my conscious mind. Lydia, I think she may be Mary Magdalene."

"Wow, that's cool."

"I don't know much about Mary Magdalene, just that she is controversial. And then what that book says about her holding Jesus' beauty."

"I think you're about to learn more, Maggie."

Next Sunday Michael stepped away from the altar and in his place remained a bright and powerful presence. It was the spirit of Jesus. Jesus stood right there, his feet in Michael's footprints, facing Maggie and looking at her. She wondered if anyone else was seeing this. Then Jesus walked to her, passing through people and pews, stood directly in front of her, placed his hand on her head, and held it there.

Maggie couldn't move, could hardly breathe. She felt as if she were made of something not flesh, something finer than liquid gold. Jesus' touch reached deep, to a clear, easy grace within her, and brought it more to the forefront. Everything settled into exquisite, simple truth, all obvious, all peace. Maggie smiled. There were no questions that mattered. There was only being this perfect serenity.

Michael had just preached about Jesus' peace, and he quoted "Be my peace." Now Jesus said to Maggie, "If you do not feel peaceful, it is not peace," and Maggie understood that she needed to do only what felt absolutely clear and right.

After the service she told Michael what had happened. His face softened into a gentle, sweet smile and he nodded, as if to say "Well, sure, these things happen." He didn't doubt it or challenge her, didn't ask, "Who do you think you are?" No peering at her to see if she had lost her grasp on reality. Just a genuine smile and trusting acceptance.

Back at home later, settled into the window seat with her journal, Maggie wrote, *"I'm amazed. He believes me. He believes in me. He trusts me."*

"Of course he does," said Nu.

"Of course he does? There's no of course here. It's one astonishment after another. Nu, I feel so good with him. I don't know if I can resist this."

She picked up the phone to call her sister.

Maggie had always thought more sunshine would do her sister good, but Caroline insisted she loves the damp of Seattle. "Think of me as an orchid," she said. Caroline was several years older than Maggie, but they looked so much alike that strangers knew they were sisters. As Maggie keyed in Caroline's number she realized that with her own hair now cut short they would look even more alike.

"Caroline, I think I'm falling in love with Michael."

"But Maggie, you were so definite that you don't want to love anybody right now. What trouble are you getting yourself into?"

Maggie easily pictured her sister's concerned face, brows scrunched low and close together, deepening the ridges in her forehead, cheeks drawn in, mouth scowling, eyes intensely fixed as she went into expert worrier mode to dig into this latest problem.

"Every time we are together, even for a minute, there is such remarkable familiarity between us, like we've known each other forever. We settle so easily into being fully present and engaged, and it feels as if nothing else matters. I want to talk with him about all that has been going on. I want to spend time together and explore this connection between us."

"Are you sure? This is such a vulnerable time for you. You don't want to get hurt again."

"I don't feel vulnerable, I feel strong. I feel great!"

"Well, if you are willing to take the risk, and you think this will make you happy, then okay."

"That's it? You're not going to talk me out of it?"

"I don't want to argue. Besides, what is the worst that can happen?"

"I could be wrong that he is even interested in me."

"From what you've said about him, he may disappoint you but I think he will be kind and want you to be okay."

"I'm going to do it. I'm going to talk to him."

Michael's voicemail answered when Maggie punched in his number. Was that a sign not to do this? She quickly hung up, grabbed her jacket, and went to visit the wolves. Again the big gray gave her the same message, "Don't volunteer to get penned in."

"Getting into a relationship doesn't have to be constrictive," Maggie said to the wolf. "It's up to me to be conscious and creative, accept no assumptions, and invent it as I go. I think Michael and I can make sure we have a partnership that brightens and expands our potential and possibilities."

She went home and called Michael's number again. This time he answered and they arranged to meet the next morning at the church.

"I'm really flattered, of course," he said. It wasn't personal, it wasn't at all about her, but he would not consider any relationship. Soon after his wife's death he had committed himself to doing the best job he could with his spiritual journey and his work, and he had found that for him a relationship took too much away from that. Living this way for almost ten years had enabled him to focus and be much more effective. He would not give that up.

"We can be friends," he said. "That would be fine, as long as you are clear about the boundary line."

Maggie left him and drove up into the high mountains, letting her mind ride the twists and turns of the road. She was numb. How could this be so real and compelling for her and yet he was not swept away by it too? How could her feelings be so strong and his so vague. How could he be so unaffected?

She stopped at a diner for coffee and wrote in her journal, *"It doesn't seem okay to even be disappointed. I am so impressed. This is a truly honorable man. His commitment to what matters is awe-inspiring. If he were willing to compromise his work or his spirituality, he wouldn't be this man who speaks to my soul, who is so beautiful to me. Ironic, isn't it? If he comes to me, in the very coming he loses who he is. If he stays back he is at his most appealing.*

"Hey, wait a minute here," she wrote. *"What about all his talk about opening to life and love and change and surprise and taking chances, and the way he looks at me as he says it, as if he is talking about us? And all those times I've seen him watching me, learning about me, being intrigued by me. That was real. I saw it. I felt it. And what about all that other level connecting? What's going on? Nu, talk to me."*

"It's all real, Maggie, the pushing away and the pulling in."

"How can that be? They are opposites."

"Just let it be all that it is. Don't try to sort it out into boxes."

"That's asking a lot, Nu. You want me to be wise and gracious and generous when I just got sideswiped? Before I've even mourned? You want me to let everything fall where it falls and be what it is, without understanding it, even though that feels impossible?" Maggie took a deep breath, settling into her center. For a while she just watched her breath flow in and out.

"Well, this is a surprise," she finally wrote. *"Now I can see that his saying no is actually good for me. I still need time alone to learn to be myself. I shouldn't get into a relationship, either. So, Michael's answer is as much for me as it is for him."*

Maggie went back to the church, hoping to talk with him again, and found him in his office. "I've been up in the mountains all afternoon," she said, "and I've come to see that it is good that you said what you did." Michael stood, but he kept his distance, watching her from the other side of his desk. She continued, "I need this time to discover and explore and stretch. I need to find out who and what I can be. Getting into a relationship now would sidetrack me, too. It's really good not to. So, thank you."

"You're welcome," he said, still wary.

He seemed so far away, over there across the desk. For a moment her chest felt hollow and fragile. It was impossible to just walk away. "I do want to take you up on being friends, though. That's important to me," she said, grabbing at the words, needing him to agree.

He studied her face, then nodded, but he stayed behind the desk. "We'll see how that goes."

As she turned to leave Maggie sensed that shadow woman again, in the corner of the room, against the bookshelves. Was she silently crying?

"He's Father Francis!" exclaimed Lydia. "Every woman in the parish was in love with Father Francis, whether they were twenty years old or twenty years older than him and had five kids. We all loved Father Francis. He got more church volunteers than they'd ever seen before. He was young and smart and good-looking. And best of all, when you talked to him he understood.

"Did you love him, too?"

"Oh, sure. I was smitten. I thought he'd fall in love with me and insist we run off to someplace far away and exotic, where he'd dote on me. Obviously it was all pure fantasy, and only happening because it was so safe. There was no way he was going to choose me over God. He was a priest! He was a holy man bound to a sacred vow. Serious stuff. We'd both have burned in Hell if anything really happened."

"But Michael is a Presbyterian minister. Presbyterians don't do that priest celibacy thing."

"Doesn't matter," said Lydia.

"Damn, you're right. He sees himself like a priest, doesn't he. He has made the same covenant with God and with himself."

"That's what he just told you, Maggie. It's official. You must have known that at some level. You're so energetically perceptive, you must have seen that in him."

"I told him about stopping myself from saying, 'I came here because of you.' He nodded like he knew. I talked about the powerful soul connection between us, and how we connect on other levels. He said he doesn't consciously experience that himself, but he doesn't doubt it exists or that I know what I'm talking about. He's not as aware as I'd hoped he might be, but he's not closed off, either."

"Maggie, he said no."

"I know," she sighed.

"Do you? It's not easy to let go of it, is it?

"I feel hollow. One big, hollow ache."

"Give it some time."

"I went for an unavailable man, Lydia. He might as well be gay."

"It's obvious, isn't it? You're not ready to be in a relationship yet. How are you doing?"

"It seems like I should be more upset. This is a lot to give up on."

"It's not like you ever had it, Maggie."

"But Lydia, what about all those looks and insinuations? I didn't imagine them. Does he realize how suggestive he is with me?"

"He may not realize, and he may very well be attracted to you, Maggie, but none of that matters. He told you where he stands, and he made it very clear."

"You may have to keep telling me that. Oh, Lydia, I already miss letting myself be in love. I hate to admit it, but it's true that I do love being in love. If I could just figure out how to be in love without having to deal with an actual person, wouldn't that be great?"

"Isn't that what Michael is doing? Being in love with God and Jesus and the church and his work and life?"

"Do you think maybe this whole thing is to lead me deeper into spirituality?"

"Those guides are so smart!" exclaimed Lydia. "Snuck you right in the side door."

Maggie grinned, then said, "I never would have been as open to spirituality as I have been if it weren't for this connection and trust with Michael. It's like Jesus and God come through him to me."

"Yeah, literally!" said Lydia, laughing.

"That shadow-woman was there."

"Mary Magdalene? Watching the two of you?"

"Yeah. She was crying."

"This gets curiouser and curiouser."

At the Spa later that week Maggie told her masseuse what had happened with Michael.

"You're not the first to hear that from Michael Cairn," said Nan.

"You know Michael?"

"I grew up here. I know everybody. My aunt dated Michael's older brother before he went MIA in Vietnam and was never found."

"I didn't know Michael lost a brother."

"Yeah, it was pretty rough. But hey, don't you give up on this, Maggie," Nan declared while kneading her calf muscles. "Maybe you're the one. You're doing great. You've got his attention, now he knows how you feel. He's going to see who you are, and he may very well change his mind."

"I can't look for that, Nan, or ask for it either. I have to honor his commitment."

"I'm not saying try to make it happen. Just be open to possibilities. Be friends. That's the best way to get into a good relationship anyway, be friends first. But don't pass up other opportunities. Go ahead and be friends with other men, too. Just don't get into anything serious. That would chase him away."

"I'm not going to strategize, Nan."

"Honey, you just be yourself, that's all I'm saying. And when you're ready, the right thing will happen."

❧

Maggie called Lydia back. "Do a treatment on me, Lydia. Help me release expectations and wishes."

"That sounds like a good idea."

At the end of the treatment Maggie spoke to Michael's other-level consciousness, "I hand you my caring for you, Michael, my dreams for us, my desires for our possibilities. I trust you to hold them, to know and to do what's right with them."

"That was beautiful," said Lydia.

"I'm really surprised how much I trust him to take care of this. I still think we would be great together. There is a very special connection between us. But I understand his boundary, and I will respect it."

"I don't think you have any choice, Maggie. If you don't accept it you could lose him entirely."

"I don't want that to happen."

"I know, Maggie. I do think this is best for you."

"I would have turned too much toward him and the relationship, and given up a lot of fulfilling my own potential."

"He has honored and protected that for himself and for you. Maggie, you weren't rejected at all. You could look at this as an empowerment, and as a freeing."

"Maybe I should do what he is doing, avoid relationship and instead commit to my work and my path. But then what do you do if you feel attracted to someone?"

"How would Michael answer that?"

"I think he would say that what you are seeing is an expression of God through that person. So, see God when you look at them. Love God in them."

"So it's all God."

"Right. I think that's how he does it. I say something intriguing and he hears God talking to him through me."

"Well, Maggie, you wanted to live as a holy person. Now you know how to do it."

❧

Stephen was eager to hear all about what Maggie had done with

Michael, and he listened intently. When she finished he sat up on the edge of his chair and declared, "This makes me certain that you are the person to help me do my work, Maggie."

She caught her breath and pulled back, startled by his intensity. "Why?" she asked.

"You don't settle for how things are, like most people do," he said. "You want to face it and explore it, you want to know, you want to get it clear, and you want to get on with it."

Glancing at him, then studying the wall beyond, she tried to consider it. "Well, I do like talking with you." She paused and he nodded. "And, whatever I try to explain, not only are you patient, waiting while I find my way with it, but then you know what I mean and you connect it to what you understand."

He nodded again. "Yes, yes," he said.

"And everything I say fits right in," she admitted, meeting his eyes.

He grinned. "That's how I know that you understand what I understand, Maggie. We're in the same place. And we've both gone through a lot to get here."

Half expecting him to grab hold of her in his enthusiasm, she took a deep breath and long exhale to slow things down, then added, "Despite our different paths and perspectives, we have ended up in the same place and understanding in the same way."

He followed her lead, took a breath too, and slid to the back of his chair. "So, Maggie, how do we enable the average person to get to where we are? Most people don't do things the way we do."

Maggie relaxed as he continued speaking, relieved to turn to practicalities.

"They choose to stay where they are," he said. "Most people wouldn't go talk to Michael, but you wanted to move forward and see where it would go. That's because of all the work you've done and where that has brought you. So, how do we reach them?"

Now Maggie leaned forward. "Stephen, you're already doing that with the grids. Your grids support people so they can reach farther, then stabilize them in that extended position so they can reach forward again."

"It's not enough, Maggie!" Intensity drove him to the edge of his seat again, feet planted, eyes blazing. "I want to take this to everyone on the planet! Maggie, I've been told I'll work with one or more people on this. I think you are one I'm supposed to work with." He stopped, keenly fixated on her, waiting.

Maggie did her best to stand up to his gaze, trying to stay open to his proposition. She took a moment to ground herself before answering. "I'll have to think about that, Stephen, and see how it fits with my own path." When his enthusiasm sank, she quickly added, "Let's keep talking."

"Sure," he sighed.

"I mean it. I do like exploring ideas with you."

He looked up, brightened, and said, "Maggie, that's all I'm asking of you now. Let's just talk and see what comes."

Seeing him across from her, his face filled with that never ending hopefulness of his, it felt as if they were always meant to sit in those chairs and say those things. It was, in a way, quite intimate. There was no pretense and no drama, just right down to raw perception and truth.

Maggie smiled and said, "You feel like an old, old friend I haven't seen for eons, and now we've come back together again to do some work. I just don't know if it will be in the form you expect."

Stephen nodded, the urgency now dissipated, his tall frame reabsorbed by the chair. "It never works when I try to figure out what's coming," he said.

He paused, looking in her eyes, then added, "Maggie, you wondered why all this has been happening this week. Well, I'm not at all surprised by it. You went through that dark time up north moving out of the house, and you didn't hide."

"I did what I had to do," she said.

"Yes, you did your work all the way through it. That sort of thing usually leads to an opportunity to raise your energy to a higher level, and that's what is happening now for you. All sorts of things are fulfilling as a result. You're taking everything another step."

"Of course!" she exclaimed, sitting up in her chair, grabbing its arms. "That trip is what precipitated all this. It seems so obvious once you point it out. I wasn't seeing that I went directly into all this right after I came home."

"I think you're doing just great, Maggie. Good for you!"

Maggie looked at Stephen again, amazed by him. He was not an energetic powerhouse in any sense of the word. He seemed always on the verge of collapse. She kept expecting him to limp or sigh, and often felt protective because he seemed so innocent and open. And yet other times, like now, she saw that he was very much like his big grids, as patient and steady and deeply supportive.

She sat back, watching him gather his papers and books, thinking about how he always said he didn't know much. He sure knew what he needed to know. She wondered if he might actually be some sort of incredibly evolved and powerful being, come to help humanity and encourage people like her.

When they hugged goodbye he stooped down from his height with what seemed tremendous effort. She always felt she should release him quickly before something strained.

"Let's keep in touch," he said as they parted.

"I think you ought to trade Michael in for Stephen," declared Lydia.

"What?" Maggie shook her head at the phone. "That would be like falling in love with your own brother. That's a whole different thing. No, I'm starting to think that if I can't have Michael I don't want anybody. I don't want to settle for less. And it's not even about Michael, it's about me. I love how stimulated and excited I feel about myself when I let myself love him. I feel so alive. I don't want to give that up."

"Then focus on being yourself, Maggie. Do your creative stuff."

"As a matter of fact, I'm starting a circle of healing and prayer. We will energetically and spiritually support each other on our paths, and join together to be a strong and clear presence of light and peace and healing in the world."

"There in Asheville?"

"Online, so people from anywhere can join. I'll write messages and meditations and reminders, and leave it open enough so that people can each find their own level of involvement."

"This sounds wonderful. This is the kind of thing you need to be doing. And I want to be part of it."

"Good. I want you to be. It will be very much like a drum circle, all of us coming together with our varying skills and talents, with the intention of creating something new and amazing together. When we each participate with sensitivity, thoughtfully and heartfully blending our contribution into what we find, together we create a dynamic, rich whole that can be truly remarkable."

"Go for it, Maggie."

"I feel good, Lydia."

"I told you that you were released."

"You did. See how much you know?"

Lydia laughed.

"Oh, that reminds me," said Maggie, "I need to call Stephen again. I'm seeing some things about the grids and patterns more clearly now."

"Like what?"

"There are deep, underlying energetic patterns which establish and support my path and who I am. These are distinctly mine, like a fingerprint."

"Fingerprint? I was picturing more like three-dimensional netting."

"You're right, Lydia, it's much more complex than a fingerprint. Let's call it a soulprint."

"Soulprint, I like that. Does everybody get to have them?"

Maggie smiled. "Yes, Lydia, you do, too. Everybody does."

Lydia laughed again. "You know me so well. Sorry, I interrupted. The grids and patterns?"

"Deep energy work I do sometimes takes place in the client's soulprint patterns. Then there are also deeper patterns that we share."

"Do you have a name for those?"

We could call them master patterns. These carry and support and affect everything that is and everything that happens."

"Like archetypes?"

"Sort of. That's part of it. Examples would be a pattern that makes a carrot carrot-like, or causes living things to mature and age, or how you and I relate to each other. This conversation we're having is supported by and influenced by the master patterns. They are the framework and foundation on which our soulprint patterns and everything that happens rest and from which everything builds. Some of the deep energy work I do is in the master patterns.

"This is feeling huge and complex to me," said Lydia, "way beyond what we can wrap our little minds around."

"I think we only get glimpses of the intricacies and power of it."

"Like with God."

"I hadn't thought of that. Interesting."

"Maggie, what does this have to do with Stephen's grids?"

"His grids are simplified versions of master patterns. That's why I recognize them. They carry the basic forms of the patterns."

"Does this explain how the grids work?"

"His grids give people easier access to the master patterns, and that's what helps them stretch farther and faster and easier."

"Maggie! That's brilliant! Do you see how powerful you've become just since Michael released you? You said he inspires you to be yourself, well, look at this! Look at what you're doing since you had your talk with him. It's awesome."

"In some ways he's still here with me, caring and holding my being, maybe even more than before."

"You're letting yourself have his true support, without the romantic complications. Good for you."

Maggie noticed Michael cautiously watching her at church for the next couple of weeks. She just focused on staying steady. She continued to speak up at the discussions, she interacted with lots of people, all as usual, and she still went for hugs with Michael after events. She was friendly and relaxed, and he saw all that. He relaxed, too, and came back to being friendly. Eventually everything went back to the way it had been.

The trouble with that was that as he relaxed Michael's flirtatious behavior toward her resumed, too. At the next discussion group Michael read several long passages about romantic love and spoke about it catching you off guard, coming when you don't want it, and messing things up. He encouraged allowing that, opening to romantic love, and trusting it. He looked at Maggie all through this, almost to the point of addressing it to her.

"Michael, what are you doing?" she wrote in her journal afterward. *"Why are you looking at me when you urge everyone to fall in love? Is Lydia right? Are you attracted to me? Are you questioning your boundary line? How can you mess with this when it is so important to you? I'm afraid that if you cross that boundary line you could end up hating both yourself and me, and even risk destroying both of us.*

"I feel you right here with me on these other levels of consciousness. Right here. Your eyes are soft and moist like they were tonight when someone else was speaking and I caught you watching me. Michael, how are we going to be friends if you keep stirring things up so much?"

Maggie stopped to stare out the window for a while. Rain and mist shrouded the city and hid the mountains, but Maggie could feel their presence. She sighed, then picked up the pen again.

"Michael, I trusted you to take care of this, but maybe you can't. Do I have

to be the one who maintains the boundary line? Do I have to build a wall between us? I'll do that if I have to, but I can't walk away from you, no matter what you do or how confusing things might be. The soul connection between us is incredibly strong and deep, like these mountains. There is no denying it and no undoing it.

"I will be here, and I will be as truthful and honorable and responsible as I can be. I will do my best to hold steady even as you try to find your way."

"And he will hold steady while you try to find yours," said Nu. "It is a beautiful balance."

"Is it? Right now all I can see is my side of it. And Nu, whatever happens, I won't go to him again. I can't. If he ever wants to be more than friends, he is going to have to come for me. That's the only way. He has to come for me."

❧

The next time Michael saw Maggie he stopped hanging a banner in the sanctuary, climbed down off the ladder, and walked all the way across the empty room with his arms open wide for a hug. Then they went downstairs together to the social hall and Maggie helped him set things up for the discussion group.

"You look tired," she said.

"It's already a long week," he sighed.

"I can easily recharge your energy, any time, Michael. Just let me know."

"But right now I need to be doing this."

"I can do it while you keep going. Hands-on is good, but it works from across the room or across the country."

"Then please do. That would be great. Thanks, Maggie."

Michael continued setting up chairs while Maggie sat down at the side of the room. She sent energy into his field, letting it go wherever he needed it to go, all the while making sure she kept any personal feelings or questions out of it. Within minutes he had perked up noticeably, and he looked over at her with a big smile.

When the room filled with people, Michael introduced the evening's discussion topic, joy. "How can we get ourselves into joy, into joie de vivre?" he asked, flinging his arms wide open. The bright red of his shirt caught the overhead light in a blaze of color. After others called out a list of ways to let go of concerns and worries, and someone said the answer would be different from person to person, Maggie said Michael's flinging his arms wide seemed like the answer to her, fling yourself wide open. Michael grinned at that.

"So," he asked the group, "if you go for a walk in the woods or play with a child, meditate, watch the sun rise, eat a bowl of fresh blueberries, take a deep breath, dance to favorite music, or contemplate a candle flame, what are you allowing to happen?"

"But, Michael," Maggie jumped in, "some of those things empty you and take you away from sensory perception, and some of them fill you up with sensation and immerse you in living the moment."

He turned to her, looking confused, and asked, "Does that matter? If we're trying to open to joy and God, can't we get there different ways?"

"It does matter," she declared. "Emptying may be a way to feel more spiritual, but it takes you out of here and now, it separates you from experiencing life. Aren't we here to be in this world? Being alive to what is happening and fully experiencing it brings us into this world, into life, into being all we can be. I think that is what we're all about, why we are here."

"But if both get you open," Michael asked, "and then you go on from there, on into your day, or into the next minute, then in the end aren't we talking about the same thing?"

He hadn't taken his eyes off her since she first spoke. He was totally focused on her, and she was barely aware of the other thirty people in the room. The energetic connection between the two of them was so vivid that Maggie could feel her body begin to shake. She wondered if she'd be able to hear him or to think or speak clearly, but in fact she was especially alert. It was very exciting.

"How can it be the same?" she asked. "In the one way you are detached, the other way you are actively, fully present." She paused to consider what he had said. "Well, maybe one way is right for one person and the other for another, and I am so much the second way that I don't get the first at all."

"So they are different, but can you make room for both to be true?"

"Paradox! This is paradox!" she declared.

"There you go!" exclaimed Michael, beaming at her. He loved paradox, and he hadn't seen that. He went on to speak more to the group about this paradox Maggie had pointed out. She sat back and watched, amazed.

After the gathering ended a small group went downtown to the Bier Garden for more casual talk. Michael came around the table to sit by Maggie.

He turned in close and said, "So, Maggie Blume, what's happening?"

She leaned on her elbow and looked him in the eyes. Despite his vow and his boundary line, he was flirting outrageously. Her mind tried to wrap around his question. He's behaving like this, and he's asking me what's happening? Maggie sighed and shook her head, still holding the eye contact as she did it, and said, "I have no idea."

"Oh, Maggie," he lamented playfully, "very uncool."

Well, if he was going to play, then she would play along. She smiled and said, "Tell me, Michael, what would be a cool response?"

He brightened and said, "Cool would be to say, 'You, sweetheart, you!'"

"Okay, I'm ready," she said, leaning in some more. "Ask me again."

He did, she smiled and delivered her line, and they laughed together, their eyes sparkling into each other's and their foreheads nearly touching.

When the waitress came around, Maggie said, "I want a beer, but I don't know beer, so will you just pick one for me?"

The waitress looked distraught, so Michael told Maggie, "You probably need to do that yourself."

"I really don't know," she said to him. "I don't do this."

Michael immediately scooped up the situation, turned to the waitress and said, "Bring her a Red Stripe." Turning back to Maggie, he said, "It's a Jamaican beer. You'll like it."

The waitress scowled and asked Maggie, "That's what you want?"

"She'll have a Red Stripe," Michael repeated. When the waitress again looked for her okay, Maggie nodded.

Later she wrote in her journal, "*That was so male! He took charge and took care of it, and I let him do it. Much to my surprise I liked that, and this is quite amazing, considering that right now I so intensely want to feel strong and independent and self-sufficient. I don't want anybody deciding or doing anything for me, especially a man. And yet this felt so right. In fact, it felt wonderful.*

"*This whole thing tonight was stunning. We're so good together. I can't believe we're not heading into a relationship. When he left he said to me, 'It's been a wonderful evening, Maggie. Have a good sleep.' So, we'll be friends who hug and touch and flirt and smile in each other's eyes, and yet we'll always know there's a boundary line one step away. Can I learn to let this be what we are? I want to. I want this.*"

Chapter Five: I Am Here

Maggie climbed onto her treatment table and asked for healing. Jesus came and laid his hand on her heart. Then Mary Magdalene stepped forward and laid her hand on Maggie's heart, too. That's when Maggie knew that Mary Magdalene had been a healer, that Mary wanted to tell her story, and she wanted Maggie to write it. It would come through Maggie, but be Mary's words.

"I can't do that!" Maggie protested to Lydia afterward.

Lydia laughed. "I don't believe that for an instant."

"Do you realize how much I'd have to open up to let it through? I can't let go that much."

"You do it in your healing work all the time, Maggie."

"Oh, I hadn't thought of it that way. Okay, I'll try."

Maggie sat at her writing desk with a pad of paper and pen laid out in front of her. She took a few slow, deep breaths and grounded her energy down into the earth, then focused on each of her chakras to clear, balance, and spin them up. Coming into the very center of her being, she expanded out through all the layers of existence and consciousness, until she was fully open and present to pure potential.

Words came. Not Maggie's words, no words she would ever say, no story she knew to tell. Not Nu's words either, nor any other guide's. These were Mary Magdalene's words. Maggie wrote them down.

Mary's Words

Most men didn't look me in the eyes, especially on the road, but Jesus did. His eyes reflected more in me than I'd felt in a long time. I had seen him before, but how could he have known me like that?

Now I collapsed right there at his feet, exhausted from the long walk in a dry, hot day. He raised me up, his hands cool in the burning sun. I could see that he was tired, too. His eyes bore that ache from too much to carry. I looked around. A crowd had gathered, come upon us from behind him. So many wanting him. They pulled on him from every direction. Yet he still made himself available.

I reached into my pouch for that soft pink stone that comforts the heart. I'd carried it for years, since Sanctuary Farm. Looking in his eyes, I pressed it into his hand. He looked startled. Then glancing down at it he smiled, closed his fingers around it, and tucked it away near his heart.

Maggie dropped her pen onto the writing pad, pushed back from the desk, and stared at the page, then grabbed the phone and dialed.

"Lydia, we did it! It worked!" she exclaimed. "It's incredible, isn't it?"

"I am so glad you did this! Yes, it is fascinating. I hope she is going to answer the big questions about her and Jesus."

"I'm still very nervous about doing this."

"That's okay. Do it anyway."

For the next several weeks Maggie resisted writing with Mary Magdalene. Finally she admitted in her journal, "I'm afraid I will get things wrong. I'm afraid what I write won't follow the New Testament, which I have never read, or it won't fit with historical evidence and detail, which I have not looked into either."

"Then they are wrong!" declared Mary Magdalene. "This is my story and I am telling it."

"Whoa!" gasped Maggie. "Mary Magdalene is right here talking to me."

She took a couple of deep breaths and got centered, then said, "Okay, let's talk. If I am going to do this I need to trust that this is really happening, that you are who you say you are, and you are talking to me. And then trust what you tell me to write. For starters, it certainly makes sense that you would know your own story better than others who were there at the time, who only saw you through their own eyes. You would definitely know it better than writers of *The Bible* centuries later, and way better than modern day historians and scholars looking back to try to reconstruct it."

"Yet you still hesitate. Is there something else?" asked Mary.

"Could the two of us just talk a bit before we start again?"

"So you can get used to me and to doing this. Yes."

"Tell me who you are."

"I'm the one they call Magdalene. I am Mary Magdalene."

"What shall I call you?"

"Call me Mary."

"What are we doing?"

"Writing down the words."

"The words?"

"My words," said Mary.

"Sometimes I only get an impression, instead of words."

"Those are my impressions. Wait for the words. I will tell you what to write."

"I don't need to try to interpret the impressions?"

"I will interpret," said Mary. "I will find the expression that will be understood. What else?"

"I want to do this, and know I am supposed to do this, but self doubts and feeling self-conscious get in the way. I need to be better at opening to it and better at listening. Will it get easier as we keep at it? When we did that little bit the other day, some of it came through as very poetic and expressive. That was great. That's what I need to aim for."

"It won't all be poetic," warned Mary. "My life has also been ordinary and boring, and it has been ugly, too. So, let's just write it all down, then see what we've got."

"People are going to have questions. For one thing, I know they want to know about the relationship between you and Jesus."

"If you come to this, or to anything else, with expectations, you will surely be disappointed," said Mary. "And more importantly, you will miss what it is. Don't make that mistake. This is my story, with its own message. Let it be what it is. Now, shall we start at the beginning?"

"I'm ready," answered Maggie.

Mary's Words

I wish I could be what Mama wants me to be. I wish I could fit my thoughts into the shapes they are supposed to be. I wish I was quieter in my head and more peaceful in my ways. No wonder Mama sighs. She's right. I am impossible.

So, they're sending me away to work in a big house in the city.

Mama put my new dress in the bag. It's too long. I'll have to watch where I step, or hold it up. Does she expect me to grow so fast? The old dress is not good enough, she says. I say it's more important I can walk straight.

Ani went last year. She was fourteen. She took herself away and we never saw her again, even when we went for the harvest festival and I looked for her everywhere. It's like in the city you disappear off the earth, I guess. I'm twelve years old. Times are even harder now, and I have to go.

You aren't supposed to be this curious, Mama told me. You aren't supposed to ask all these questions or make all these faces or try to understand. You're supposed to bow your head low and be pleased and honored and grateful and do what's expected. You're supposed to be cooperative and glad to be cooperative. You're supposed to go to the city now and be relieved there is a place for you at all. Take yourself away from here so your family can feed one less mouth and clothe one less body, and so your mother won't be so worried about you.

That was the one that got to me. She worries. She frowns at me when she thinks I won't see. She puts her face on when I'm looking, but the worry shows when I turn sideways and peek. I see it.

I try to be the person she wants me to be. She truly believes that person is in me. She searches and searches for her in my eyes. I search for her in my quiet times. Is she in here? Can she come and be a better me? Nobody else I know has this problem, being the wrong one, needing to find the right one. They just go ahead being right from the start. I need this other one. Now!

My brother Aaron is taking me in the morning. This is the last night in my bed, last dinner, last of being here in this house I've lived in all my life. The last hearing the sounds, last hand on the doorway, last drink from the cup, last voices, last being this. Tomorrow, all change, all motion, all questions, all new.

We're going to walk for days, Mama said, and then arrive. I am to be respectful and obedient, keep my head low, not stare in eyes, not ask, and not wiggle. I am to keep my shoes on and my mind to myself. I am to be careful what I say and do and think and imagine. I am to wrap myself tight and still. Because this has to work.

There is no coming back. Eight mouths to feed here, no bed for me, no room, no me here, as if I disappeared, as if I am over with, as if I died. It is because I couldn't fit to what I was supposed to be. I tried, they tried, we all tried. They brought seven men to look me over, and not one stayed to marry me. That greasy, fat one, he thought he could take me until I asked, "Would camels stand and wait without ropes?"

"She talks entirely too much," he said. "Can't you quiet her?"

Mama sighed a loud one that time. I'd promised her, but I couldn't help it. He had said certain beings are meant to serve, they live to meet the needs of others. He said it is their purpose and satisfaction, as if they choose it and want it, as if they are grateful for the opportunity, as if he is doing them a favor! And he thought that I should be all that? Me? Live to wash his feet? Be grateful for the opportunity? Feel fulfillment at his feet? He is a fool.

It won't be long now. I've lain awake all through the night, wondering where I will be tomorrow evening. If I'd agreed to marry any of those men I would still be nearby. There would be only known places and happenings, and familiar faces at the well and in passing moments. But I am going far away to unknown ways and people, to strangeness and mystery. Well, at least it is out there, where the questions seem to come from.

—∾—

I was a slender girl, barely impressing my clothing. Everyone took me for weak and fragile, but under that hanging fabric I was strong in spirit as well as muscle, because I knew I had to be. No one else was going to be there for me after I left home.

One time during the first year in the city I had to run from thugs after I'd bought milk at the market. I dropped the jug on the street and back at the house I was beaten for stealing the money. There was no one to take my side. All I could do was work hard, be careful, watch and learn, and store up whatever I could for some day, one day, when I would leave there. I seemed destined to be one who moves on.

The children of the house left their things lying around for others to straighten. When I got the chance I studied the boys' school exercises and listened in on lessons, soaking it all up. I began to ask questions after hours of the tutor, Rav. At first his eyes opened wide, but he soon became accustomed to my inquisitiveness and took pleasure in showing off his knowledge. He spent many hours late at night taking me down avenues of learning as I explored and questioned and tried to understand. I learned history and philosophy and religion. I learned about thought and deed and spirit, as it had been recorded through the years by educated people. Some of it was very different from my own experience, and some familiar, and the distinction was not always predictable.

After a while I was able to spend some of my time assisting Rav.

I loved working with the children. They simply would not tolerate less than everything. I learned to express myself clearly, and expect it of others. It wasn't that I loved to argue, but I would tear apart a person's words, trying to find the truth in them. Most people didn't say what they meant or what they knew. They tangled words around vague impressions, and tossed it all out there like a puzzle for the listener to decipher. Then they were frustrated when others didn't understand it any better than they did themselves and that the others didn't explain it in the reply. I wanted people to think. I wanted them to try. Don't speak nonsense to me. Say what you mean. Work at it!

Preachers could be the worst, meandering all around in a subject hoping to hit a point. Meanwhile everybody grew so tired of trying to make sense of it that they went into a trance and heard only rhythm and tones. If the preacher was clever he made use of that, carrying them along on the music, then finishing with a grand, rousing declaration that woke them up implanted with good intention. Perhaps that was the plan all along, to frustrate reason to the point that it abandoned the person, then deal directly with their emotions and vulnerability. But had he really taught them anything?

I missed Rav terribly when he moved on. The new tutor did not want to bother with me, so I returned to household chores. At night I read what I could from the master's library. I read about far away places and strange customs. I read letters and poetry and mysterious texts forbidden to women, often late into the night.

One time after being up late the night before, I fell asleep at work in the middle of a hot afternoon. The old father of the mistress found me and shook me awake before anyone else came. He was kindly, with a bright twinkle in his eye. I suspect he knew I borrowed items to read in my room. Certainly someone knew, for I would regularly find an extra vial of lamp oil on my bedside table.

Maybe I did have someone on my side through that time, but if it was the old man there wasn't much he could do but watch while I was treated harshly. He had little position or authority in the household either. He had to be grateful for his son-in-law's generosity.

I stayed there for seven years. It seemed forever.

The master had another, older son who, as soon as he was grown enough, had put on a uniform with gold braid and cording and gone off to far and exotic places. An injured leg meant he was unable to keep up, so he returned, lost and angry. He wandered late night drinking places and brothels, looking for himself.

One night this son came home early, well before dawn, drunk as usual, and saw my light. I blew out the flame when I heard him near my door, and pushed the chair against it. That did not deter him. His pale, soft hand muffled my cries. The old man slept soundly in his far-off room, and it was a long time before his grandson left my bed. If anyone heard my struggle they did nothing.

I finally slept as dawn came, awakened in full light by a rough shaking when Indaya, one who worked in the kitchen, came looking for me. "You have missed the entire morning!" she said. "Now you are in for it." The beating did not release the beginnings of a child in my belly. She insisted on being birthed nine months later.

They took her as soon as she was born and gave her to a woman anxious to be a mother. I never held her or even saw more than a glimpse. I barely heard her cry out before she was gone. For a while my breasts ached for her. My heart never stopped aching. I rarely spoke with God, but I begged that she have an easier way with life than I did.

As soon as I was able to leave that house I went as far away as I could.

The sun went down fast in the desert. Its fiery ball grew, then flattened and disappeared quickly down a burrow to hide till dawn. With the sun went the heat. At first the remaining warmth of sand and rocks felt comforting to cooling hands and feet. But the heat quickly vanished as chill absorbed everything. Then the only warmth was around a fire or wrapped in a blanket. I had no blanket. And a fire was a dangerous place for a woman alone. Other women had their men to guard them, even to fight off a drunken brawler. I had only my wits. Sometimes it worked, sometimes it didn't.

In the desert night, when the sky is clear and the stars bright, sound and heat seem to rise right up to the top of the sky. Without shelter, plenty comes disguised as distance and beauty and mystery, and echoes in return as smallness and solitude and silence. Never have I felt so meaningless, or so at peace, as in the desert night.

I learned to disguise myself as a man so that I might slip into places easier. In the places I went, the laws against dressing as a man did not matter. Besides, it was rarely discovered. One time a man made a grab for my genitals and to his surprise he came up empty. There was no fixing that. I slipped out before he recovered from his surprise. Another time my sleeve caught fire so that I had to fling aside my shirt. It could have been plain to all that my breasts were bound tight within a length of cloth wrapped around them, but half the crowd had already fallen asleep, and the rest had drunk enough wine to cloud their impression. I was long gone before it came up in the morning.

Among the men, I learned that a man can be more than he seems to be. And that he does not always say what he means. Roughness of exterior is practically irrelevant. The eyes tell more than any demeanor or costume. I learned to listen differently, and to hold precious those small gems of secrets shared in cautious trust. Men do not share much. When they do, they risk humiliation and even ruin. Consequently men appreciate trust much more than do women. They count on it, where a woman can compensate and still do what needs doing.

—~—

The man jerked me around to face him, then slammed me into the door frame. "You lying bitch!" he growled. "I'll show you what a man is!" Blood filled my mouth; I spat it in his face. He smashed a fist into my jaw and I lost consciousness. For that I was grateful, but my abandoned body continued to bear the violence and then it carried the beginnings of another new life. This one made it only as far as a shallow grave at the side of the road. Despair engulfed me.

Where is this God who is supposed to be father? Where is compassion? Where is help? I wail to the moon, Mother Moon! I sob to the depths of the earth, Mother Earth! My belly rocks with each surge of anguish. My heart rips open and shrivels to a knotted cord. I CANNOT DO THIS ANY MORE! I CANNOT BE THIS. I cannot bear one more hand on me, one more lascivious look, one more sneer, one more self-conscious laugh, one more lewd gesture, one more question or want or grimace.

God, if you are there, take pity on this woman. Take a moment's interest in this woman. Lead me somewhere, tell me what to do, anything, anywhere, now. Take me out of this!

—~—

The dancer spun in her brown dress, a flower tucked at her waist. Light on her feet, she floated more than touched earth. I sat on the dirt, cross-legged, planted in the dirt, holding onto the earth, safe now, among the women. They let me simply be there, alone in the midst of them, silent and still, for as long as I wanted that.

It had been months before I would even speak, months of watching the days to see if they would keep coming anyway. Each night I challenged the sun to return, to dare to prove to me that it would do it again, despite all my anger, all my condemnation, all my doubts. It did, day after day, until I began to believe it might, and then that it would. Until my shoulders softened, my head rose, my eyes met the dawn, and there was Rebecca.

She stood there every morning, waiting for me to acknowledge her. She came again and again, seeming to believe there would be a day when I would respond, seeming to believe there was something left in me that would care enough to notice her. Day after day, she came, her smile soft, her eyes gentle, her hands open. It wasn't enough to hide in my darkness. She found me anyway.

Sweet, patient Rebecca. Lighthearted, tender, believing the best, even as life battered her as much as it did the rest of us. Once my eyes met hers she pestered me. She would not leave me alone. She brought me food and drink, she washed me, she changed my clothes—I do not know where she got new clothes. She talked, she sang. She urged me up onto my feet until finally I came to work the grinding stones and do my part to feed the women.

I had found myself in a women's place, a sanctuary and farm, where women lived together and healed together. It was a place of safety and caring and life. My body healed in the rhythm of the stones and grain, rocking and circling and releasing its hardened places. The melodic sound of women's voices sharing over work began to comfort, and then to release, my fear.

—∾—

Minha always took the young ones with her to fetch water, and she taught them all along the way. She pointed out berries and leaves, dug roots and offered a taste, brushed scents across their faces, and rubbed balm on scrubbed knees. The world came alive along the way. And each child returned with a favorite to share. That way everybody learned and the old ways continued.

Minha told stories of clouds and rains and surprises and comforts, she spoke of gathering in and of adventuring out, she entranced the children with exploration and discovery, she raised questions in their minds that would draw them along for their whole lives.

The children adored Minha. Her hair lay down her back in a thick gray braid they tweaked and teased. Lines and creases shaped her face, brown from the sun and wind and rain, and ran down her hands onto busy fingers that never rested. Her smile lit up their faces, and her voice drew pictures in their minds.

The children ran to see what she carried in her pocket. One day she handed them a ball of soft fur gathered off low shrubs near a nest.

Another day it was sticks that burst with sparkling flavor in the mouth. Or flat bread still warm from the baking stone. Once it was a baby creature with large eyes and tiny feet, left behind when its family fled. The children gathered sticks and leaves to build an enclosure for protection, and fed it bits of their own food until one morning it was gone.

Minha herself disappeared for hours at a time, telling us only that she was out exploring. Some saw her up a tree or down on hands and knees in grasses or wading in shallows. Occasionally a young one would take to following her, first at a distance, then they'd be seen with heads together or rushing to and fro in some great endeavor, until the child remembered other play and wandered off.

I followed her myself one morning. It was a gentle day in earliest spring. On this day I woke in darkness and did not drop back to sleep. Soft voices already rose from the kitchen, bakers busy since well before first light. From my bed I heard a remarkable bird call. I listened for others to react, but heard no change in nearby sounds. There! Again! Still no one reacted. Perhaps only I heard it. Perhaps it was calling to me. There it was again, as if confirming. "Yes, yes, yes," it called. "Come!"

Minha passed by the door of my tent as soon as I stuck my head out. Again the bird called. Was I supposed to go with her? Wait! Hurry!

I caught up with her at the edge of the settlement. Without a word, as if she had been expecting me, she handed me a bundle to carry, and headed off. It wasn't that I chose to go with her, I just did it. We headed toward the call of the bird, our sandals crunching on loose stones, unable in the predawn darkness to see ahead of our feet. The ground rose. I labored, my body unused to the exertion. She didn't look back, didn't speak, but her steps slowed and I kept with her.

We walked that way until the sun came fully into the day. As we emerged out onto a ridge, there it was, a great circle of brilliance rising from the land before us. We weren't the only ones watching it. Wild goats stood on outcroppings, all facing the sun, as if honoring its return and asking for blessings on this new day.

Minha went to a broad, flat rock and set down her things. She gestured for my bundle, and untying it, spread the fabric upon the stone. From other sacks she brought out objects, one by one, tenderly placing them in the center. A corked bottle of liquid, a shallow clay bowl into which she poured grain from a small bag. A wide, flat seashell for bright golden powder, and another for green granules. Stones and bones, a piece of twisted wood, a bracelet of opal and jade, and a simple band of gold. All these she arranged as if knowing where each belonged. She sat down on the blanket, facing east across the altar, straightened her spine and closed her eyes, then gestured for me to sit.

Grateful to settle my weary body to the ground, I found a smooth indentation within the stone and joined her meditation. It had been a long time, but it came easily, like breathing. Drawing into the center of my body, resting there for a minute, then binding myself to Mother Earth, who freely gives all life and takes us to her body when it ends. I felt her presence, her power, her generous spirit. I felt the sun on my skin, the breeze in my nostrils, the breath in my body. I let life come into me. I grew taller and straighter. I rose up from despair, from weariness, from collapse, from the edge of death. I lifted up from all the troubles of my life. I let the love of the Great Mother come into me and fill me with her sweet essence. I became the dawn and the new day.

A gentle touch on my shoulder roused me. In the distance I heard the call of the bird, I heard bells, I heard the voices of goats, I heard a song. The bright sun already stood high overhead. "We must return," said Minha. I nodded. Her precious objects were gathered into their pouches. I bundled the blanket and followed her off the ridge. The stony path wound back and forth down a steep slope I had only known in the earlier dark by putting one foot in front of the other, trying to keep up. Mountains rose around us as we descended to a river and then followed it downstream. The valley opened, and there were the women working in fields ahead.

Some of them glanced at me, then greeted Minha cautiously, others merely nodded in our direction. They must have been surprised to see me with her, and didn't want to make much of it for fear of chasing me back to my bed. How would they know there was no risk of that? How would they know it was truly a new day? I smiled. I knew.

—w—

Fourteen women living together and making a life together at Sanctuary Farm was the best thing some of us ever needed. There was gentleness, a low-pitched murmur, a quiet encircling. Even when the one called Elisa growled and told us what to do, we knew there was caring behind it. So many of us had been wounded. It was understood that no wounding would take place here.

Outbursts erupted, but no one fought them. Everyone knew they came from fear and from memory of other times, everyone knew they came from the woman's own mind and body, and were hers to experience and resolve. We learned to watch and wait. Others stood by, ready to support, ready to catch the falling woman when she could allow it. It was good for me to see this so that I would accept it myself when it was my turn to go that way. And we all did. No one escaped their past, in memories, and dreams, and reminders.

—w—

Soon after I began to actively participate at Sanctuary Farm the woman named Magri began coughing up blood. She had arrived the previous spring, alone, beaten and bruised. They told me she had been terrified, like I was, and cringed whenever anyone came close. Yet even as she relaxed she never recovered her strength. By winter she was unable to lift the jugs of flour or carry water from the well, and needed to rest often during the day. Her body lost its way with life.

The women were so kind to her. There was always someone paying attention, always someone taking care. Caring seemed to flow out of their nature. It seemed instinctive.

When Magri could no longer keep up, someone stayed with her, close by, gently surrounding her with soft song, soft hands, soft eyes. And two or three times a day women gathered in a circle around her, sang to her and through her, and comforted her with their touch. They lifted up her attention, up from pain and fear to a peaceful place of love and support. They shared their joy of life with her. They brought tears of relief to her eyes and peace to her face.

I'd forgotten they did the same with me, back when I was so lost in the dark that I gave up on life, back when I waited to die, when I expected to discover I already had. Back when I did nothing to care for myself. I did not clean myself, I did not eat, I did not watch the day, I did not leave my bed to void, I scarcely breathed.

They had come around me, too, surrounded me with beautiful sounds and images, touch, and comforting peace. I truly thought I was in the midst of angels. It wasn't until I saw them do the same for Magri that I realized those angels were these wonderful, gentle, sharing women. Each of them was bruised herself, each of them knew full well the cost of living the life we found ourselves in. Each of them respectfully offered me the life-honoring choice we all have, every day, to go on to death or to stay to become an expression of one's own being despite the hardships and cruelty we endure.

It was in this loving embrace of women's circle that I chose. There I found the strength to continue, to thread my way through whatever may come. It was in this gentle and yielding but powerful and tenacious web of support that I discovered my right and my yearning to find out what I can be. There I began to see myself as I can be, as I will be, as I am. It was within that circle that I recognized Mary Magdalene.

Magri died peacefully in her sleep one quiet morning after the others left her bedside. The woman who stayed to sit with her through that morning had turned away to tend the fire and did not see her last breath. Magri ended her life alone, but she had a beautiful smile on her face.

Another woman named Jaliel lived out her whole life at the farm. She died in her sleep on the night of a new moon, after gathering all of us around her in the evening to hear her vision of a life of peace and prosperity. Only later did I learn that the land was hers and she was the last of her lineage. The women did not know what would then become of our sanctuary. It would be safe at least until the tax time. I learned later that one of the women impersonated Jaliel for years to come, keeping the sanctuary in their hands. No official ever knew the wiser because for so many years no man had really looked at Jaliel and could not have recognized her anyway.

I lived among the women at Sanctuary Farm for three years. Women came and went, some remained. Magri and I had arrived on very similar roads and our lives were equally impossible, yet, we left in opposite directions, on very different paths, Magri to ending and me to new beginning. The women of Sanctuary Farm saw in us the grace, and the importance, of supporting both roads.

Not Far

Not far from dreaming is awakening,
through stirring, through hesitated breath.
Not far from fear is curiosity,
through question, through resolve.
Not far from closed is open,
through turning, through a shrug.
Not far from frozen is warm,
through sunlight, through touch.
Not far from doubt is faith,
through wondering, through release.
Not far from loneliness is love,
through a smile, through giving.
Not far from grief is renewal,
through tears, through passion.
Not far from me is you,
through recognition, through acceptance.

Not far from all of this is God,
through dreaming and awakening,
fear and curiosity,
through closed and open,
frozen and warm,
through doubt and faith,
loneliness and love,
through grief and renewal,
through me
and through you.

As simple as a stirring, a shrug, a recognition,
as simple as breath or wonder or tears or acceptance.
We reach out and everywhere touch the sacred.

Chapter Six: Not Far

"It is almost a month since my boundary line talk with Michael," Maggie wrote in her journal. *"I've settled into being cautiously friendly, but he is all over the place, ranging from blatant flirtation to outright avoiding me. And yet, when I open at all to the deeper levels of consciousness he is looking for me there, not at all confused, clearly wanting to connect. On those levels I am the one who worries and resists. How can we openly connect on the other levels and not expect to express it in the everyday world? I don't know how to do this. I don't know if I can keep it all sorted out."*

"Stop trying to sort, Maggie," said Nu. "Just let it all be what it is. Trust it."

❧

"Here's how I see it," Michael was saying to a young woman at the far end of the buffet table. "There are many levels of existence, and each of us is like a string hanging down through them all, touching each level on the way." Maggie could hardly believe her ears. Michael was talking about the levels as if he was totally aware and comfortable with them. He glanced over at her, just for a moment, then he went on speaking to the young woman. "But we are only conscious of a few of the levels," he said. Then he looked straight at Maggie and said, "We block the others out, and we go on as if they don't exist." Maggie and Michael stared at each other as his words echoed through all their levels of being, and Maggie knew that whether he consciously realized it or not, he was asking her to allow more connection.

She called her sister Caroline when she got home. "He's supposed to be the one who isn't sure about our connecting on other levels, but now he's blatantly coming after me about opening to that part of relationship."

"Maggie, you know I'm skeptical about this whole thing, but I'll ask this anyway. Do you think he really is interested, despite what he said?"

"I think Michael is confused and doesn't know what he wants. I can never predict how he will be when I see him. Most of the time he is relaxed and friendly and affectionate, and sometimes I could still swear he is falling in love with me. But other times when he sees me he runs the other way, avoiding me entirely, turning to anyone but me. And then sometimes he intently immerses himself in being holy, insisting that everything is about God and that's all any of us needs."

"It sounds like he is trying hard to find his way with this, and he hasn't yet or he would settle on something. Maybe you have to give it more time."

"I don't know if I can take this much longer, Caroline. I really like the good parts, but then I'm devastated when he shuts me out. It begins to feel like that passive aggressive stuff Alex did."

"But Michael doesn't play games, Maggie. He has been very honest with you all along. He's just confused."

"He really is thrown by this, isn't he? There's an innocence about what he's doing."

"Yes, there is."

"Okay, Michael, I'm still here. We'll keep doing this, whatever it is."

For the next several weeks Michael continued to be unpredictable. One morning Maggie wrote in her journal, *"Stephen would say my difficulty with this is evidence that I need to stay with it and open my heart. So, okay, here goes..."* She brought her attention to the middle of her chest, to the heart chakra energy center, and held it for a moment, then gradually spread it open.

Maggie gasped for breath. "Damn, this hurts way more than I've admitted. My heart is in agony." She put both her hands on her heart to support it. "I can't go on like this with Michael. It hurts too much."

She climbed onto the treatment table, and as soon as her back touched the cushion Maggie burst into convulsive sobs. All she knew in the world was that her heart hurt more than was possible. Then she noticed Michael right there next to her, as real as if he stood there in person. She wanted to push him away, but everything in her stopped her from doing it.

Giving in to a powerful sense of what is right, she let herself go deep, reached up to lay her hand on Michael's heart, and following guidance said, "I know who you are." As she did that she knew this was about him, too, not just her. She felt him know he was hurting her. She wanted to reassure him, but just then her heart tore wide open and more sobs ripped out of her. All she could do was repeat over and over, "I know who you are. I know who you are."

Maggie let everything they ever may have been and ever could become fill her, she let it all exist for her, and at the same time kept her hand on his heart and repeated those words, "I know who you are." After a while he pulled away and she lost the connection with him, so she called out, "Michael, look at me. Look at me!" until he did, until his eyes came right into hers. Then she said again, "I know who you are," and he heard it and he stayed with her.

She had no idea how long they went on like that. She had to bring him back several times. Then, still following guidance, she said to him, "Feel this, right here, this is me, feel me. Now feel this other. Feel the difference. That is you. Feel you." And he did, too. He felt his own true self, which was what he needed to do.

After all the pain and intensity calmed down, Maggie was exhausted. As she rested she wondered if this was happening because of Mary Magdalene. In her journal she wrote, *"Am I having to experience all this with Michael to prepare me to write down Mary's story? Well, then my answer is no, I can't do it. It goes too deep and hurts too much. I quit. Somebody else has to write this."*

But she moaned, then sighed. "No, I have to do it," she admitted. "I am the one." And she sank under another wave of pain and tears.

Later that week, while getting a massage at the spa, Maggie told Nan, "I know Michael wants me to open to him on the other levels of consciousness, to let us have that and let it be all it can be, and I still don't do it. I don't even open when he so strongly comes for me there."

"Did you hear what you just said? He comes for you? Comes for you, as in come for you?"

"Oh, Nan, I didn't mean that."

"No? You said it. Isn't it true?"

"Okay, yes, he does come for me that way, on the other levels. But that's not real."

"I thought you said it is real."

"It would be so much easier to have an ordinary relationship. In this there is no going step by step. There are no handholds. There is no holding back or place to hide. This takes real commitment to fully being who we really are, commitment to living deep in our souls. Look how much pain I already have. This terrifies me."

"Hang in there, Maggie. It's an investment."

"Are you strategizing again? I shouldn't even talk with you about this."

❧

In her next morning meditation Maggie focused on releasing fear. As that began to work, she sensed an energetic presence nearby. It was Michael.

"No," she protested. "He's not really here." But he was there. Tentatively reaching out her hand, she felt him start to take it and she instinctively pulled it back. Then she took a deep breath and let this be happening. Michael stayed with her while she worked at releasing what she could of old blocks and messages and influences that kept her masked from expressing her true self.

At the end Maggie opened herself to Michael's other level presence and went deeper and deeper until there was nothing between the two of them, no line, no separation, no caution, no doubt. The connection was strong and clear and complete. It touched everything in her, every sense, every awareness, every emotion, every expression of her existence. She stayed like that for a long time, letting herself be in it, until resistance gradually, insistently reclaimed her, bringing her back to questions and wariness.

❧

The next morning Maggie went to the church to donate healing sessions for staff members, knowing that Michael was not expected to be there. While waiting for the first appointment she wrote in her journal about how it had been to open that way to the connection with Michael. She looked up and to her surprise he was there after all, across the room walking toward her.

He smiled and said, "Good morning!"

Startled and feeling very awkward, wondering if he was aware of all that had been happening between them on the other levels, Maggie scrambled for something else to talk about. Mary Magdalene. She breathed a sigh of relief.

"Do you have a few minutes?" she asked.

"Sure, what's up?" he said, grabbing a chair to sit down. She told him about the writing. He smiled and exclaimed, "You've found another Mary!"

"I think she found me."

Michael nodded.

"I didn't believe I could do this writing with her, but I am, and it is amazing. Michael, would you just know that I'm doing this? You don't have to do anything, just know. Just hold it."

"Sure, I can do that."

Maggie felt the responsibility of writing Mary's words shift and the load lighten. "Thank you," she said, then added, "Do you have time to get on the treatment table?"

"I've got to write a whole bunch of stuff to meet a deadline, so I can't."

Maggie spent the next four hours working steadily on other church staff members, then found Michael still typing at the computer in his office. "Last chance," she said.

He got up and hugged her. "You're going?" he asked. He kept hold of her arms as he explained that he had a wedding at two and too much to finish before then. Maggie just smiled, happy to spend a few minutes talking and looking into each other's faces and feeling so comfortable.

Later that day she wrote in her journal, *"He doesn't know, does he? He responds to the other level happenings as if he knows, but he's just being influenced by them. He doesn't consciously know what happens there."*

"Maggie," began Nu, but she interrupted.

"Nu, I know, you're going to say that I close myself off so much that it's nearly the same for me. But at least I can get there when I allow myself to open to it. I don't think he knows how to do that, or even that he can. Yes, he's very responsive to what happens there, but I doubt he could explain why he says what he says or does what he does. And he seems fine with that. He doesn't need to figure it out. He accepts the confusion, calls it mystery, and he actually enjoys that. I'd like to be like that."

"Be yourself, Maggie," said Nu. "Be in your own mystery."

On the next Sunday Michael preached about letting God come through. "God comes to us through little moments and little gestures that might seem insignificant. He reaches through them to touch us and enliven us, to transform the ordinary into extraordinary. All we have to do is be willing. All we have to do is to open to allow impressions, impulses, and inspirations. All we have to do is take a bit of a chance.

"Reach out and you might just touch the holy. Or you might bring it to someone else. We can let these moments, these gestures, these openings, be what they can be. Go ahead, be amazed! Open yourself to let God's light shine, in you, around you, and through you. You never know what may happen. Life is a beautiful, blooming mystery!"

Maggie waited after the service to catch Michael for a hug, but someone distracted her. When she looked for him again, he was gone, probably already went upstairs to his office and she had missed him. Then to her surprise, there he was, coming around close behind her, wrapping her into a hug. As she turned into his arms, it reminded her of when he ordered the beer. He gathered her up, taking charge, she followed his lead, relaxing into it, and she liked it.

"He came and found me for a hug today, instead of leaving for his office like he usually does," Maggie told Nu. "And he smiled that joyful smile."

"You know why. Because he holds your beauty, just like you do for him."

"I've been letting myself enjoy this familiarity and affection, and it's wonderful, but I don't think he realizes how intimate he is with me. It's hard not to fall for it again. Are you sure I'm supposed to be doing it this way? Not being more careful?"

"Yes. Don't try to organize it, Maggie. Simply allow it and marvel at it."

Caroline flew in from Seattle to spend a week with Maggie in late June. They hadn't seen each other for nearly a year, and dove right into that mystical sister-dance of talk and play and laughter and tears and stories and understanding. They didn't even get to most of the things they planned to do, because they so enjoyed just hanging out together. They fell asleep talking and they started right in again in the morning.

To Maggie's surprise, Caroline wanted to meet Stephen. They drove out past Waynesville and he took them up the mountain to his big, two-acre grid. This was the master grid on which the smaller, simpler installation at the Montford Center was based. This one contained over 1500 buried crystals laid out in geometric patterns within the larger form of a golden mean spiral. The spiral itself represented our solar system, with nodes at each of the planets. This was the first time Maggie had been there.

The three of them entered the grid at the farthest out point, at the top of the meadow, stopping at the first planetary node, TransPluto. Maggie immediately felt light-headed and she began to shake. She tried doing a simple clearing of her energy field, but it did not help. She tried to ground herself, and couldn't. Becoming concerned now, she lay flat on the ground, but even that wasn't enough.

"Are you okay?" asked Stephen.

"No, I'm not okay," she said. "I feel like I'm going to fly off into some vast expanse somewhere far away."

Voicing it made her realize she was in serious trouble. Maggie asked her guides to hold her in place, and they did. Then she wrapped each level of her energy field with a layer of gold. This was a technique she discovered several years earlier, which she used to anchor herself here in the physical world while working very deep in the patterns of existence. Fortunately it did that now, too, and when she finished Maggie felt solidly connected with earth and meadow, surrounding forest, and mountain.

"Now I'm okay," she told Stephen. "I can go on into the grid."

Stephen nodded, and led the way. Coming in through the planets of the solar system, the spiral contracted into an ever-tightening curve toward the sun near the lower end of the meadow. The patterns in the grid's energy challenged Maggie at each planetary node along the spiral. She needed to spend time at each one to adjust. Changes and reconfiguration were happening within her own energetic patterns. Maggie didn't know what it was about, but it felt important to do. The adjustments became easier as she moved deeper into the spiral.

Stephen considered the sun position to be the main focus of the entire grid, so Maggie was surprised she didn't feel more intensity when they got there. It simply did not attract her interest, nor did it challenge or impress her. She looked up the middle of the meadow they had skirted on the wide part of the curve. There was some place out there she wanted to be.

Rain began to fall. Thick clouds had come over the mountain, heavy with rain that would not pass quickly. Stephen said, "Let's go back to the house. I made lunch for us."

"You go," said Maggie. "I want to stay here for a while." Stephen looked anxious. "I'm okay," she assured him, though she wasn't at all certain of that or of what was going on. She saw by his face that he wasn't convinced. Maggie looked firmly in his eyes and said, "I really want to do this."

"Okay," he said, "but if you're not back in half an hour, I'm coming to get you."

Coming to get me? Maggie smiled, astonished that Stephen would say those particular words to her, so clearly pointing out the contrast between Michael's caution and his own willing presence. But this was no time to be distracted by that.

Stephen was right to be concerned. It felt like just about anything might happen. Maggie had faced risky situations before and her guides had always kept her safe, but it didn't hurt to have back-up. She took a good look at Stephen. It would take considerable power and skill to help her if she got into more than she could handle. Was Stephen a lot more than he seemed? He was probably just being chivalrous, but perhaps he did have resources he hadn't demonstrated yet.

"Okay, I agree," she said. "Give me thirty minutes from when you get to the house. If I'm not back by then, come get me."

Then Caroline surprised her by saying, "I'd like to stay with you, but I'm going to the house, too. I don't want to get soaked. Are you okay here by yourself?"

It had not occurred to Maggie that either of them would stay with her, and she didn't want them to. She looked at Caroline, wondered if she had any awareness of the real situation, doubted that, then just nodded.

"Here, take my watch," said Stephen, handing it to her. It began to feel like they were preparing her for an expedition. She checked the time and put it in her pocket.

"I'm fine," she insisted, wishing they'd leave. "Go ahead and go. I'll be fine."

Stephen and Caroline started down to the road and Maggie headed up the middle of the meadow, up through the center of the grid. She found the right spot about fifty yards up. It was the place she needed to be. Turning, she saw that Stephen had waited at the edge of the meadow, watching until she settled. Now he hurried down the road to catch Caroline.

❧

Maggie looked around. Every tree, every raindrop, every wildflower, every leaf, every color, every texture, every line, every edge was bright and clear and vivid. The meadow felt lifted up to the top of the world, like Machu Pinchu, like the Himalayas, raised up to the sky. She wondered if it would even be noticeable from outer space.

She felt part of this place, built into it, she belonged here. To be here she had to completely open herself; she had to let go of all resistance and effort and control, let them peel off and fall away, leaving the clear, naked wholeness of who she is. She had never felt so unencumbered, so comfortable, so right.

She sat on the ground and the summer rain became a downpour. It soaked through her shirt and pants and hair, it penetrated pocket and seam and collar, it saturated her underwear, it ran down her face and neck and body. She was totally drenched. She had never been so wet. The distinction between her and the rain disappeared. She was one with rain, one with meadow, one with mountain. She was vividly here, in this rain, in this place, in this moment, in this life, rooted into these mountains and into the earth. She felt supremely alert and alive and present.

Maggie let her awareness expand. She was wide open now to all that is beyond our meager knowing, to holiness so vast and profound and full there is no way to relate to it. Then she opened more, differently, distant and deep. She saw a place, bright with light, full of patterns of being and beings. She could not see them clearly. If only I were more visual, she lamented, but quickly let it go. How wonderful it felt there! It felt so good that a yearning welled up in her, flooding through her. The yearning overcame her.

"Home!" she wailed. "I want to go home!" That bright place felt powerfully and clearly home, even more so than these mountains. She cried into the rain, she sobbed. Free-flowing tears blended with rainwater to run down her body and sink into the soil. She cried for all the disappointments of her life, and the missed opportunities; for all the letting go and the hanging in there she had had to do; for all the pain and loss and sorrow; for all the wrongness. She cried because she knew, somewhere in herself, that here in this life she was not home, she was not where she could be at ease, where she could release completely and simply be. She cried, finally, for the hard work of living her life, of being the person she continually evolved into and through. She cried tears of relief that all the many feelings and impressions and reactions and desires that had seemed so misfitting were actually truth, were real, were of this, were her own, and were understandable. She cried with joy and laughter that she could feel so right, so accepted, so absolutely fine.

Thunder sounded from just over the mountain, following the path of the rain, approaching fast. Stephen's wristwatch, dug out of a soggy pocket, said it was time to go. It was not easy to leave, not easy to return to the regular world. More thunder came fast on the heels of a bright flash. She leapt up and raced the storm down the road, cutting across another meadow and around the back of the house.

On the porch Stephen handed her towels and dry sweats to put on, and he was so eager to not miss a word that she had to insist he leave while she undress and dry off. Then they ate and talked until she had told everything she could remember.

"That place, Stephen, where is it? What is it?"

"You tell me."

"I don't know. Only that I wanted so much to leave all this and go be there."

❧

Caroline rarely went to church at home in Seattle, but she wanted to see the place Maggie spoke so much about, and she wanted to see Michael. As they walked there on Sunday, Maggie realized this might not go well. She fidgeted all through the service, and a whole chorus of critics railed in her head at everything Michael said and did. She was very sorry she'd agreed to bring Caroline with her.

Waiting in line to get to Michael, Maggie was quiet and withdrawn. After dutifully introducing her sister, she immediately turned to go, but Caroline was already commenting favorably to Michael about a point made in the sermon, and Michael began discussing it with her.

"I was sure you hated it," Maggie told Caroline when they finally left.

"I know how to be polite," Caroline chided. "Actually, I found it interesting. I hadn't ever thought about comparing the Jewish Diaspora and the desert in that way."

"I didn't know you ever thought about the Diaspora at all."

"A lot happens that you don't know about, Sis. Come on, let's go get some dinner. All that praying made me ravenous."

Twenty minutes later, busy in the kitchen, Maggie couldn't stand her sister's smug silence any longer. "What about Michael?" she asked. "What did you think of him?"

Caroline took a deep breath before she spoke. "To be truthful, this really didn't change a thing for me. I know you wanted it to, but he's pretty much as I expected, except for the Jimmy Stewart thing he's got going, which no woman can resist. You didn't tell me about that."

"Michael doesn't sound at all like Jimmy Stewart."

"Not the sound, the mannerisms, the style. That awkward, boyish, ducking the head, bashful style."

"I hadn't noticed. So, you are still skeptical?"

"Let's say cautious."

"I'm disappointed."

"Of course you are. You want me to tell you what I think you should do so that you have that to bounce off of. I'm not going to do that."

"But you always do that. Why not now?"

Caroline shrugged. "I don't know. I just don't feel like it."

Stephen had given Caroline and Maggie materials to take home so they could each create a small manifestation grid, and the two of them did that together on Maggie's kitchen table the next morning. Caroline focused hers on finding a new career. Maggie set the intention that hers bring what she needs to fulfill her life purpose. With each crystal they glued in place they each wrote a related element of their intention.

"I connect spirit to ground," wrote Maggie. "I am open to messages and guidance. I feel and trust the presence of God as father and his loving support at all levels around me. I feel and trust the presence of God as mother and the connection from my heart and essence to hers. I effectively carry out what becomes clear to me. I heal what needs to be healed in me. I allow and accept and welcome expansion. I allow and accept and welcome new patterns. I am ready to be whatever I am becoming." When they put the generator crystals into place, both Maggie and Caroline felt their lives shift.

"This is very exciting," said Caroline.

"Get ready for a wild ride!" Lydia exclaimed later when Maggie read her list of intentions. "You've asked for a lot, and you'll have work to do to get there."

For a moment Maggie shrank back, afraid she'd been foolish. But then she knew she had followed her instincts and guidance and deep knowing, just as she had up in the grid on the mountain. She would be fine.

Two weeks later Stephen asked Maggie to come back out to the mountain grid and help him mark the spot where she sat. A psychic friend told him that an energy vortex opened there as a result. Stephen wanted Maggie to validate this and to tell him what she could about it.

Maggie had heard there were energy vortexes in Sedona, Arizona, but she didn't know what they were. Instead of looking for a vortex, she walked out into the meadow looking for that same sense of right place, and again she found the spot. This time Stephen piled stones there, and she sat on the ground while they talked.

"There's definitely a flow here," she said. "It seems more like an opening than what I picture as a vortex. More like a passage through to someplace else."

"A portal?" asked Stephen.

"I don't really know what these words mean, but portal seems more like it than vortex. There is a lot of energy coming through. Can I sit here again for a while?"

"Sure. I have to go to work, but stay as long as you like."

Maggie had come prepared this time, with blanket, book, water bottle, and travel clock. She sat for two hours and never opened the book. This place provided respite she had never experienced, time out from fitting into anything, a time to let go of every effort and to finally be able to simply be. What a pleasure it was to feel so totally accepted and valued, just as she is.

Stephen called a week later and asked her to come out again. He'd been told that the portal had doubled in size while Maggie was there, and a second portal had opened. When she got there, he led the way up from the bottom, past Maggie's spot. She wanted very much to stop there, but he continued on up through the center of the grid, urging, "Come spend time in the new one, Maggie. It's even better. It's more powerful."

Maggie followed him and stood in the new spot where he had piled more rocks. "This one does feel very strong," she said. "It's insistent, it's pushy strong. I'd rather go sit in the first one."

"Maggie!" interrupted Stephen. "Just while you've been standing here, this new portal has doubled in size." He stepped back four feet to the new outer edge. "Look at this! Somehow your mere presence facilitates these openings."

"Believe me, it's without any effort or understanding on my part," she said, looking back down the field at the first pile of stones. "Stephen, I know you really like this one, but I just don't feel much connection with it. I like the other one. It's gentle and supportive. This one is more intense."

"Well, I like this one," he said, "and I don't feel much at all in the other one. Maybe this one is mine. That first one is definitely yours."

Stephen left her in the first portal and went back to the house. An hour later Maggie stopped by on her way out.

"When I sit in that first portal," she told him, "I get a strong, clear sense of home and being more fully myself. I know who I am. It's wonderful. And then when I settle into that, I get the impression that there in that portal I have access to everything that is mine to know or understand. It's awesome, Stephen. Do you get any of that there?"

"Not that I can tell, but you are much more in tune to this than I am."

Later that week Maggie called Stephen. "I know more now. The first portal is about knowing and the second portal is about expression. Expression is putting things out there, ideas, creativity, who you are, and taking action. That's why it feels more forceful."

"That fits with what I experience there," said Stephen. "I have news, too. I've measured and found that the first portal is exactly one-third of the way up the middle of the grid. And the second portal is exactly another third of the way to the top. Don't you just love this?"

Stephen started referring to the portals as hers and his, and as the feminine one and the masculine one, and every time he did it Maggie winced. The labels carried too many associations and invited too many assumptions. They would direct people's expectations and limit their fully experiencing the portals. Maggie could already see that happening in how Stephen spoke of them.

He listened to her concern and came up with other names, the Earth Portal and the Sun Portal. That felt better, but Maggie still suspected that any naming narrowed perception and understanding.

Stephen began to sit in the portals for twenty minutes each day, alternating between the two of them. Twenty minutes was as much as he could be in the grid without becoming overwhelmed and disoriented. A few other people he knew came to sit in them, too, and none of them could stay more than twenty minutes. Maggie was the only one who could stay there longer.

Everyone preferred the Sun portal, commenting on its power. Maggie felt sad for them. They were missing the more subtle treasures of the other portal. She told Stephen it was good that he alternated even though he preferred the power.

Chapter Seven: Reach Out

When Lydia came for a visit Maggie took her out to meet Stephen and to experience the grid and the portals. Stephen brought them in at the low end of the meadow and up through the middle. Maggie stopped for a few minutes to sit in the Earth Portal while Stephen and Lydia walked on up. She immediately received a series of messages:

- There are no answers; there are only questions.
- Just be.
- Be fully present in each moment.
- There is no past or future.
- There are no fences or boxes or assumptions or rules.
- Have no commitment beyond just being.
- Be open to whatever happens.

Again she felt that she came from some other, faraway place, or some other way of being, and that this spiral grid and its portals connected her there. Again a tremendous, aching yearning overcame over her. She wanted to be home.

Maggie caught up with Stephen and Lydia at the Sun Portal, and together they continued to the top of the meadow to walk the spiral. They followed the path of its planetary nodes from the outermost point, curving around the far edge of the meadow. It seemed to Maggie as if she entered the solar system itself, as if she remembered spiraling in from space, long, long ago. She was a young adult and very attached back to that home place very far away. She remembered changing her mind about coming here, wanting to go back home instead. By the time she reached the grid's Uranus and Saturn nodes, Maggie felt profoundly depressed. She wanted desperately to go to the portal and connect with home, but the guides insisted that she finish following Lydia and Stephen around the spiral. There was something to complete.

Maggie continued, spending enough time at each node to adjust her energy. Again this walk was transforming her. As she approached Tiamat, then Mars, she became more grounded and present and willing to continue.

At the Earth node she no longer felt that strong desire to leave. Moving on, deeper into the solar system and the grid, Maggie even forgot what had been so compelling. And from then on it was simply easier to be here.

❧

Lydia and Maggie talked late into the wee hours that night. Finally Lydia asked, "Maggie, you haven't said anything about the Mary writing for a month or more. What's going on with that?"

"Oh, well, nothing really. I haven't done any of it for quite a while."

"Why not?"

"I guess I'm still awkward about it. Even with all those pages already done, I still don't believe I can do it."

"You're not quitting, are you?"

"I hope not. Keep asking me, okay? Give me a nudge once in a while."

"Sure, if only because I want to read it myself."

❧

Maggie couldn't wait to hear what Lydia had to say after they went to church. "Come on, come on! Tell me!" she urged.

"It's sure different from Mass!" exclaimed Lydia. "Don't you miss the ritual and the incense?"

"No, I don't miss it," said Maggie, laughing. "I never had it."

"Oh, right, I always assume everybody grew up Catholic."

"So, tell me, what about Michael? What did you think?"

"He's kind of cute, but he doesn't do much for me. He's not my type. Sorry."

"Lydia! I'm not asking you to fall in love with him, just tell me what you thought."

Lydia laughed. "Okay. I'm not surprised that you like him so much. He's exciting. He's a damn good preacher. He sure knows how to engage a congregation. I only saw one old guy asleep and I suspect he's hard of hearing."

"Did you catch how he looked at me when he spoke about God challenging us to reevaluate our assumptions and open to living life more fully?"

"Yeah, I noticed that."

"Doesn't it seem like he's telling me he's considering changing paths? Except then nothing changes. He says it and then he goes right back to stay firmly and safely entrenched behind his boundary line."

"So he talks the talk but doesn't walk it?" asked Lydia.

"Is that what it is? Mismatch between public presentation versus private reality is a very bad pattern for me, and painfully familiar."

"Yeah, for starters there are your parents."

"They came across in public as open-minded and liberal, but in private they were tight and controlling and judgmental."

"Michael's not like that, is he?"

"He does have everything pretty much under control, and keeps it that way," said Maggie. Then she sighed and added, "Lydia, there's a lot more of this public-private disconnect in my history."

"Your husband."

"Dan seemed to be a bold adventurer when I met him, but in private he turned out to be very insecure and always worried about other people's expectations and judgments."

"And then there was Alex."

"Yes, him, too. Alex seemed to be all about healing and light, but in reality he lived immersed in constant fear. Lydia, I've been drawn to a whole string of people who repeat this pattern."

"I suggest that you take that pattern one step farther, Maggie."

"To myself? Okay, yes, this definitely points out my resistance to being more of my true, whole, powerful, brave self."

"I told you that manifestation grid was going to challenge you."

"There's an irony here, Lydia. My being more of my potential means opening myself to all levels of being, and that would include allowing fuller expression of the other levels of connection with Michael. As it is, out in the world both he and I barely acknowledge all that. If I start letting it be as extraordinary and marvelous as it seems to be, there will be even more disparity between the other levels and this one."

"Paradox!" exclaimed Lydia. "And the two of you do just love paradox!"

"Damn. I hadn't seen that."

"But it doesn't surprise you, does it?"

"Lydia, this whole thing is so complex and confusing!"

"Only when you try to make sense of it, Maggie. When you let it flow, it all falls into some pretty interesting patterns."

"Why am I even considering this? When I left Alex I swore to myself that I would never again get involved with anyone who didn't proclaim that I am the best thing that ever happened to him."

"And Michael?"

"The bottom line is that he said no. He may seem confused about it, but he said no. If he wanted to be with me he could find a way. He doesn't. And this whatever-it-is we've got going on may be magical and amazing in parts, but it's not enough. It really isn't. I deserve more. I deserve a loving, happening, complete relationship."

"I totally agree with that last statement," said Lydia.

"I don't think either one of us is ready to have a real relationship. We continually alternate between intriguing and frightening each other. I am no more willing to deal with a real man than he is willing to deal with a real woman. We're both scared to death."

"So it's a good match!" declared Lydia, laughing.

❧

When Lydia left the next morning, Maggie spent time writing in her journal. *"I wish Lydia had either said, 'Oh, yes! Michael is definitely the one for you!' or, 'Forget it, Maggie. It's all wrong. Move on.' It doesn't help that she is staying neutral."*

"She's not going to tell you what to do," said Nu.

"No matter what I say or do, when I open to my heart, there is Michael. I'm opening right now and I feel such full and tender love from him. I know he won't allow this on the worldly level, but he definitely wants it on the other levels. And yet I resist. I'm so afraid of getting hurt."

"On those levels there is no getting hurt," said Nu.

"Why is he doing this, Nu?"

"Because he does love you."

"Yeah, sure, he loves some sort of reflection of God in me."

"You say that with such sarcasm, Maggie."

"Isn't he saying, 'I can't love you as you are, but if I see you as a purely spiritual being and we stay on intangible, spiritual levels, then okay, I'm willing to love you'?"

"What is it Michael says about this every Sunday?" asked Nu.

"That we are all images of God, just as we are."

"Yes, and Michael therefore sees you as who you are, an expression of all that is sacred. And as that unique, stunning image of divinity that you are, as that beautiful, true expression of God's desire that is you, Michael loves you."

Maggie sighed. "Okay, Michael, keep coming." Maggie reached out and felt his hands take hold of hers.

Three crows landed on a chimney a hundred yards across from Maggie's window as she wrote in her journal. She watched them, thinking that in ancient nature symbolism the crow reminds us to look for the magic in what is happening. Suddenly one crow flew straight toward her window, cawing all the way, insisting she pay attention. It flew right at her. Only at the very last possible moment, as Maggie gasped out loud and ducked her head, did the crow finally veer sharply up to land on the roof above.

"Okay, God," she said, still shaken, "that certainly got my attention. If you're really telling me that everything is magical and mystical and more than it seems, let's make it really clear. Have another crow do the same." The two remaining crows turned and walked away from her to the far side of the chimney cap.

Maggie laughed, "I am outrageous! How dare I demand confirmation from God? Can't I believe the message I already got?" Just then she heard another series of caws, looked up, and a second crow was flying straight at her. It, too, nearly hit the window glass just before swooping up.

"Damn, this is for real." Maggie stared out the window for several minutes, stunned. The third crow was gone. "You're telling me the world is amazing and mysterious and jam-packed with meaningful messages and signs. And that life is absolutely full of extraordinary, mind-stretching, mystical happenings. I want to get this. I want to know it."

"Jesus said, 'I've come that you might have life and have it more abundantly.' Faith is not about holy thoughts of God or Jesus," said Michael, preaching from the pulpit on Sunday. "Faith is not about going to church, or reading the Bible, or praying, or trying to please God. What makes God happy is when we're living as we're made to live, in the fullness of life. Faith is living as if fullness of life is there for us every moment of every single day. And the way to experience it is through simple acts and experiences of love."

After the service, after they hugged, Maggie kept her hand on Michael's arm and looked into his eyes, and said, "Thank you for being you."

"You're welcome," he said, with a warm smile.

"And thank you for being in my life," she added.

"You're welcome. And thank you for all that, too." He took a few steps away, turned back, and said, nodding, "Yes, all that right back at you, Maggie."

Another Sunday Michael spoke about being and receiving God's treasure. At the end Maggie said to him, "I always hope you listen to yourself on Sundays."

He smiled a tired smile and said, "I do, too."

"Did you listen today?"

He laughed. "Actually, I'm talking to myself up here, and if anybody else gets anything out of it, that's great."

"The messages you offer are so important and helpful. I hope you allow them to work for you, too."

He took hold of both her hands and nodded. But was that a sigh?

"Oh, Michael," she exclaimed, "I don't mean to suggest more for you to take on. I was thinking this would help lighten your load."

"Yes," he said, smiling and squeezing her hands. "I know that. I heard that." He started to move off, then added, "You always give good advice."

❧

The terrorist attacks of September 11 overwhelmed everyone's lives. Maggie did what she could to calm, support, stabilize, and heal. She worked alone and she joined with other healers in the effort. Most clients she saw had a lot of clearing to do, releasing current fears and reactions, as well as older wounds shaken loose by so much threat and insecurity. Maggie went to the church to do treatments for the staff, and called Michael to arrange a session for him.

He arrived a few minutes early and by the time Maggie was ready for him he was on the phone in his office. She smiled, he smiled; he pointed at the phone and shrugged. She said, "Anytime," and she went down the hall to talk with others while she waited. When he did not appear, she went back to his office and now he was working on the computer. She said, "I'm going to put you on the treatment table and work on you, and you can join us anytime you want."

"You mean I can stay here and you'll do your thing while I get work done?" he asked. When she nodded he said, "That's great! Let's do it!"

His field was thick with congestion. She worked to clear it, but lost the energetic connection several times when something back in the office caused him to withdraw his energy. Moving her hands to his heart, she said, "Come on back here, Michael. It's me, it's okay, it's safe." He responded immediately each time, and she easily resumed the work.

She did a lot of clearing and then simply held his heart for quite a while, saying, "Michael, trust me. Let some healing happen." He relaxed and she felt the energy flow until he had drawn quite a lot through her. When it was finished and she moved to release, she could tell he still needed help to maintain the flow. She set it up so that for now he could easily draw more energy through her until he could do it on his own. Then she went to the office to talk with him.

"It's arranged so that you can fill up with energy whenever you need it. It's very easy. Just allow. Just open to it," she said.

He nodded and she knew that he understood. He trusts me, she thought. He's not closing off in the slightest. She decided to take him one step farther.

"When you allow the energy to flow, let it clear things," she said. "Let go of whatever you don't need to hang onto and the flow will carry it off." He nodded vigorously. She could see that he realized this would be very good.

"There was another thing," she said, then stopped and laughed, "but I have no idea what it was." His eyes danced and he started to say something, but she interrupted. "Oh! Oh! I've got it!" He smiled and waited. "It's about my working on you regularly, especially for now. If it's okay, if it doesn't feel invasive."

"I'm not feeling that at all," he said, shaking his head.

"Then that would be very good to do."

"I don't have to physically be there, right?" he asked, looking for her nod. "Then that would be wonderful." He got up and hugged her, looked in her eyes and said, "Thank you very much, Maggie. I really appreciate this."

Later in the day she did a quick remote check on him and found that he was pulling energy through. It was working, and it was good.

"Now that you know how well it works to do it remotely, I don't suppose I'm ever going to get you to physically lie on the treatment table, am I?" she said to his other level self. They both laughed.

❧

9-11 took everybody down, like a strong undertow. Maggie's friends who were usually steady became fearful and depressed. Maggie tried to stay clear and balanced so that she could help others, but eventually she sank into depression, too. She even went late to church on the second Sunday and the only seat was way in the back where Michael never even saw her. She cried all through the service. At the end Michael crossed the sanctuary quickly and was gone before she could catch up to him. How could she leave now? Everything felt wrong. So she stayed for the later service. This time he found her and he kept looking at her as she cried all the way through this service, too.

When she went to him afterward for a hug, he held her tight and long. He asked how she was, but he couldn't hear her answer because his ear was so firmly pressed against her cheek and he would not release his tight embrace. Finally she managed to shift her head just enough so they were cheek to cheek and she could speak into his ear.

"Not so good," she said. "I'm tangled in all my dark stuff."

He looked closely into her face, and then he sighed, "Yes, we're all in it." He seemed lost and exhausted.

"It's okay," she assured him. "It's life. We can do this."

He nodded, then repeated some of what he'd said in the sermon, more to himself than to her. "We just have to settle for not knowing the answers," he concluded.

"You know you're talking to the one who insists on answers," she said.

"I know." He nodded and still held onto her.

"What you said this morning did help me some," she said, trying to encourage him. "Thank you."

"I'm glad." He looked closely at her. "You know we can't expect to make sense out of it."

Maggie nodded and smiled weakly. "I know," she said. But everything seemed so heavy and impossible. She let go of him and turned to leave, not knowing what else to do.

She was several steps away when she barely heard him say, very softly, "I love you." Time stretched and it seemed that nothing moved. The words hung in midair between them. They were so soft. Did he even know he said them out loud? He couldn't have been sure she heard them.

If she reached for those words all the grief of the past twelve days would collapse in on her. More than that, if she looked in his eyes, with those words hanging there between them, how could she not cling to him?

No, she couldn't do this. She had to go. That was clear. She had to go.

She did not turn back. She did not look at him. Gently, with a sigh, she kept walking and left his words there. They were safe there, in the church.

Near the front doors she passed the shadowy form of Mary Magdalene, intently watching her. Maggie shook her head no, and kept walking.

She never told Lydia or Caroline or anyone else what Michael had said. It would have helped her keep hold of it if she had. This way it was so easy to doubt and then to lose it, the way she lost all sorts of extraordinary things. Maybe she didn't tell because she was scared and she was running away from it. Whatever it was, by the next day Maggie came down with a bad cold, and the illness swallowed up the words. She never remembered he'd said it, not even during times she wondered how he felt about her.

The cold worsened fast, burrowing deep into her chest. Thoughts and emotions plummeted in the exhaustion of being ill. Maggie's mind spun with outrageous fears about money, terrorists, Iranian neighbors, the oven catching fire, and dangerous creatures coming up through the drains. She finally asked herself how miserable she needed to get before she would stop all this fear and negativity.

"I don't want to have to hit absolute bottom," she declared. "I want to stop now and say that I won't live feeling this miserable and pathetic. I want to turn back to knowing who I am. Now."

Suddenly she was a creature made of starlight, walking through her rooms, bright and beautiful and magical and clear. None of the worries mattered, none of the details mattered. There was no struggle; there was no need to be in fear. She looked for solid ground to anchor into, expecting the mountains, and instead Michael was there. She didn't remember those words he had said, they were long gone, but as soon as she touched on his energy she knew who she was and everything began to fall back into place.

She set about clearing the illness. Within five minutes the thick, colorful mucus dried up and the coughing ceased. Sinus pressure dissipated and nasal flow ended. The cold completely cleared. Twice later that day she caught herself going back into feeling needy and scared, and the cold symptoms began to return. But when she stopped the attitude, and shifted back into claiming her choices, the cold cleared again. It was really quite remarkable and impressive.

"*I'm stunned by how undeniable this healing is,*" she wrote in her journal. "*There is no choice but to admit it. If I want to be pathetic, I can do that. If I want to be sick, I can be miserably sick. If I want to forget who I am and get lost in a tangle of fear, I can do that. Or I can decide to get clear and move forward. It works. It truly is up to me to claim my strength.*"

Maggie went into another big shift. Again it seemed that everything was new and brimming with discovery. All choices were thrown wide open, all habits and usual responses in flux, and nothing was obvious.

She asked herself what did seem steady. The mountains absolutely did, and the spiritual connection they made easy for her. So did having Michael in her life, and her daughter Rachel, and friend Lydia. After that, and not nearly as solid as the first group, came Caroline, Stephen, a few other friends, the church, and her work. Everything beyond that was uncertain.

One thing definitely shifting was her involvement at the Montford Center. She and the director were not getting along. Teresa's style of leadership was unfocused and lax, and when Maggie tried to clarify or resolve anything, no matter how gently and tactfully, Teresa quickly became defensive and irritated with her, even suggesting that Maggie was being difficult.

It took a while for Maggie to realize that Teresa had begun to deliberately undermine her. Teresa was telling people she was concerned about Maggie. She said Maggie seemed troubled and needed to get some help. She even talked some of Maggie's clients into switching to other practitioners. Maggie realized that Teresa was being passive aggressive and doing things uncomfortably similar to what Alex had done to her.

"Didn't you tell me she flirts with Stephen?" asked Lydia. "I bet she's jealous of how close you and Stephen have become, and that's what's behind this."

"If that's true, what do I do?"

"Whatever it is, your part is the same. Stay in your heart and stay in your integrity. The goal is to not even notice Teresa doing something. If you don't take it on, it has no power."

"But Lydia, she is messing with my clients and ruining my reputation. How can I ignore that? And, why do I have to go through this again?"

"You're going through it again because there is something more to learn. Be grateful that this time at least you're not in love with the person. Being in love with Alex made it much harder, so this is a big improvement. It'll be easier to hang in there till you get the lesson."

Maggie listened, but Lydia's perspective on this just didn't feel right. She wondered to herself if the thing to learn was not how to be in it, but instead how to say, "I deserve better, I don't have to do this," and leave.

"Stay in your heart," echoed Stephen. "Don't get into your head. Trying to figure it out only recycles the problem and invites in lower vibration energies. Stay in your heart and you'll know what to do. You'll advance in your journey."

"But Stephen, I need to figure it out, and it's hard to figure it out without figuring it out!" Maggie declared, laughing as she made fun of herself. "Okay, I'm listening." She took a deep breath. "I am breathing and coming into my heart. I am a model of peace and generosity. Yes. And from here I can see that Teresa is on her own journey, caught up in her own stuff. I can stay centered in who I am."

"Sounds good," said Stephen.

Chapter Eight: Everywhere Touch the Sacred

Maggie began hiking every Tuesday with Jackie Winslow, a new friend from the drumming circle. They went up into the high mountains to follow trails along ridges, up peaks, beside creeks and rivers, to waterfalls and vistas, through wild rhododendrons, fields of blueberries, meadows, and woods. It was marvelous to get out into the mountains so regularly. They made discoveries, told stories, had adventures, and became good friends.

Jackie was earthy and wise. Her sharp blue eyes demanded honesty and presence, and strong facial features along with a firm jaw backed that up. She wasn't interested in delusion or fakery. Maggie liked that.

They enjoyed spending time together along the trail, sitting by a stream, or weeding Jackie's garden, but their favorite thing to do was to talk endlessly at Jackie's kitchen table, in the heart of her home in south Asheville. They talked about anything and everything, and spent enough time at it to even figure some things out. And their very favorite thing to do while talking was to drink lots of good, fresh-brewed coffee way too far into the day.

Robert, Jackie's husband, was the practical one in their family, the organizer and problem solver. He rarely failed to see right to the heart of a matter and offer impressively targeted suggestions. He was the one who convinced Jackie and Maggie to go hiking in the first place. Now he and his family took Maggie in. She often spent an evening at their house for dinner and videos and more talk.

One Sunday at church Michael told a joke about a man falling off a high cliff and catching hold of a root on the way down. The man hung there, two hundred feet above sharp rocks, calling for help. "I'm here," answered God's deep voice. "Let go and I'll catch you." Maggie was riveted. She felt she had been hanging from that root for several months, trying to keep everything under control, unable to trust enough to let go.

The joke was that the man thought about it and then yelled, "Is anybody else up there?" Maggie nodded her head. She had gone through all her friends, asking them for answers. It didn't work. She was still hanging onto the root.

She told Robert and Jackie about the joke, then said, "I don't know what to do. It's as if I've heard God and I cannot let go."

"What if you did let go?" asked Robert. "What would happen?"

"This is the crazy thing. I know that if I let go, not only will everything be fine, life will open up to wondrous things. I still can't even begin to let go."

"What if the rocks and the two-hundred foot drop are an illusion? What if it's only a foot and a half to soft earth?"

She stared at him for half a second, then burst out laughing. The whole scenario, the whole drama had dissolved. "Robert! You just blew the whole thing apart!" she declared. "It's gone."

Later she realized that the cliff and root and rocks, along with looming disaster and needing miraculous rescue, were just one perspective of many possible perspectives. She did not have to stay in it, and she didn't have to play it out either. She didn't have to prove anything. She could simply know what she knows, trust that, and let it go. Then the root and cliff and rocks and falling became irrelevant.

Did this mean that the all tests, dramas, trials, and challenges in her life were unnecessary? Did none of them have any real substance? Could she simply change perspectives, step out of any of them, and go directly into faith and belief and trust? She had done exactly that before, simply left complexity behind and headed onward. Was it really that simple?

"If you can abandon Dad and move to the south, then I can go out west," declared Rachel on the phone.

"One thing has nothing to do with the other," Maggie told her daughter.

"The south, Mom? What were you thinking? Bigotry, anti-Semitism, racism, slavery, sexism, rednecks, lynchings, the Civil War?"

"Everybody thinks this is such an awful place! It's wonderful here, honey. The mountains are beautiful, I love the city, and there are plenty of good people here, like anywhere else. Don't let blind negativity and judgment influence you. Come and make up your own mind. I think you'll really like my new friends. Come check this place out before you decide."

"It's already decided. I sent my letter of acceptance. I'm taking the job in Santa Fe."

"For one year, right?"

"Tenure track. Could be forever."

"You don't want to take the offer at Penn?"

"Too high pressure, and teaching all freshman classes. No, I'd rather teach small classes of upper level students who are actually starting to design buildings. This way I can be more creative. You're always telling me to listen to my heart. That's what I'm doing. Are you doing that, Mom? Isn't your heart really always going to be with Dad? It's not too late to work things out, you know. He's so sad. He just wants to go back to the way things were."

"I know, and that's exactly what I can't do. I can't go back."

"You won't even try!"

"I've tried, honey, more than you'll ever know. More than he'll ever know."

"I don't believe you. And I'll never forgive you for destroying our family!" Rachel slammed down the phone.

Maggie sighed and laid the silent phone into its cradle, her eyes filling with tears. She never meant to leave her daughter, too.

Maggie called Rachel again a week later. "How about coming here for your winter break, Rachel? You can meet my friends and check out my new life."

"I thought you were going to Aunt Caroline's to do Christmas again."

"No, that's not working out. If you come here I'll skip all the Christmas stuff."

"Does this mean you'll come back to being Jewish?"

"I doubt it, Rachel. Certainly not right now."

"Is this some sort of passive aggressive way to get at Dad? Damn it, Mom, I just don't understand you any more."

"Come spend some time with me, honey. We can talk."

"If you're not going to Caroline's, then let's both go to Dad's for that week. We can talk there."

Maggie sighed and didn't know what else to say. She had said no so many times.

"Well, then," declared Rachel, "I'm going to the beach with Joan, and Dad'll be all alone."

"That strategy is not going to work, Rachel. You're not thirteen any more."

"Fine. Have it your way, then. Ruin everything." Rachel hung up on her again.

By the time Maggie met her, Amy Wilmot had been through two years of surgeries and chemo and radiation that had done a lot of damage. She was scheduled to go to Texas for more abdominal surgery in August.

Amy was beautiful inside and out. She was 42 years old, petite, with a pretty face, large, clear honey-brown eyes, a strong chin, and bouncy, shoulder-length, blonde hair. Her deep-south accent grounded her into the land. Amy loved anything about real people: music, stories, folk art, faces, family, hopes, gatherings, sharing. She had been a high school English teacher until her illness interfered. She loved teaching. She loved the kids and she loved the adventure and discovery of working with them.

Amy didn't show her fear to many people; she didn't want to worry them. But her body betrayed that just as it had other intentions. Her blood pressure rose too high now whenever anything medical was happening. Amy didn't want to take any more drugs, so Tory had asked Maggie to see what she could do to help.

They did the sessions at Amy's house in North Asheville's historic Manor House neighborhood. The rooms were too crowded with antiques and artwork to bring in a treatment table, so they cleared the clustered candle centerpiece off the dining room table, spread out a quilt, and Amy climbed up to lie on it.

Amy was surprised she could feel what Maggie was doing when Maggie wasn't even touching her. "And now how can your hands still be at my feet when you're up here at my head?" she asked.

Maggie chuckled and said, "I'm not sure how that happens, but people are always telling me I've got extra hands."

"Well, I can't believe how relaxed I feel."

"Good. That's what we want. Take a couple of deep breaths and really get into feeling that. Get used to it."

After several weeks of working with Amy, Maggie asked for Lydia's advice. "I can clear her fear and stress, get her really relaxed and calm, and get her blood pressure down. I can balance her energy so that it flows well and it seems that she is fine, but I can't do any substantial work. I don't know how to explain it. I can go deep, but I'm not getting access to much. I still don't know anything about the cancer. I can't get to it."

"She's on her path, Maggie."

"Are you saying I can't do anything that might alter her path? All I can do is make things a little easier for her as she walks it?"

"How are you with that limitation?"

"It's humbling. It puts me face to face with my role in this work. I expect to fix things, and when I can't I assume I'm failing."

"It's not about success or failure, Maggie."

"Right. Let go of expectations. I hear you, but you know how I love validation. There's no validation in this."

"The validation is just different. It's more subtle."

"It's so subtle I don't get it at all."

"You know how to hold the space for something, just supporting it, paying gentle attention to it, allowing it to be what it can be."

"But Lydia, that's not enough here. This is serious stuff. I need to make a difference. I need to fix this."

"This is more complicated than that, and hard to do. You're in grad school now, Maggie. Congratulations!"

"Not fixing it is grad school?"

"Come out of the physical and into the higher levels. Don't you see it?"

"I see it, but...let the cancer...accept it?"

"Yes, Maggie. It's her path. If you were meant to heal it you'd already be doing that."

"That does explain why I can't get to it. Damn. This is really tough, Lydia."

"Welcome to my world."

"I feel very drawn to her. I've been spending three or four hours, day after day, just being with her whenever she's in the hospital while she waits for the Texas surgery. I simply, strongly want to be there. She and her husband, David, totally accept whatever I want to do. They say come whenever I feel like it and stay for as long as I want, so I go when I feel the pull. I'm wondering if this may somehow be as much for me as it is for Amy."

"You are on your path, too," said Lydia.

One day Maggie picked up Amy at her house to take her for a session at the Montford Center. Amy wanted to see and experience the place where Maggie usually worked. She seemed so frail out in the world, and Maggie wondered if this outing was a mistake. But when Amy was determined about something, and she was determined about doing this today, everybody better make way because she was going to do it.

"I just need to drop off this basket at a neighbor's on the way, if you don't mind," Amy said as she lifted it into the car.

"What is this you're doing now?" asked Maggie, with a smile.

Amy had baked twelve dozen blueberry muffins and was distributing them around the neighborhood.

"You're incredible," said Maggie. "You're always thinking of everybody else."

"Oh, that's not true. You know that."

"Well, I'm going to try to convince you to be more selfish."

"It's all selfish, Maggie. I'm doing what I want to do. Nothing gives me greater pleasure than someone's appreciation. That's selfish."

❧

"How's Amy doing?" asked Lydia a few weeks later.

"She's out in Texas, getting settled in. The surgery is in two days. She sounds pretty good on the phone. I keep working on releasing stress for her."

"And how are you?"

"I feel like I've prepared her as well as I can. I made an audio tape for when I'm not around. We're hoping the sound of my voice will soothe her the way my presence does. I recorded a meditation, a grounding exercise, and some guided relaxation. I also sang a couple of songs from church that we both love."

"You didn't answer my question. I just thought I'd point that out. It's easier to talk about her than yourself, isn't it? So, how is she feeling about the surgery?"

"She so much wants to live. She loves life and she is very brave. She's an amazing person. Pray for a miracle, Lydia."

"I already am."

❧

Amy's surgery took all day, fourteen hours. David called after it was done to tell Maggie that she had come through it well. She was in recovery and would go up to the room soon. The doctors told him they felt good about the results.

Maggie had been praying and singing and doing what she could energetically since the night before. She sat in silence long after hanging up the phone, thinking about Amy, this remarkable woman who had become such a presence in her life. Then she whispered, "Thank you, God."

It would be three months before Amy came home. They kept her in Texas for radiation and chemo and careful observation. Maggie turned to her own life, and her days filled up.

Strangers gathered in the middle of the big grid. Stephen's psychic sources had told him that the two portals would eventually join to form one large energy vortex, and from there the stabilizing influence of the grid would spread to touch every spot on the earth. Stephen wanted to go ahead and create that now. He set the group's intention to calm worldwide tensions and promote creative problem solving.

Everything felt weird, not at all Maggie's familiar experience of being there. She recognized a few people, but most of the eighteen participants were strangers, and none could be mistaken for the country club set. There were spacey ones, trailing floaty scarves and long tunics and speaking loudly in flowery, complex language. There were intense, dramatic ones dressed all in black, one all in white carrying a single flower, and a few more earthy types. Many were trying to impress each other, while a few were simply watching and waiting. Maggie unobtrusively scanned their energy fields, checking for anything negative or menacing. She wondered if anyone noticed her doing that. Although there was plenty going on in their fields, nothing was dangerous. Maggie settled into being one of the quiet ones. When Stephen began speaking and referred often to her experiences with the grid and the portals, she did not add to what he said, just nodded and stayed focused on him.

The ritual was powerful. Maggie and several of the others had difficulty moving though the energy changes so quickly. She wanted more time to adjust, and sometimes it seemed nearly impossible to continue, but Stephen kept everything moving fast and she didn't want to interfere with his concentration, so she didn't say anything. He was totally focused on facilitating the process, and did not seem at all aware of anything but that. It was left to each of the participants to keep up.

They buried crystals in a circle around the center point of the grid, and each person charged each crystal with intention and movement. Then they joined the two portals to the center, anchoring it. When they completed the ritual back at the center, Maggie felt streams of energy spread out through the earth, drawn to specific points and areas.

By the time the ritual was finished it had lasted well over an hour and she was exhausted. Many of the others seemed disoriented and some almost panicky, but Stephen felt great. He wanted everyone to stay right there to talk about what had happened. When the group elected to leave the grid now rather than stay any longer, Stephen was clearly disappointed. Maggie just wanted it to be over.

❧

A few days later Maggie called Stephen. "This morning I went back into the energy of the grid and clarified some places left uneven or incomplete. I couldn't do it that day with so much going on."

"Thank you for doing that. Have you noticed anything else?"

"The two portals are still distinct and basically unchanged. The new center is very powerful. Maybe it is some sort of generator or transformer."

"That's interesting. Keep me informed as you learn more."

"Stephen, it was difficult for me to move through the ritual at your pace. I wanted to ask for more time, but it didn't feel right, so I concentrated on keeping up."

"I'm glad you didn't say anything. It would have influenced others and thrown the whole thing off."

"There is one other thing, and I hope you are okay with my saying this. My impression is that the effects will be gradual. The changes will come up from underneath and grow rather than burst out and quickly take over."

Maggie wished they were speaking face-to-face. Stephen had such boyish enthusiasm, always wanting fast, impressive, widespread results. And he really wanted it. He would have given everything he was to have their work dramatically change the world for the better.

"You know," she added, "if everything suddenly did change, we'd be looking at it from within the change, changed ourselves, too. I'm not sure we'd be able to tell."

Stephen laughed, then said, "I know it's ego, this wanting to make a difference. A big difference! No subtlety for me! But I'm already letting go of it,

Maggie. I've done what I was supposed to do, and now it will be what it is. It's out of my hands."

Stephen built a circle of large stones around the new center and put a bench there. That became the place where he and anyone else who came to the grid chose to spend their time. Maggie wondered if anyone but her ever went to the Earth Portal.

Several weeks later Stephen asked Maggie to try a new elixir he had charged using the energy flow at the portals. He was told that it would help people work through and clear whatever was holding them back from being all they can be. He gave Maggie one of the bottles charged at the Earth Portal.

"Put two or three drops under your tongue each day," he said, "and let me know what you notice. I'm eager to hear what you can tell me about it."

Maggie was cautious. She'd had bad experiences trying other people's techniques or treatments, and she never would have considered trying anything like this except that it was to help Stephen and it came from the grid. At first she simply held the bottle in her hands and allowed it to gently influence her. She felt some clearing and releasing. Impressed, she repeated this a few times over the next couple of weeks.

One day she decided to take it farther. She squeezed one drop of elixir into a quarter cup of apple juice. With the first tiny sip, she asked to release fear-based perspectives and come into her heart, into love and trust. Again there was clearing. She took another small sip, asked for more releasing, and felt completely peaceful. With the third sip she asked to release any doubts that the results of this would hold, and with the fourth said, "So be it." She left most of the mixture in the glass, taking in less than a quarter of a drop of elixir with the four sips.

Maggie felt so relaxed by this time that she couldn't remember what had needed releasing. She smiled, recognizing this sign of a good release. Maybe this elixir would be an effective tool. Could she write up directions for someone else to follow? How exciting for Stephen.

Then that night she slept badly, and the next day she felt achy and muddle-headed, getting worse fast as her thoughts ran rampant with self-criticism and increasing negativity. By midmorning Maggie realized that her energetic patterns were alarmingly out of sync. She could have corrected this on someone else, but she was never as effective working on herself, and especially not while in this condition. Unfortunately Lydia had just left on a two-week trip to Europe, and this was no time to take a chance on a less familiar healer making things even worse. She was on her own.

Focusing as much as she could, Maggie realized that the elixir speeded up some things and not others. Stephen always wanted things to move fast, and he probably asked for certain quick results when he developed this. Now Maggie's energetic patterns were jarringly mismatched. She had to get herself back to harmony and balance, but from within the turmoil she couldn't see how. Frightened and trying not to panic, she felt vulnerable, like a baby bird fallen out of the nest, lying exposed on the sidewalk.

I need to go sit in my meditation chair and breathe, she told herself. I can at least do that.

It was a good move. After a few minutes of conscious breathing, a message made it through to her. Ask the guides to help. As soon as Maggie asked, a familiar crew of energetic beings encircled her, eager to help. Relieved, she realized once again that we always have to ask. They never just come in. Now they busied her with doing basic balancing on herself, while they got to work on reestablishing her field. An hour later Maggie was fine, and very grateful for it.

"The elixir may be really good," she told Stephen, "it may be amazing stuff, but I can't use it."

"Maybe it is too good."

"I often can't tolerate treatments that are fine for other people. I can't even receive Reiki, and everybody loves Reiki, so don't decide based on my experience. Maybe it just needs fine tuning."

"Well, whatever is supposed to happen will show up. I appreciate your feedback, as always. Keep letting me know."

❧

The next time Maggie visited the big grid it felt familiar again. The other people's influences had cleared. She spread a blanket and spent the next couple of hours in the Earth Portal. Stephen came up after work, and she went with him to sit on the bench in the center. They spent the next hour and a half there, talking about their lives and what was going on for them. Stephen was thrilled he could stay in the grid this long and feel fine. They both left when Maggie needed to get back to the city.

By now Maggie knew the energy patterns of the grid so well that she could enter its energy remotely from anywhere as easily as remembering a familiar place. The process was similar to doing remote healing or connecting with Michael on the other levels, a matter of opening to it and allowing herself to be in it. She didn't need to go to the grid to spend time in it, so she did not drive out to Stephen's for quite a while. Their phone conversations grew less frequent, too, when Stephen became involved in a new romance. Lydia still thought Stephen would be a good partner for Maggie, and urged her to seriously consider it before it was too late. For just a moment Maggie wondered if she was missing her chance to create a real relationship. No, she shook her head. That was not what she and Stephen were meant to be.

Michael's love for Jesus and the Jesus story was dazzling during the weeks leading up to Christmas. Two weeks before Christmas he spoke about Mary's initial visit from the angel. "The archangel Gabriel came to a young, teenage Mary. She was a peasant girl, barely past childhood, and the angel told her she would give birth to the son of God. Imagine it! You're fourteen years old and an angel knocks on the door saying, 'God has a job for you.' At first Mary was frightened. Who wouldn't be? And she asked, 'How can this be?' But then she just knew she would do it. She said, 'Yes, let it be for me to do.' Thank God she said yes.

"Messages come to all of us, saying, 'Open yourself, God is about to happen here and you are the one to carry it into the world.' We may be frightened, we may feel inadequate, we may delay and resist and deny. The angel told Mary, 'Do not be afraid.' Can we have the wisdom and the courage of a teenager named Mary? Can we say yes?"

Amazing things had happened all through Maggie's life to show her that there was more going on than seemed obvious. She had learned to put them aside so that she could go on coping with practical matters. She heard other people talk about spiritual awakenings, describing experiences very much like hers, and how their lives completely changed as a result. Maggie wondered why her experiences didn't dramatically transform her life like theirs did, but she put that aside, too, and kept going.

When Maggie began working with energy, she realized she was on a path, being led, step by step, lesson by lesson, toward a new away of being. She was aware that powerful spiritual forces watched over her. Still, she refused to admit the full reality of all this. She still tried to keep things practical and ordinary.

Now Michael asked, "Can you allow an angel to knock on your door and say, 'God has a job for you'? Can you summon your courage and stand up for what you know you should be doing? Can you be a womb through which God comes into the world? Can you say, 'Yes, let it be for me to do'?" Try saying it with me. 'Yes, holy one, I will do it. I will be a vessel for divine fertility and give birth to God's love in the world.'"

Maggie couldn't stop her tears. She felt an unusual pain, an exquisite pain, as if it was very high-pitched, like sound out of hearing range. Was this spiritual pain?

Sometimes in the shower, with her head under the running water, Maggie opened herself to the divine and really felt it. And sometimes when she did this she found herself saying, out loud, "I am yours." She never knew what it meant, or how she dared to say it, but she knew, when she said it, that it came from deep in her core, and at that level of her being there was no question or hesitation.

Yet out in the world she still resisted. She put aside anything that stretched ordinariness too far and lived as if none of these unusual things ever happened. This time she had not done any more writing for Mary Magdalene's story for months, avoiding it, resisting. Michael's words were an insistent and compelling message to face Mary and all of the other remarkable things that were happening to her. This was a call to pay attention and be responsible to them. It was a call to be brave and full of faith like that teenager Michael spoke about. It was a call to stand in the fullness of her life and say, "Yes, let it be for me to do."

Michael kept looking at Maggie all through this service. Some of the time he looked at her every time he looked up from his notes, as if she were the only one there. She stayed for the late service, too, moving way to the back so she could be alone and cry, but he found her there and still looked at her. She went to talk to him afterward.

"Everything you said today...was..." she choked, tearing up again, and tapping her hand on her heart. He finished her sentence with her, both of them saying in unison, "right there," as he nodded and tapped his own heart.

"I suppose you're totally booked this week?" she asked.

He nodded, looking even more concerned, and asked if she could talk with another person who counseled church members.

"I really don't want to start from scratch explaining everything to someone I don't know very well."

He was already nodding, and he said, "I understand."

She looked in his eyes again. There he was, looking back at her, caring and supportive. She took a deep breath, then said, "Okay, I'm doing this."

He looked hopeful. "Okay?"

She nodded and said, "I need to do this myself."

He gathered her into another hug. When they separated she looked in his eyes and took another deep breath, really being there, letting herself feel it and know it. When she reached down for her bag and coat, he kept his hand on her back and said, "You'll be okay." Facing him again, she nodded and smiled, and squeezed his hand as she left.

"Lydia," Maggie said later on the phone, "I've cried all through two services and I'm a wreck. Tory told me I am having spiritual birthing contractions."

"What are you giving birth to?" asked Lydia.

"There's Mary's book, but that's not ready yet. I think it must be me. I must be birthing myself."

"Congratulations, Maggie."

"Lately I've been so sensitive. I do okay for a while, then things start to be overwhelming. Suddenly I just have to stop, right then, either immediately sit down and stop, or go straight home and write in my journal until things sort out and ease."

"Sure does sound like birthing to me," said Lydia. "I can tell you, having gone through three childbirths myself, that tensing up is just going to make it harder, cause more pain, and even do damage. Letting go allows it to happen easier, though nothing makes birthing truly easy or painless."

"Rachel was a c-section. I never did that part."

"Well, welcome to the club now. Hey, Maggie, didn't you tell me you've been doing nesting things in your apartment, cleaning and clearing and simplifying? I hadn't thought about it before, but females of all species instinctively do that when they're preparing to give birth."

"Yes, and I remember doing that before Rachel was born. You're right, it was just like this," exclaimed Maggie. "It's very compelling to clear out everything I don't absolutely need and organize what's left, all before something—I haven't known what—happens. Yes, this is a birthing."

PART TWO

RISING

Sun Rises

The sun rises reluctantly in the mountains.
First light eases in, muted, spreading behind the eastern ridge,
backlighting the sky,
a subtle drama of understated luminescence.
It is an hour before the sun itself appears,
an hour as soft glow graciously invites morning to begin,
before the fullness of light streams across meadow and forest and city,
before day surrounds all, bringing even the shadows to light.
It's an hour before undeniably golden brilliance enters the room,
wakes everything in its path,
and dances through crystal prism rainbows into your eyes.

In the desert,
where the land runs for miles without respite,
the sun materializes on the horizon,
blazing molten ore,
naked, demanding,
it burns sharp in eyes and harsh along edges,
glare and heat ignite the air.
No embrace, no coddling ease, no forgiveness here,
only confrontation.
Insistent reveille.

The earth turns, and the sun rises,
no matter where we are,
no matter what we think,
no matter what we fear.
It turns no matter what we do,
no matter what we need,
no matter what we want.
Another dawn, another time,
welcome or demanding, subtle or severe,
the earth turns and the sun rises
and the light appears.

Sit on the steps of a downtown parking building
with a raggedy man who hides his bottle,
and look in his beautiful, bleary eyes
as he holds your hand and prays for you.
"Can I keep this string of bells?" asks a friend, "I really like it."
"Sure," you say, "if you like it you keep it,"
and you smile at each other's delight.
A visitor settles deep into the chair, wanting to talk,
you release expectations and plans for the evening.
All this, instead, rises before you,
like sun into day, like morning light,
no matter what you might have anticipated,
coming anyway.

The earth turns and the sun rises
on rock and sand, on mountain and desert, on ocean and city.
It rises slow and sudden, harsh and kind, joyful and intense.
It rises on past and future, on courage and pain and death and grace.
The earth turns,
the sun rises,
the light appears,
and we find ourselves in it.
And we find ourselves,
in it.

Chapter Nine: Sun Rises

"Maggie, why are you calling so late? It's Christmas Eve, I just got to bed, and you know we have to be up early with the grandkids."

"He's gone, Caroline. It's over."

"Who is gone?"

"Michael."

"Stop being so dramatic and just tell me what happened."

"Okay," she sighed. "For the past two weeks, everything has been absolutely wonderful. Best ever. Michael has been acting like I'm the most important person in the room every time I saw him, very attentive, focused on me, kind, smiling, and laughing. It was irresistible. I gave in and let myself believe we were going to be together. I opened my heart." Maggie's voice broke into sobs.

Caroline let out a big sigh of her own, then asked, "But Maggie, what about the boundary line and honoring his vows?"

"I thought he must have decided he could handle it. I thought between the two of us we could deal with just about anything."

"So, what happened?"

"With no warning at all, day before yesterday, Sunday morning, he wouldn't look at me. I mean not even a quick glance. And he rushed out of the sanctuary so fast I couldn't get to him."

"Maybe something happened."

"I tried to think that, except he did it again tonight at the Christmas Eve service. He never looked at me, not once. And it was just me. He was looking at plenty of other people just fine. He had to work at it, too, deliberately, to completely avoid me like that. It was awful. It was cruel, Caroline. He set me up these past two weeks of being super affectionate, and then he slammed the door right in my face, brutally cutting me off. At Christmas!"

"Something must have happened, Maggie. There must be an explanation."

"Nothing that I know of. Damn, I feel abandoned in an endless, lifeless void with nothing solid to hang onto. This is a nightmare."

"Take a couple of breaths, Maggie."

"I'm devastated, Caroline. I took a chance and opened my heart, and now it's left out there between us, shredded and bleeding. Damn!"

"He must have gotten scared, Maggie. You know, during the holidays people get really emotional and vulnerable. People do things they wouldn't do otherwise."

"He really does not want to love me, Caroline. He wants to stay with his vows. He's working very hard to do that."

"Sounds like it. Oh, Maggie, I'm very sorry it's turning out this way."

"So now I'm the bad guy, threatening the sacred promise. Caroline, I don't want to be that! I'm not a bad person."

"Of course you aren't. Nobody is saying you are."

"He is, isn't he? When he runs away from me like he did tonight, when he treats me like I'm toxic? He's being good, all focused on God and Jesus and responsibility, and I'm threatening to ruin everything.

"Can you give this some time?"

"You mean so we can go back to doing our bizarre little dance along the boundary line?"

"You're hurt, you're confused—"

"Yes, I'm hurt! And I'm confused! I really don't understand how he could be so cold to me tonight if he cares for me at all. I was so happy just a few days ago. How can such fullness turn to such emptiness?"

Caroline sighed and asked, "When will you see him again?"

"Next Sunday, I guess. If I go."

"Why don't you take this time to get yourself really centered and strong in who you are and what matters to you. And then see how things are on Sunday."

"I don't have much choice about that, do I?"

"I mean don't make any decisions, Maggie. Don't do anything about it for now. Just let it ride for the rest of the week. You don't want to burn your bridges at this point."

"I don't think I have any bridges."

"You know what I mean."

❧

The next morning was Wednesday, Christmas morning. Maggie picked up her journal to write, threw it back down, and cried out loud, "God, why did you even show me what Michael and I could be? Why did you get me to open my heart? Do you want me to be this alone and raw and hurting today?"

Maggie left everything and drove up into the mountains. She walked along an icy river and sat on cold rocks watching the low, solstice sun through bare-branched trees. She let the beauty of nature gather the pieces of her wounded heart and hold them for her. Her tears became part of winter and her cries scattered into the unforgiving cold of this sacred day. Her body shivered, but her soul found solace in the mountains, and her mind found resignation and acceptance.

"Okay, Michael," she cried out, "be closed if that's what you choose. Be careful, be afraid, cling to the false security of what is familiar. Be whatever you choose; do whatever you do; I release you."

Back at home in the afternoon, she picked up the journal again. Words were coming and she didn't know whether they were Mary's or her own.

"Just write them," said Mary. "They are mine, and you need them now."

"You've been watching all this?"

"Yes."

"You watch Michael and me whenever we're together. Why?"

"Write. This comes from a while after Jesus died. It is from when I had to find my own way with life and with becoming who I am."

Mary's Words

I stood in the early morning sun and felt myself renewed. The sun's light entered my body, my form, my being, as it enters a leaf, revealing its essence and patterns, illuminating vein and inner beauties. It came through me, glowing, warming, making me a bright light. God came through me as light, shining into my crevices and dark passages, through doubt and anger and hesitation, through each intersection with confusion, through every smallness and constriction, through fear and sorrow and loneliness and memory, through all I was and am and will be, until there I stood, naked and empty before it and in it and of it. Until I was but a reflection of pure light and nothing more.

I began to shake. It was as if my mortal body could not contain such purity, could not bear such beauty, as if its material could not be of such an essence. I shook for a long while, as my body eased into new being, new essence, new clarity, new hope.

I would be me now, the voice told me, a new, no, a real version of who I am and had always waited to be. And in that realness I would carry this same light, this aliveness, this wholeness, to whatever I do, to whomever I touch. I would be this light. It would come through me, as it does this morning, to touch others, to spread through more confusion and darkness, until there is light everywhere, until there is no more obscurity, until there is nothing but peace.

I stood in the early morning sun and let it teach me who I am.

I stood in the early morning sun and let myself become who I am.

I stood in the early morning sun and transformed into what I had always been. I found my true being. All else fell away but that light and that knowing. All else. It was the most peaceful and the most complete I had ever been. No other wants or wishes or needs or hopes or questions. Just this. Completed. I was completed.

On this day, the light of God entered me and I was completed.

"Mary, I want to work," declared Maggie as soon as this passage was written. "I want to immerse myself in writing your words. Let's do it. Now. Please. You told about the years at Sanctuary Farm, what's next?"

"This next part comes several years later. Some of it I shared before, but let's put it all together now."

"Okay. Go."

Mary's Words

I met Jesus on the road. I had been walking to the house of someone I once knew, hoping there would be a place there for me to sleep and stay for a few days. Some would take me in, at least for a while, until whispers created uneasiness, and then their faces scowled and words shortened.

Most men didn't look me in the eyes, but Jesus did. His eyes reflected more in me than I'd felt in a long time. I had seen him before. I had heard him speak once at the edge of a marketplace, but how could he have known me like that?

He was an ordinary-looking man with sharp eyes and full lips, dark curls fell onto his forehead, his long fingers traced words in the air. He was of slight build, but his feet lay snugly onto the earth. There was a brightness to him, in his mind, yes, but also a sense of brightness that surrounded him or came from him. It was quite appealing. And compelling. That was what drew the crowd. That and his words. He spoke words that came right into our hearts and into our minds, that took hold of us. We couldn't ignore them. At least I couldn't. Others stayed away or wandered off, but many were as captivated as I was.

He spoke at the marketplace about being the person who did the right thing for the right reason at the right time, no matter what else was going on. The person who stands firm, knowing it is the thing to do, and the way to be. Afterward I felt brave and strong and able to do better at life. I remembered the feel of that afternoon through many days that followed, and it helped me find my way.

And now on this summer afternoon on the road, I collapsed right there at his feet. I'd fallen because I was exhausted from the long walk in a dry, hot day, but it was more than that. I surrendered into a place to be, a given place. It was such a relief! I wanted to be there. It had been a long time since I wanted to be somewhere. He raised me up, his hands cool in the burning sun. I could see that he was tired, too. His eyes bore that ache from too much to carry. I looked around; a crowd had gathered, come upon us from behind him, so many wanting him. They pulled on him from every direction, yet he still made himself available.

In my pouch I found that soft pink stone that comforts the heart. I'd carried it for years, since Sanctuary Farm. Looking in his eyes, I pressed it into his hand. He looked startled, not used to receiving. Then glancing down at it he smiled, closed his fingers around it, and tucked it away near his heart.

I followed at the edge of the crowd. We walked to a knoll where everyone sat on the ground and listened while Jesus spoke. He was talking about children this time, except we were the children, children of God, and God is our father. He spoke about God loving us like a father loves us, attending to us, watching us, following us, knowing us, caring and providing, loving, holding, cherishing. I felt something wrap around me, embracing me like a thick blanket on a cold day, bundling me into safety and peace and love and joy. I felt it come into me, filling me up, filling empty places in me. Others felt it, too.

We all sat there, our eyes shining, not wanting to move when it was over. Jesus sat there, too. We stayed right there as the sun dropped low and the breeze picked up and you'd think we'd have been cold, but we weren't. Not at all.

Finally two men built a fire and some people left while some stayed and slept by the fire. And that's how I came to follow him. I never left.

—

Did he mean to say there is grace for everyone? There are those who are righteous, who carefully follow the religious laws. What about those women who prepare two days for Shabbat and a month for Pesach? What about those men who never miss shul and live lives filled with holy reverence? What about the boys who study all day every day? What about the Talmud? What about the rabbis? Is he saying none of that matters? How can he say we are all the same in God's eyes? Is he saying I can be me and still be in God's grace? How? Why?

I don't understand this man! He baffles me. He takes all I've been told to consider all my life and throws it into turmoil.

What about all the mistakes, what about all the wrongness, what about all the out and out bad things I have done and been done to and fell into and become? What about all those wrong choices, or when I had no choice, when I had to survive, when I had to do what was in front of me? Is he saying I can have done all that and still be God's beloved child?

He said blessed are the ones who follow their noses into that which presents itself in pain and despair. He said grace loves the one who lifts up her eyes to see the moment in the midst of anguish. He said ugly truth is beautiful. He said God is in ugly truth. He said fortify your will to stand tall even as you wallow in the sins of the earth, for it is there that the light of God's love shines strongest. He said I—me!—I am the light in God's eyes! Even as I am wracked with the sobs of hopelessness. He said there is no place without God. He said there is no heart without acceptance and love and hope and possibility. He said there is no darkness without light, or light without darkness, and it is all—ALL—blessed with holiness.

Can we believe this?

And yet…I cannot dismiss it. I cannot dismiss him.

He touched my head, again, and I felt so peaceful. He takes me to a place where there is no hunger, there is no hurting, there is no fear, there is no violence, there is no hatred. Where I can be still, where I can breathe, where I can rest, where I can imagine a life of more than surviving. Just being near him I can find my own mind, I can find my own thoughts and yearnings and dreams, I can find my own being.

Does he bring with him some knowing the rest of us only imagine? I long to know like that, to walk with burning feet in the hot sun and feel only coolness, to let go the crowd and know only their goodness, to trust the forgiving heart of holiness beyond holy, love beyond love.

Sometimes I know what he means. Sometimes I glimpse what he

says. Sometimes I am there.

When I was a girl I was the one to draw and carry water from the well at the center of town in the early morning before and as the sun rose. It was solitary and quiet, even as we gathered to wait our turn to fill our jugs. The men and boys passed by, close to the wall, heading for shul to pray. We kept our faces turned away to not distract them. We kept our voices low. It was a quiet time, a special time for us too, gathering at the water while they gathered at the words.

I imagined God there in mysterious first light, in soft flowing water, in bare feet padding on dry earth, in coming together, in touches and muffled tones and reassurance of another day beginning. I imagined God there with us as much as in the shul, God within precious water and dawn and women and children as much as in holy words. I felt the Shechina, Mother-God, bless our daily rituals of earth and water and fire and air, filling them with as much holiness and presence as God did the praying of the men and boys.

It was just another kind of holiness. To tell the truth, I would rather feel my feet in the dirt and hear the water splash and watch the light illuminate the world in that coming-from-within way dawn brings than stand in shul chanting prayers—even though it is at the holy of holies. Perhaps if I were a boy I would understand that, but I was always relieved to be in the water line instead of tying phylactories and marching off to shul. I was relieved to be a girl among brothers and among those who came to the well.

That was before I knew what it meant to be female in the rest of life. You can't stay a child fetching water at dawn. You have to go out and do the day.

But I wouldn't change it, even now. Even after all I've been through. I'd still rather know the dawn than the shul. I'd rather know morning's gentle kiss of newness than lose myself in chants and ceremony. They speak the prayer thanking God for the dawn, and they may truly mean it, but do they let the dawn enter into who they are? Do they become renewal? Do they become newness? Do they feel the hope and possibility in each birthing day the way we do as we stand with our feet in the dirt and let the light grow in our eyes every blessed morning? Do they let the Mother-God surround them and be with them and within them in such an intimate way?

Now I remember it! I felt precious! A precious one within the new light and soft beginnings of day, within the re-beginnings of life each early morning at the well. I felt safe and loved within the awakenings, within the potential for newness, within the renewal itself. I, too, did know what this man Jesus says is how things are. I was there.

—~—

Following Jesus in those early months, I did not know how to be with all that was coming to me. I had to find my way with it. God was such a mystery to me then. There seemed to be no boundaries.

I went to where no one has ever been there with me. And there you were, God. I went to where I thought there was no way to be there with me. And there you were. It seemed that no matter what, there you were. Out in places where nothing can touch, nothing can bear, nothing can exist, nothing can stay, nothing can hold. Just you and me. That was it. Just you and me, out there alone.

So now I put one foot in front of the other foot and I keep on walking out there, even though nobody else can even see me, let alone be there with me. And I go and I go and there I am, out there, out there, out there, and there you are, keeping right with me. Even though nobody else will even look at me, nobody else will even acknowledge me, nobody else will even take a breath with me, nobody else will even imagine me out there where I really am. And then I know. I am me and I am there and I am who I always was and will be and it is what it is. It is what it is. It is what it is.

I look far into the distance and close into tiny spaces and, doubled up again within myself, I pour anguish into joy into despair into brilliance into bitterness into mirth into dark holes of emptiness that call my name, and God, you draw me there and farther and more, collapsing within impossibilities that break open my soul and cast it beyond dreaming and contemplation. You take my tiniest bits of resistance and make them the greatest tools that ever came through me. You open me to such vastness, such ecstasy of expression, such blissful resonance of simple, expansive existence. And you fill that, you settle there, you become all that and you are all that, and you are me in that, and I know you then. I know me then. And I know being.

I cannot take one step now without knowing it is right. Without first feeling that sureness that comes with your presence. I cannot take for granted anything that preceded this vision of your face in mine. Every moment is new exploration of aliveness and being and truth. Every movement is fresh clarity of expression. Every breath is an exquisite experience of absolute, tender perception.

"Why" doesn't matter. It doesn't mean a thing in this hovering moment of pure being. It doesn't have a place to settle, doesn't manage to claim any space to push its persistent, nagging neediness. It drops away, along with the trials and efforts and concerns of past moments, along with the ancient warrior ways I learned to live through, along with the desperation of one recognized on the road, walked around, left, abandoned. All practice drops away, all need drops away, all claims and taking and grasping and holding and carrying and searching and seeing. All that I was, that I thought I was, that I thought I must be, that I thought precious and necessary and mine, all that drops away. I stand there on the road bare to the bone, vulnerable, open, defenseless, cracked open to depths I never knew existed. There in the fiery sun's strident brightness, I reveal all, to the core of every strand of being, until there is nothing there but pure being. And it is perfect. I am exactly what I am meant to be. I am home. I am bliss. I am everything I ever imagined or dreamed or imagined imagining. This is who I am. This is being me. This is finally, finally yes. Finally yes. Finally yes.

Thank you, holy one, source of all being, provider of breath, one who pours water on wounds and light into questioning. Thank you, holy one, mother, nurturer with milky-breasted richness of life, love, lover, loving arms wrapped around my innocence, golden eyes moist with tears of compassion for my foolish, prideful arrogance. Do you ever miss me when I wander?

Thank you, holy one, who feeds me truth and carries the balance through every portion of being human. Thank you, holy one, who patiently waits while I struggle to let go of struggling, while I ask questions without answers, while I arrange tiles in endless designs that do not matter, while I parade and shout and gesture and demand, while I watch for clues and imitate those mistakes made endlessly before me, while I circle and dive and ask and figure and try, while I hollow out yet another spot in the midst of plenty, while I organize myself in patterns that merely entertain petty wants, while I alphabetize ideas and sort thoughts and try and try and try again.

Thank you, holy one, for your infinite patience, for your infinite love, for your infinite being, for your infinite oneness in which I exist despite my ignorance of its reaches. Thank you for this bit of knowing that I have managed to wrap myself around. Thank you for this miniscule awareness to which I expand. You are all that can be, all that is, all that ever was and will be, all of all. I am of you, in you, through you, with you. And in that I am all. For that I am gratitude and I am humility. I am awe and I am emptiness. I am expansion and collapse. I am everything that ever was and is and will be, all at once, all present, all come together in this that is me. And I am less than nothing. I collapse into all that is.

Yes, we were close, Jesus and I. Others were jealous of that, so I was not always accepted. But they wouldn't dare treat me badly, only whined sometimes to him that they did not get what I got. But they did not give what I gave.

Yes, they loved him, they listened and heard him, they followed him, they devoted themselves to him. But sometimes a woman knows a man in ways another man, or even another woman, cannot. She sees into his heart and into his mind and into his soul. She knows him, and she cherishes that complete being he is more than any other can understand, as a holy wondrousness straight from God. There is no doubting, no hesitation, no selfishness, no wandering, no questioning. There is only loving and being there. Always being there. Through whatever happens.

I never wavered. From then on I was there. Whether he looked for me or just knew, I was there. And so was he there for me, in my awareness and experience and understanding, in my knowing and in my body and in my being, always. I knew his presence, knew his love, both with me and in me, every moment. It was this way. It never differed.

He depended on me. He talked things out with me, he looked to me for confirmation and encouragement. Sometimes he used me to know he was doing or saying the right thing. Somehow he knew through me if he was. Somehow he saw in me what he needed to see.

And I learned from and through him to be a person who walks in God's ways. I learned to know right steps and to listen for guidance and to allow grace and love to come through me. I became a better person. I became that beloved child of God he spoke about. It was a beautiful time of my life.

We were camped out in the desert, just three of us with him, when he found out he was going to die soon. During those seclusions, when he needed to get away, only a few of us would go with him and we left him alone to do whatever he needed to do. We just stayed there, holding the place, there for him when he wanted us.

We hadn't seen him for days and we were all unusually anxious. No one could sit still. I couldn't take my eyes off the hills to the west. Finally Simon leapt to his feet, stared at me intently, and then strode out toward the hills. The next day he came staggering back, carrying Jesus over his shoulder. I watched them come, not able to move, not knowing if he was alive.

He was so weak it was two days before he could talk. Then he told us what was going to happen. It was brutal. Simon cried out, "Don't go, just don't go." All I could do was look at him and hold his fear and his courage. I knew he would do what he had to do. There was no question of that. And I knew I would be there. For him, with him, always, no matter what came.

Not that I didn't cry. We all cried. Jesus cried, too. We cried together, there in the desert under the wide, dark sky. We stayed there another eight days. Sometimes we tried to understand, sometimes we were resigned, sometimes we raged at God and begged for another way, sometimes we bargained, sometimes we prayed, "Dear God, please get us through this. Please help us do what seems impossible. Please hold us even as you tear us apart."

"I will tell the others," he said as we headed back. We nodded, glad to be free of that burden. Usually we returned from seclusion with new energy and enthusiasm and we spread it among all the other followers. This time we came back solemn and cautious. Things were never easy after that.

I held him at night and sometimes he cried against my heart. I cried with him. He clung to me as he clung to each moment of life left to him. And I clung to him, memorizing every sensation, for he would soon be gone from me and I would never hold him again. My mind could hardly imagine it possible, but my heart knew, and my body knew.

The rest was a nightmare. I scarcely realized what was happening around us, so intent was I on him. I knew every nuance of his emotions and of his efforts. I knew every word before he spoke it. I knew every step before he took it, and how heavy it would be. I knew every blow and every wound, every puncture and bruise and tearing open of flesh and emotion, every humiliation and degradation. I knew his fear and his shame and his despair. I knew his loss of faith and the overwhelming darkness that thrust him into.

I stayed. I was with him through it all. To the end.

At the end he turned completely to God and a radiance came over him and over us all. God's peace came, God's love came. It wrapped his broken body in a shroud of golden light. It gathered up his spirit, lifted it off the cross, and brought him into God's heart.

I watched him go.

I watched him go.

I watched him go.

I did not get to say goodbye...

I watched him go.

—~—

It was impossible to go on without him. We were embedded in each other's awareness for so long. We had a trust neither of us had known before, trust beyond deed and action, as if the other were built into our bones. We knew each other, simply knew, and knew the other was there. Always.

Now he was gone. I felt unbearably alone. As if the sun had gone from the earth and left a pale substitute. I looked across the land and felt a chill of cold emptiness. He would never walk here again, never set foot on soil or raise his face to sky. He would never exclaim in loud surprise at some revelation. Never lay a hand on furrowed brow or anxious crown. Never peer into puzzled eyes. Never murmur soft praise. Never nod in solemn agreement. Never laugh with spirited delight. How empty the hills felt now. How silent and still, as if life had abandoned them. As if now they would only, always, wait.

I sat waiting, watching, listening for some sign of continuing life. Was that a footstep? A shadow? A movement? A whisper? Nothing. We waited, the land and I, waiting.

He was even more of an absence than he had been a presence. Every bit of creation spoke of loneliness. It was so profoundly still! I wondered if breath would continue to come automatically. I wondered if life would wither and end. Would all I saw fade into nothingness, void, empty waiting for some stirring? It was so still! I sat waiting in the waiting land, waiting, waiting...

Time was endless. I did not know how long it was. The light came and went, and that was all that moved. Nothing else did, or if it did I could not tell. And it mattered not. No sensation, no perception, no movement, no presence, no impression, no need. There was only nothingness and nowhere, no experience, only waiting. No being but waiting. Not even any sense of anything to wait for. Just waiting.

The women came for me on the third day. They lifted me, prepared me, dressed me, like it had been at Sanctuary Farm when I first arrived. I recognized that. Women caring, taking care, in the face of desolation, in the midst of despair, and now in the emptiness. They lifted me up and prepared me, and I began to feel a sense of a slight stirring. It seemed a far off whisper from across the void. A feather's movement? A silent step? The turn of a hand? I could not tell.

We walked in the early morning light along a rocky path. They had handed me cloth to carry, and several small bags of herbs. I followed in silence, once wondering where we were, but not needing to know. The stirring had ceased. I searched for it with my heart and could not find it in the aloneness. Stillness stretched out all around me, more real than the women walking before me, more real than the path underfoot.

I walked, but that did not change the waiting. The rocks, the shrubs, the insects, the small creatures hidden in their hollows all waited. The sun, rising now, waited. The crisp, still air waited. My breath, such a shallow presence in time with my steps, followed in the vacuum.

When the women exclaimed out loud it drew me from my separation. They made way and I saw the stone rolled aside, the guards asleep, the empty tomb. Then I knew where we were. This was his tomb. They'd brought me here to prepare his body for proper burial. And it was not here.

Now the stillness bore into me, painful in its clarity. Even his body was gone. All I could think was that without his presence there would be only emptiness where there had been life and breath and being, where there had been inspiration and love.

Again I felt that movement, a whisper, a suggestion. I looked around. Nothing. No one. Not even a quiver in the air. Only stillness. I sighed. Was it my imagination?

He had spoken to many of us about what would happen after he died, but we took his words as metaphor, as urgings to keep his messages alive in our memories and hearts. No one believed he meant he would actually rise up from the grave and leave it. He spoke to me again, separately, late one night, insisting I listen. Because he always spoke the truth I gathered the words and held them to me. And yet what was I to think?

When the women took to the road again I followed. I did not know if we headed onward or back. Footsteps followed footsteps through the void. It did not matter. Did we walk long or far? It did not matter. We walked.

Someone approached from behind, soft footsteps, barely noticeable. I wondered if the others would step aside to let this person pass, but they did not. The footsteps came in line behind me. I felt comforted by them. We continued thus for a while.

"I am here," he said. His voice did not surprise me. I did not turn to look, I did not hold up my steps. I knew he was here. I felt his presence.

"Just as I promised," he added.

"You meant that? Literally?" I looked at the women's backs ahead of us as they continued on, and knew they heard none of this.

"I will be here always," he said. With that he touched my heart, and I looked in his eyes and knew he was right and my eyes filled with tears.

"I am love, I am light," he said. "I am your connection to all life, to all that is. I am that God-goodness-aliveness-sacred-being that is within you. Do you hear me? You are everything I have ever said and ever been. You are the expression of all that is in me. It is in you."

"This stirring," I said, "it comes from the mountains, it comes from the land. It comes right into my heart."

"Yes," he said.

A breath came around me and there appeared ahead on the path a presence that became form. The first woman took a few more steps, then looked up, startled, and stopped. "Well, there you are!" she began, then faltered, gasped, and collapsed against her companion. The two women held each other, shaken, unable to move or speak.

"I want you to tell the others that you have seen me on the road," he said. "Do as I say. It is part of the whole. They will have difficulty believing you, but hold steady. You know what you know, and you are strong women. They must realize that what was prophesied has come to pass. God has raised me up out of my death so that you will know that you are raised up, too. You are as I am. We are the same.

"I came to bring God's love to life and this is the most important part of his message. God gave me, his son, so that you may live in my footsteps. I walked among you as flesh, now I walk among you still. Believe! Be in your hearts! Know the true miracle there."

As he spoke I felt his touch again in my heart and the waiting was over.

Once the women realized he no longer stood before them they chattered excitedly, coming repeatedly to ask me did I see this, did I hear that? I nodded each time, and went to sit on a rock while they fluttered about.

Across the valley the sunlight blazed on a far ridge. A hawk soared above it, watching the bright rocks below. Movement caught my eye. Sheep searched for sprouts grown in pockets of soil among the stones. Two lambs scampered onto a high boulder, looked out for a moment, then quickly disappeared beyond it. A shepherd boy clamored over the ridge, his arms full of the day's supplies. He called out to the hills and to the rising sun.

The women insisted we go on so that they could tell everyone what had happened. They would say, "God is with us. He walks with us on the road and speaks to us in our hearts." They hurried ahead of me as we continued along the road. Every so often both of them turned to urge me to keep up and to join in their excitement. They could hardly restrain themselves from running ahead to tell what they had seen.

I walked behind them, absorbed in my own thoughts. "I am with you always," he had said, "know me in your heart." Maybe I did feel him there now. Maybe the ache and sorrow had lessened.

He spoke again, "I am more with you now than I ever was."

I stumbled on an unevenness, and catching my balance stopped to sit on the roadside. "Where are you?" I insisted.

"I am in your heart and in your mind. I am in your being, in who you are."

"I don't understand this. Where are you?" I cried.

"Remember how it was when we talked last week when you were so weary from the long day, yet we spoke late into the night. You drifted in and out of sleep, with my words and yours mingling into impressions, not at all sure whose were whose or what was what. It all danced around and through you, and just was whatever it was."

"Half dreamy, half here?"

"Something like that," he said.

"A different way of being?"

"Yes, this will be a different way of being. Being open to more of who you are. Let yourself go into it, as a river current, allowing it to take you where it will."

"I think I understand what you mean."

"Of course you do," he said.

I looked at him and saw him and felt his presence settle deep into my heart and my knowing. It was a homecoming. The home I had never found, and forgotten to miss, would be within me. Rather than a place, it would be a different way of being and knowing.

Suddenly, one of the women took hold of my shoulders and shook me. "Are you all right?" she demanded. "You gave us such a start when you disappeared. We walked clear back to the narrows looking for you! What were you doing?"

"Figuring out some things," I said. I followed them on for a while, and then took their leave and turned toward the mountains at the crossroads.

Chapter Ten: Light Appears

Maggie called Lydia. "When Mary and I wrote about the emptiness after Jesus died, it was unbearably painful, as if I was living it myself. I know I let it come through me more clearly because of what happened this week with Michael."

"You certainly are whole-heartedly into your work," said Lydia with a chuckle.

"I don't seem to have a choice."

"Well, good for you for being open to it."

"Do you think all that happened to prepare me for writing Mary's story?"

"I don't know, Maggie."

"There are so many similarities and interconnections going on."

"It's pretty amazing."

"Lydia, I think Mary is intensely interested in my relationship with Michael."

"How so?"

"She watches every nuance. I'm more and more aware of it"

"That's intriguing. I'm sure you'll eventually find out what that's about. Meanwhile, how are you doing?"

"I still hurt a lot."

"I know. I can feel it."

"That terrible desolation Mary experienced... At least Michael is alive. I am grateful for that."

"Well, yeah."

"In some ways Mary's aloneness was temporary. Jesus came back and told her he would always be with her, but in a different way of being."

"Yes, isn't that interesting? A different way of being, like you and Michael on the other levels."

"That's what I'm thinking. And if I'm living similar patterns, which is what seems to be happening, then maybe that other level connection is how

Michael and I are supposed to find a way through this."

"Are you okay with that?"

"Not really. I don't know if I even want any relationship with him any more. I have plenty of concerns."

"I agree."

"Except, what about our soul connection? Even in the worst possible circumstances, I don't see how that could ever be truly gone."

"I agree with that, too, Maggie. So, what are you going to do?"

"I don't know. Give it more time, I guess."

In the afternoon of that Friday after Christmas Maggie wrote in her journal, *"I like my role in the writing collaboration with Mary. I write down what she says, and then point out anything that does not feel clear. I don't try to fix it myself. Mary gracefully takes care of it. Sometimes we start out just talking with each other about the writing and before I know it she slips into telling more story. I just follow along. I don't have to make any effort; I simply hold the space. I'm learning to do that."*

Maggie paused, and then wrote, *"I might not go to church on Sunday."*

"Why?" asked Nu.

"I don't want to get hurt any more."

"What *do* you want, Maggie?"

"Well, I don't want to hide, either. I don't want to feel like I did something wrong. I want to be fine just being who I am. And that means going to my church to get spiritual validation and inspiration and to be with my friends."

"Then go!"

"It is so painful when he avoids me."

"He needs to do that," said Nu. "Give him that."

"What are you saying? He needs to do that for himself? Is this really not even about me?"

"Of course it is about you, but you take care of you and he'll take care of him."

The next afternoon Maggie sat at Jackie's kitchen table and for the first time told her the whole story about Michael, from the beginning.

"I don't think his resistance is about his spiritual journey or his work," said Jackie. "I think he is afraid of losing control of things and letting his emotions loose."

Maggie stared at her, astonished. "That's what you see? He's scared of losing control?"

"Yes, especially with his own emotions. He doesn't trust himself with them."

"This is a whole different way of looking at it."

"Maggie, the best thing you can do is to stay steady, like you said. That's good for you, and it's good for him, too. That will reassure him that it's okay for him to be himself."

"Be himself? Jackie, I've been trying to support him in exactly that all along."

"I know, and it is working. As for you, Maggie, you need to stay in the soul love. Don't go off into romantic love. That way no matter what happens, everything will be fine, because that soul love is the real love and that will never fail."

Back at home, Maggie put an energetic representation of herself on the treatment table so she could work on releasing any unclear connections with Michael. As part of the process she checked on him and found that he needed some work, too. Could she do that now without her own emotions entering into it? Planting her feet and grounding first, she dropped into that altered state of being where she becomes part of the work and tried a simple, general clearing of his field, watching both him and herself for reactions.

He needed reconnection with his own core energy again. Guidance told her to get him there by bringing him right through herself to experience her own awareness of his core self. To do it they'd both have to trust each other. Maggie barely breathed as she carefully led him through. She watched him recognize his own deep self, then very gently she let go and left him alone there.

Afterward she realized this was the best possible thing they could have done today. She had put the hurt aside and stepped into her strength. From there she had trusted him. And he had trusted her. They had connected in an energetically intimate way with no discomfort or suggestion of crossing any boundaries, and it had gone very well. This would make Sunday a lot easier.

Late that evening Maggie checked on him again and to her surprise they immediately connected on the other level. She took a deep breath and let it be happening. He was exhausted and just stood there looking at her, so she spoke.

"Hi, Michael. I'm glad you're okay."

"Yeah, tough week," he replied. "Remember Easter? When you came to every service?"

"I remember I couldn't even talk at the end, just stood there looking at you."

"This whole week has been like that for me, way too much going on. About church tomorrow, I don't know, I'm still..."

"You do what you need to do," she said, shaking her head, not really wanting to get into it.

"Believe in yourself, Maggie. Believe in what you know."

"I know that the work we did together earlier today was extraordinary."

"It was a remarkable experience. Thank you."

She got her journal and wrote, *"This is certainly challenging me. We still connect easily and completely, despite my caution. Even as I stand back, being careful, I stand inside of us. It may be that there is no leaving this because it is an essential part of who we are."*

At church the next morning Michael preached about wanting to be where we belong and the challenge of finding our way there. She could see he was still groping for solid ground. When she approached him at the end he told her he had gotten away for several days of vacation with his kids and grandkids, and that he really needed that. Then he hugged her like Christmas hadn't even happened and everything was just fine.

"I saw him today at church," Maggie said to Caroline later, sighing. "It's painful just to look at him. We talked a little. He doesn't seem to even know he hurt me."

"That's disturbing," said Caroline.

"I guess we're going to act as if it never happened."

"Is that what you want?"

"I don't know what I want. This has changed things for me."

"I'm glad to hear you say that, Maggie."

"I may be able to be his friend and support him, but I swear I'm done with the romance. I want that boundary line now, more than he ever did. And I'm turning my attention to the work with Mary."

"Sounds good," declared Caroline.

On Monday over coffee, Jackie asked, "You're not ending the whole thing with him, are you?"

"I don't think that's an option," Maggie answered. "But I'm sure backing off."

The next day Lydia laughed at that conclusion and said, "Are you taking bets on for how long?"

Maggie growled at her, and then asked, "Lydia, I don't think he realizes what happened for me. Was this whole, painful mess only in my own perception? Is it possible that it only happened so I would feel Mary's loss?"

"I don't know, Maggie. Strange things have occurred throughout this adventure. Could be, I suppose. It is shocking that Michael seems to have not noticed he was having any impact on you."

"I keep making excuses for him."

"I noticed that."

"That's not good for me."

"True."

"And it's not okay that he leads me on, then shuts me out. Even if he doesn't realize he's doing it."

"That doesn't seem okay to me, either," said Lydia.

"For now I just want to turn away and focus on the work with Mary."

Maggie reread the last section of what they had written. "Mary," she declared, "this is amazing. I was wondering if now you want to go back over earlier parts to elaborate on anything or fill in gaps."

"Gaps?" asked Mary Magdalene.

"You haven't said much about being with Jesus while he was alive. I know people are very interested in that."

"But I told you, this is my story, not his," said Mary. "The important parts for me were after he died, when I came into my own fullness. That's what I need to talk about."

"Okay. We can always do it later if you want to, when you've finished telling the main story."

"Listen to me, Maggie. The important part, the part people can personally relate to, is after he died. Neither you nor the readers can ever expect to spend time with the live embodiment of Jesus, right? But that non-physical presence that I knew after he died is available to everyone. Jesus is as much with you right now as he was with me then. Do you see? That's why this has to be about afterward. It doesn't matter what he and I were. What matters is what you and Jesus can be."

"Now I understand. Let's get to work."

"The beginning of this next part is what I told you to encourage you when you were so devastated at Christmas. This is where it fits in the story."

Mary's Words

After I left the women I went up on the mountain and stayed there while time stood still, or did not exist at all. There my heart opened until there was no resistance or hesitation, until there were no boundaries, until it dissolved completely into all that is. And there it stayed. I experienced life and death, spirit and flesh, love and abandonment, despair and hope. I knew sorrow and joy, anger and peace, tranquility and anguish. I became, on the mountain, every experience and every possibility. And there I stayed. Simply, fully, wholly being all that.

Then one day I stood in the early morning sun and felt myself renewed. The light entered my body as it enters a leaf, revealing its essential patterns, illuminating vein and form and inner beauty. It came though me, glowing and warming me, making me bright. It came through me as God shining into my crevices and dark passages, through each intersection of confusion, doubt, anger, and hesitation, through every smallness and constriction, through fear and sorrow and loneliness and memory, through all I was and am and will be. Until there I stood, empty before it, being it, in it and of it. Until I was but a reflection of pure light and nothing more.

I shook. It was as if my mortal body could not contain such purity, such beauty, as if its material could not be of such sacred essence. I shook for a long time as my body opened into new being, new clarity, new hope.

I would be me now, the voice told me, a real version of who I am and had always waited to be. In that realness I would carry this same light, this aliveness, this wholeness, to whatever I do, to whomever I touched. I would be this light. It would come through me to touch others, to spread through confusion and darkness, until light is everywhere around me.

I stood in the early morning sun and let it teach me who I am, allowed myself to become who I am, and transformed into what I have always been, and I found my true being. All else fell away but that light in me and knowing it. All else. It was the most complete I had ever been. No other wants or wishes or needs or hopes or questions or doubts. Just this. Complete and completed. On this blessed day the light of God entered me and I was completed.

God said to me, "You shall be a healer." I saw myself surrounded by people. "You shall go out among the people and in the land," God said. "You shall know in your heart, this heart, truth and righteousness. You shall touch all with my hand."

"Righteousness?" I asked.

Jesus answered. "Righteousness is such a difficult word. I, too, always had trouble with that word. Understand that with it God speaks of deep, sacred harmony and beauty, of a profound fitting together."

"Is it that deep knowing, when everything settles into place and feels right?"

"You understand," he said.

"I will have this deep knowing?"

"How can you not, once you have experienced such an open heart?"

"And I will touch everything as if with the hand of God?"

"Yes," Jesus said. "This is your calling. Do you accept it?"

I looked in his eyes and knew. "It can be no other way."

"Yes, you are ready. Go be God's emissary."

"Will you be with me, Yeshua?"

"I am always with you. Forever."

—ᴡ—

Through the following days I learned to make choices different from any before, and to follow, rather than make my own, fierce way. Struggle ended. There was only peace, only fullness of being, only that beautiful wholeness within and through me.

This new sense of myself gave me courage and inspiration to go do and be all that was asked of me. At first it was simple, like Sanctuary Farm, simple living, moment by moment, rise and tend to the simple process of living. I came down from the mountain. There was peace in me now, wherever I went, whatever I did. For I knew that every thing was held in the heart of God and touched by God's hand. I knew that whatever existed was part of that fullness of being, and rooted in the intention of truth and wholeness.

I found myself caring for others without thinking. My heart stayed open. Each encounter entered there and was bathed in the beauty and brightness I had come to know on the mountain. Spontaneous, simple reaching out, touching, offering a hand, and sharing a smile flowed effortlessly, until it became what is, as if it had always been, and I forgot how to be otherwise.

Everywhere I went, healing blossomed. When God said I would be a healer, it was not only to ease pain. I was to heal people's hearts and heal their fears. I was to bring to them this deep knowing from my time on the mountain, this truth in all that is, and it would open their hearts, too, so that they would know the beauty and light and peace in all that is. They would discover that all of this is within them, too. It is who they are.

Words could not do this. How difficult it is to bring a new vision with words, piling words upon words, hoping that somehow from the whole there will emerge understanding. Instead I was to be a loving presence, a calmness at hand, passing comfort, and in doing so draw others into harmony with my peace and knowing, draw them into the patterns of God's presence.

The light continued to fill me. The more I gave, the more it came, in endless supply, until I believed it would always be so and I forgot to wonder. It simply was.

In the old writings God said, "I am and always was and always will be. I am being. I am what is. I am is." This was what filled me. I was filled with the essence of sacred being, with the huge wondrousness of the wholeness of being, until I knew that I, too, am being itself. I, too, am the pure, sacred, absolute being that fills and illuminates all that is. I became that essence. I am that essence. As are we all.

God, the holy oneness, is in us all and through us all. God is the life force in all that is, the aliveness within life, the breath and blood and sap and patterns of light and form and sound and being. God is heartfelt knowing and heart-filled knowing. God is meeting yourself in that early morning light, alone before all that is holy, facing yourself in the face of God. God is honest, clear, complete grace.

Thank you, Holy Oneness-of-All-That-Is, for this experience, for this blessing of grace that fills me. I offer myself, all that I can be, with humility and awe. Accept me, anoint me, take me into you. I am yours. I am your servant.

For a time I went from place to place, repeating the story of Jesus' resurrection to anyone who would listen. In some I saw understanding or wonderment, but in most either confusion or disappointment. Many refused to believe. Many were angry with Jesus and with God for not keeping him here among us to continue to deliver inspiring messages. They felt betrayed. They wanted to say this proved there is no God, no revelation, no hope.

Even the most ardent followers resisted, even those who had smiled smugly when unusual things happened around Jesus, as if they had already known such things were possible. It was one thing to accept a healing or a miracle. It was entirely another to admit that Jesus had risen from the tomb, had talked to three women on the road, and had truly offered us the light of God within us. This challenged even the true believers of his words and deeds. They could not go that far based on my story alone. Each one had to come to the truth through his or her own experience of it.

And yet, even as they protested something touched their hearts and changed them. A spark of knowing caused hesitation, even in their angry grief, even in their hopelessness. Jesus had touched them and he was still with them, bringing God to them. And it changed them.

After a while I did not need to repeat the story. I just looked in their hearts and when I did I felt the touch come into them there and knew it was done. From the most pious to the most generous to the weakest, most hungry, or lost one, it was the same. A touch in their hearts and they were changed.

"This is how it will be," Jesus told me. "Let me come through you to enter their hearts and together we will rescue them from their fears."

I went wherever I felt drawn to go, and then kept myself in that knowing, with my heart open. Soon I realized that I no longer made judgments. Anyone, a filthy, diseased beggar, a simple worker, a wealthy businessman, a liar, a child, a priest, a politician, a fisherman, a laundress, a teacher, a wanderer, they were all the same. All waiting to know God within them, wanting to open their hearts, to trust, to receive, to allow their empty places to fill. And so we came together.

I moved with ease, apart from any concerns. No one questioned me, no one asked for papers or justification or authority. I passed through roadblocks and census taking and lines and barriers without hesitation. There were always accommodations and offers of food and whatever else I might need. I never went without the basics, and needed no more.

I went wherever I was led, and I did not need to know where I was or with whom. Only that my heart was open and God was with me.

My sense of Jesus' presence changed. I felt him more than knew him now, as if he were part of me, as if in experiencing my own being I experienced his also. Oh yes, there was a great brightness when I focused directly on him, and everything became clearer, easier, and more expansive. Then I felt a great boost. But even in the most distracted moments there was an element in me that reminded me of him. I felt him here within me, beyond the knowing, beyond all the changes in me. He was more than with me, he was bound into my being, melded into who I am. He was within my soul.

I traveled the land, meeting people in every place. I became known as a healer, and so they welcomed me and trusted me. They took me into their homes and let me enter their inner places. And as I came close, that sacred touch passed through me to them.

It felt different with different people. Sometimes it was so cool it made me shiver. Sometimes it burned through me and I knew this was powerful and likely to cause a striking change of direction. The touches could be melodious, or jerky, or slip easily through. They could be loud or heavy or playful or solemn, but in the end they were all the same, leaving that touch in the heart, undeniable, insisting on new awareness.

So, I went from place to place and person to person enlivening the holy, leaving wonderment in faces and change in paths. I traveled in close circles, not far, but the message spread as if winged. "Open your heart and let it be filled with the God within you. Let God's love flow through you."

—~—

"How do you know you're not making all this God-stuff up?" a man asked me one day. "How do you know your mind is sound? How do you know you're not losing touch with reality?" His questions followed me, then danced around me as darkness fell and stars filled the night sky. By the time the fullness of the moon rose, I wasn't sure of anything.

Now, under this moon and stars, I was Mary, just Mary, this moment, this night, nothing else. I had no words to answer those questions. I had no words at all. I was flesh and sensation. I felt the moonlight on my face and arms. It illuminated me as if from within. I was moonlight flesh and star-sparked eyes and the river of life. I was heartbeat and hope and inspiration. I stood by the stream as the moon crossed overhead, opening myself to the sky, dissolving into the earth, flowing as water into timeless wonder.

The high, bright sun woke me. I'd slept long and hard after the late night. Small, golden leaves scattered across the water, swarming like a flock of birds through the narrows of the stream, crowding between rocks in the fast flow, cascading into the swirl below, then lazing on over easy waters. Sunlight gleamed off the water's turnings and glowed through the leaves above, warming air and rocks. I drank in its warmth and the water's delicious chill.

The morning seemed so peaceful, so clear, so simple. The sun was the sun, the water was the water, the trees were the trees, and I was simply me. And yet those impressions had new meaning. Now my sense of me included moonlight and starshine and lively water and dancing leaves and morning sungleams and breath spinning through endless impressions of what is. And it changed me.

I did not need words, proof, evidence, explanation, convincing reasons. What were they in the face of a spray of stars across the sky? Or a bird's morning call? Or the sprinkle of rain's first drops on parched soil? Or the swelling in my heart at sunrise? Or the deep sense of grace that followed?

Words are so petty. So limited. So confining. Put a word on something and immediately that word is all you see. Call a leaf "gold" and you look no further for the slight crimson tinge along its edge, the remnant streaks of green that follow its veins, the rusty brown stem, or even the many shades of gold among its neighbors. Call it "gold" and all you see is confirmation of your declaration, and you settle into complacent misperception, letting go of your deep wonderment and your yearning for sacred mystery and magic and the holy in everything. The word is a mask, turning the leaf finished and gone out of consciousness, and you have closed yourself down one more time, one more degree, until you, too, ask, "How do you know that mystery is real?", for you cannot see for yourself any more.

I stood on the bank of that stream again in the light of day, and let myself feel and know the mystery in all being, in all perception, in all knowing, in myself, and in all that is. And I knew the best answer to the man's questions was no answer. Leave unanswered questions bright in someone's mind and perhaps my willingness to not answer would shake open some tightness there.

Naming Flight

A large, majestic bird soars silently
through bare-branched trees just over our heads,
riding the contours of the mountainside
on broad wings feathered gray and white,
slow, graceful, serene,
accepting us
despite our gasps and unrestrainable exclamations.
An eagle! A hawk? A great owl!

Naming dissipates.
This glorious flying creature lets us be part of its forest.
And we are.
For those expanding, expansive moments of awe
we are more a part of trail and sun-lit shadows
and arching branches and mountain vista
than we have ever been.
Shape and texture and pattern and light
enter our senses, stir knowing and being,
and claim us.

Watch for direction pointers,
said the Sunday morning preacher just hours earlier.
They may come in any form,
and their message may not be obvious.
But if it makes your body tingle,
she said,
and your heart sing,
that's the one.

God…
do you want me to be like this bird?
Do you want me to take wing on your currents and contours?
To step off from ground and naming and effort?
To let be,
serene and graceful and accepting,
in harmony with whatever comes?
Do you want me to fly?
Do you want me to be the stunning mystery
that soars through a magical afternoon
in a world more fertile and surprising
than I ordinarily allow?

Do you see majesty in me?
Can my flight evoke awe?
My presence hush chatter and halt breath?
Do you want me to find my feathers,
discover what they are
and who I am
with wings spread wide
among the trees
in the sunshine
of this day?

I am the bird
and the mountain and the trees and the trail
and the day and the awe.
Identity dissipates into a yielding glide,
aloft in the breath of spirit,
trusting your direction.

Chapter Eleven: Naming Flight

Amy Wilmot had barely returned from Texas when she went back into Asheville's St. Joseph Hospital for surgery on her gall bladder. Her husband David got up every morning at 4:30, took care of things at home, then went to the hospital to get Amy started on her day before he went to work. He helped her into the bathroom so she could shower, style her hair, and put on makeup while he changed the bed linens, got clean towels, and took care of all her dressings and connections and equipment. He straightened up the room and got her all set to feel good about the day. Later, he called or stopped by at lunchtime. After work he went home briefly, then came back for the evening. Before he left he made sure Amy was ready for the night. David knew where the patient supplies were, and he knew what needed doing when. The nurses loved him; he made their job easier.

Everybody at the hospital loved Amy. She learned their names and where they grew up, all about their families, their hopes and dreams. She talked with the nurses, the techs, the food service people, the guy who collected the trash. She loved people, and she loved hearing their stories. She'd get people to talking and sit there looking at them with her eyes wide, asking encouraging questions, and it would feel as if this telling was all that mattered in the world.

Soon after the gall bladder surgery Amy went back into St. Joe's again with another complication, and it continued like that, one thing after another. Each time Maggie found out that Amy was in the hospital she went there to do whatever she could to help. When Maggie arrived Amy's mind eased, her blood pressure came down, her brow softened, and she relaxed. Often she would sleep for the first time in way too long.

Maggie spent hours there, day after day. Sometimes they talked, sometimes they went for a procedure or test somewhere in the hospital complex. Sometimes Maggie just read or wrote or stitched stars onto the quilt she was making, or she simply watched Amy sleep. David said he was grateful for the peacefulness Maggie brought.

"I seem to stay endlessly," Maggie told them both, "so you tell me whenever you want me to leave, okay?" They nodded, their faces filled with amazement.

"You be here whenever you want," said David.

"I love having you here," said Amy.

They never asked why she was doing this. And she couldn't have answered if they did. David told her later that they just figured it was all God's doing.

"Amy loves you, do you know that?" said Tory one day in the hall outside Amy's hospital room. "The very first time she met you she loved you."

"I just know I need to be here," said Maggie, her eyes filling with tears.

Tory nodded. "It's good for both of you."

Amy's home was filled with pets and folk art angels and sunlight. Books were tucked and stacked everywhere, and so were candles and plants and colorful curiosities. Amy loved being home. She always wanted to leave the hospital and go home. At home she settled into a corner of the living room couch with all her favorite things gathered around her, the cats curled into her afghan, and their big dog, Dooley, sprawled out on the floor between her and the door.

Each time Amy went home from the hospital, Maggie went home too, to her own home and back to the rest of her life. Sometimes a whole week passed, then Tory would call or see Maggie at church and tell her Amy was in the hospital again. The next time it was a problem with Amy's kidneys. The doctors tried to do more surgery, but her belly was so full of scar tissue from the radiation that they couldn't get in. Things kept going wrong, and Amy spent more time at St. Joe's than at home, and the doctors couldn't solve the problems.

Maggie couldn't get into Amy's belly energetically any more than the surgeons could with their scalpels. She couldn't do anything at all substantial to help Amy.

"Imagine an apple is sitting on the table and you reach for it," Maggie explained to Lydia. "As your fingers come close it's there but you just can't get to it."

"Like there is a force field around it?"

"No, I don't feel something in the way. I don't know how to describe it. I think it is just that I'm not supposed to touch it. So, Lydia, why am I there?"

"You do help her."

"But only in the most simple ways. A beginning energy work student could do what I am doing."

"So what is happening, Maggie?"

"All I know is that I need to be there. When I feel like going to her, I go. And when I feel like staying there, I stay."

"Maybe that's all there is to know right now."

"Maybe for me this is about not knowing," Maggie wondered out loud.

"That and not being as effective as you are used to being."

"That has been so weird, Lydia. I can hardly do anything for her, and then I just hang around, wondering why I'm there but not wanting to leave."

"Maggie, are you going into an altered state when you're there? You are! I bet there is work being done at some other level, either by you or through you."

"Oh! Like when the guides come through us to do work and we cannot move until whatever is going on is finished? I bet you're right. That's what this is like. Very good observation, Lydia. The difference in this is that my whole presence is being used, not just my hands."

"Awesome. No wonder Amy likes to have you around."

"Now that I look at it this way, yes, something definitely is going on. I wish I could tell what it is. I don't think it has anything to do with physical healing."

"I'm not surprised, given all you've said before. You're still doing the writing with Mary, too, aren't you?" asked Lydia.

"Oh, yes. I'm not stopping now."

"I'm very glad to hear that."

Mary's Words

"Eli!" I shouted. "We have to go!" The barely-turned-four-year-old boy had run out into the field chasing colorful movement. "Leave it," I said.

His dark curls tossed sunlight in all directions as he shook his head no. Then with a swoop of his bag and a squeal, he came up with his fist carefully closed around the top and he started back toward me.

"I got it!" he shouted with a wide grin. Cautiously opening finger by finger, we both peered inside. It was empty.

I laughed, "Ah, you've caught another mystery. This one is very interesting. What do you see?"

"This one dances and twirls as it flies!" he declared. "And it sings, too!"

"How wonderful. Let's let it go now. We need to get back. Goodbye, beautiful mystery."

Eli opened the bag wide to the sky and we smiled big smiles into each other's faces. This child's enthusiasm and trust never failed to delight me. I took the bag, he took my hand, and we walked back down the narrow road. In the distance houses nestled close together next to the river in a small, rural town, their pale stone walls gently muted by the bright afternoon sun. Birds gossiped, an unseen small animal rustled in the hedgerow, a few soft, light clouds hovered low on the horizon. That warm little hand in mine completed the peaceful moment.

"Thank you, God, for this richness of being alive. Thank you for bringing me to this," I said out loud.

"Why do you do that?" Eli asked.

"Do what?"

"Talk to God."

"Because it reminds me to pay attention. And to remember what really matters."

"Okay," he said, grabbing a stalk of long grass that hung out into the road. We walked on past the next bend before he spoke again. "Thank you, God, for Mary," he said, "and for mysteries, and for fun afternoons."

I smiled, my heart full, and gently squeezed his hand.

—~—

Eli's mother had died trying to give birth to a second child, and the child died also. Reuben, Eli's father, was devastated. Now he was left with this young son to care for alone. Reuben's parents lived nearby and they did what they could. When we met they asked me to help.

I shared a room with Dena, the cook, a woman of few words and vast curiosity. She urged me to talk late into the night, telling stories of my travels. Through them she learned to expand her own horizons. She had saved every coin she ever earned, and now she asked for time off and she set out for the city to experience it for herself.

The house seemed hollow without her. Another woman came in to prepare food once a day, and we ate simple meals otherwise. Reuben stayed mostly to himself, only going each day to teach at the school for boys, and otherwise secluded himself in his library. I rarely saw him more than briefly. He was a quiet, pale-skinned man of small stature, with graceful hands unaccustomed to physical labor.

This was a peaceful time for me, a time of rest and contemplation, a time to settle after moving from place to place for so long. And this child! What a blessing! Every day was one miracle after another as he discovered life and himself and others and the world. I delighted in sharing it with him, seeing with my own freshly opened eyes, seeing astonishing things that would have passed by unnoticed had I not been sharing a child's perspective.

—w—

"Mary, Mary, come! Hurry!" Eli's panic flew at me. I dropped what I was doing and rushed to the doorway. He was at the very back of the courtyard, gesturing under a shrub.

Once there I peered into the dusky undergrowth. A cat lay on its side, eyes half closed, barely breathing. "Come on, Alef," I urged, "Come on out of there. You don't look so good. Let me see you." He barely raised his head to look at me, then let it sink again into the dirt.

"We need to get him out of there, Eli. Run and get me a cloth to wrap him in."

"Here! Take my shirt!" Eli exclaimed, pulling at it.

"No, get me a cloth. It will be more comfortable for him."

The child ran toward the house and I turned back to the cat. "Now let's see what's going on here, Alef," I said. I slid my hands carefully under the small body, and brought him out into the light. His tan fur was dark and matted with blood. He cried out as I lifted him, but relaxed in my arms. Nasty wounds on the side of his belly and leg explained the blood, and the leg hung at a distorted angle. A gouge just missed one golden eye, and a piece of ear was gone.

"Well, Alef, you have tangled with something bigger than you, haven't you. Will you never learn the wisdom of retreat? Come, let's get you cleaned up and see what we've got."

Eli emerged from the house with his arms full. When we met halfway I grabbed a cloth to quickly cover the cat, and said, "Let's bring him into the kitchen."

"Good thing Dena is gone," he said. "She would never allow that."

"You think so? She is pretty fond of this cat."

"One time I needed to give a frog a bath," said the boy. "He was all slimy from the river, and she wouldn't let me do it in the kitchen. She made me get a tub and take it outside."

"Well, we're going inside. And I think if Dena were here she would agree." I laid the cat on the table and brought hot water from the stove, then carefully began to clean the blood from around the wound in the cat's side.

"Eli, you can sit by his head and hold your hands like this around his body. That's it. Now think about Alef, about things he has done. See him strong and healthy and happy. Can you do that? You can tell him what you're thinking, too. That will help."

"Sure, I can do that. I have lots of memories with Alef."

With Eli's gentle murmurings in the background, and my hands busy cleaning the wounds, I prayed. "Dear God, this cat is one of your creatures; you hold him in your care. If I can be of assistance in whatever is meant to be, I am here. Please help me to do what I can. If there is to be healing, guide my hands to do your blessings." I laid my hand across the belly wound and Alef did not object. The other hand went to cover Eli's. "Careful to keep a light touch, Eli," I said. He nodded. We sat like that for a long time while the boy told Alef's stories.

"Remember the time, Alef, when you brought that baby rat into Dad's library? And you played with it all afternoon until it collapsed right in the middle of a mess you'd knocked off from the table? By the time Dad found it, you were sleeping peacefully next to the kitchen fire after a whole day of fun. Dad was not happy!

"My favorite thing you do is how you follow us when we go for walks. You're always getting distracted off to the side, usually chasing or pouncing or climbing up some place to see what you can see. Then you race to catch up before we get too far ahead, and you get all tangled up in our feet because you can't stop in time.

"You're a great cat, Alef. I love you, Alef. God, thank you for Alef. Please make him okay."

"Amen," I added.

The leg was broken. I closed and wrapped the wounds, then set the bone and used small, light sticks to make a splint. "He's not going to like this, Eli, but we need to make sure this leg heals straight so he can walk easily."

"Okay, Mary. I'll help him with it."

I left Eli explaining the splint to the cat while I cleaned up and washed the rags.

"You are teaching this child well," came Jesus' familiar voice. "He will be gentle and kind because he understands."

"I just share with him what I know myself."

"Exactly," he said.

I turned back to the kitchen. "Eli, can you find a basket in which we can make a soft bed for Alef?"

"I know just the one!" he exclaimed, and rushed off to get it.

"But this is your collecting basket. You want Alef to use this?"

"Yes!" he declared.

We lined it with cloths and set it on the floor near the heat. Alef slept the rest of the afternoon. By nightfall he sat up and began grooming the parts of himself he could get to. A week later he was up a tree in the courtyard and daring Eli to follow.

—w—

"God, what do you want me to do?" I pleaded.

The young woman lay dying. I had done all I knew to stop the internal bleeding. It was as if a spigot locked open, refusing to turn closed. It was as if no effort was meant to rescue her, as if her death was inevitable.

"Can we not save her? She is much loved and her newborn child needs her."

I thought of Reuben's wife, Eli's mother, dying this same way. This young father's drawn, gray face and wide, frightened eyes haunted me.

"God! Are you going to do this again? Take a young mother from her family? Set them adrift in pain and grief? If so, why?"

Tears ran from my eyes as old ache seized my heart. Why is there such grief? I turned away from the bed, went to sit on the floor against the wall. It was not good to bring my own anguish to the bedside. No one noticed I had moved away, each one lost in their own response to the day's turning from anticipation to despair.

"Come outside."

I followed his voice. We had not talked in a long time.

"Thanks for coming here, Yeshua," I said, and smiled to feel his close presence.

"I am always here, you know that."

"Sometimes I need reminding."

"Tell me what is going on for you, Mary. You've been in these situations many times and usually you are fine with it."

"This time it feels closer to home. All the losses of my life opened up."

"Ah, yes."

"I ache for the future these young ones face. I want to protect them!"

"You know—"

"Of course I know I can't," I broke in. "I know they must live their own lives, discover their own wisdom, build their own strengths, and my protection would interfere, and maybe even cripple them. I know! But still…"

"Your heart aches."

"Yes! My heart aches for them. And for me too." I turned away from him, then spun back. "Tell me, why did you have to leave my life?"

"Look at all you have become!"

"But there is still this aching 'why?'."

"And if there is no answer? If you are called, in this deep crisis of faith, to simply, wholly accept and trust that all is as it must be, all in perfect order, then what?"

"Do you never lose your way?" I blurted, exasperated. Then I looked in his face and remembered. Of course he did. I was there.

"Not any more," he softly replied.

"Not any more," I repeated, realizing what that meant. "I used to hold your beauty and grace for you, knowing you, remembering who you were, even when you forgot. You no longer need that. You are not mine any more. You belong to everyone now."

"I am yours still, and I am everyone else's, also. It is all possible, and all true. I am in every heart; I come through every soul. I am the eternal love there, the faith, the knowing God's grace. Come back, Mary, to helping me open hearts to that inner wholeness. Come back with me to that important work you used to do."

"Travel again? I do remember how it was, touching all those hearts."

"We need to get you back to knowing without asking. Will you come?"

—~—

Dena brought a friend with her when she came back from the city. Rua was a sweet and gentle young woman with an eager mind. Eli took to her immediately. Dena and I made space for her in our small bedroom, and she helped in the kitchen and with other chores. She always did a little more than expected. She had such energy!

I watched life pass day by day, aware of my choosing to stay here, and aware of a discomfort underlying that choice. One early morning I walked alone by the river, remembering what Jesus had said to me about moving on. It had become easy to live in this peaceful place, to know what would happen later today, to expect comfort and companionship and familiarity. I had settled in and learned to want it. In doing so I had compromised, I became what this place asked of me and forgot who I am. In staying here in the comfort I had lost hold of purpose. I found myself clinging to superficial reassurance rather than craving deeper knowing.

All this musing took me far along the riverbank. I came to an abrupt stop in front of a familiar figure seated on a large boulder. Reuben had been watching me approach.

"Was I talking aloud to myself?" I asked, chuckling.

"No," he shook his head, "but you were rather animated."

"Reuben, do you feel you are doing what you are supposed to be doing?"

"What do you mean, Mary?"

"Your work, your life, your son…"

"I do my best. It's difficult alone. Why? Do you see something?"

"Oh, no, I do not mean any criticism. I was really looking for my own answers, but if you are asking for suggestions…"

"Any suggestions would be welcome. Go ahead."

I began, "Eli is such a capable boy."

"Yes, he is!" burst in Reuben. "And I've been wondering if I spend enough time with him."

I smiled, watching the way open so easily. "What would you do with more time?" I asked.

"You and he do such interesting things, Mary. He tells me about your exploration and fun. I could do some of that."

"What a good idea! I'm sure Eli would love that."

"I'm entirely too serious, you know, since my wife died."

"Perhaps it is time to change that."

"Yes!" he declared, and he leapt off the rock onto the path.

I laughed. "You and Eli are more alike than I realized!"

"I like this, Mary! It makes me feel full of life, full in my chest, like my poor shriveled heart is expanding."

"Like your heart is opening up." I said softly, smiling, knowing. There it was, that familiar sensation coming through me, and then I knew it had been there all along. I had come to this place to help God touch a grieving man's heart and to keep a little boy's heart from closing. The results were obvious in Reuben's glowing smile.

There was one more thing to do. I visited the family of the woman who had died in childbirth. There I told them what God told to me. "We do not open our eyes expecting to see only light. We see patterns of light and dark, colors and forms. Altogether it makes a whole picture, a whole world, the whole of life. So it is with experience. We experience joy and faith and fulfillment and pleasure. And we also experience absence and fear and disappointment and confusion. Together they make a whole, the whole of life. It is all life. There is no wholeness without it all. There is no richness or dimension or distinction without all of it.

"I asked God, in my own grief, 'How can I live with this?' God told me to open my heart. And in this I see that if we open our hearts to the miracle in every moment, from a new day's sunrise, to a tree completing its cycle of life by providing its own body to nurture new life, from a conscious breath, to the sweet juice of a melon, to a baby's cry, to a poetic line, to the soothing music of a rock-strewn stream, then we know that life goes on, and we go on, and there are riches and beauty left to be discovered, and joys to be felt, and all is as it should be, all is life, all is one wholeness.

"Your wife-daughter-mother-sister is with you in that open heart that welcomes life. Feel her in the sunlight and in shadow, in the moon's rise and disappearance, in the flower's bloom, in the hawk's cry, in winter's chill, in satisfaction and confusion and frustrated repetition. She is as much in everything as you let yourself be in everything. As you open to life, as you let it be in you, you will find her there and you will find yourselves there, too."

They sat in silent breathing for several long minutes, until one-by-one they began to stir, and to look at each other, and to see each other for the first time since that painful night.

"Let's go for a walk outside now," I suggested.

"Down by the river," someone added. "She loved walking there at this time of day."

I left them there and went to pack my things.

It was not easy to leave Eli. But already Rua had begun to step into my place, and Reuben would follow through on his promise to be a more active participant in his son's life. I left them much healed from how I'd found them.

"Maggie, there is a painting of Mary Magdalene at Grace Cathedral in San Francisco you have got to see," Tory declared one Sunday after church. "I have a poster of it. I just need to find it. I've looked everywhere for it."

"That's okay," said Maggie, relieved that Tory could not find it. Early on in the writing with Mary, Maggie had realized she should not read anyone else's ideas about Mary, and she felt uneasy about looking at this artist's view. It felt important to get all her Mary Magdalene impressions from Mary herself.

"No, it's not okay," said Tory. "I want it myself. So, here's what I'm going to do. I'm flying out there next week for a class. I'll buy two more, one for me and one for you."

Maggie considered objecting, but left it alone instead. She didn't think she was supposed to see that image until the writing was finished, but it felt like it would all work out.

Maggie's days were full. She wrote in her journal and with Mary every morning for as long as she could. She saw clients scattered through afternoons and evenings, taught classes, and around all that fit time with Amy and with Jackie. Last thing each night Maggie typed the new, handwritten pages of Mary's words into the computer.

Time spent with Jackie was very grounding and Maggie needed that with everything else that was going on. One afternoon she helped Jackie gather neighborhood children into her kitchen to make paper mache creatures. Each of the kids soon dropped out, but Jackie and Maggie were hooked. From then on they spent their time together with their hands in flour paste and newsprint. Maggie sculpted a cat with wings and its tail curled into a spiral, while Jackie created a whole herd of seahorses to hang in her bathroom.

One evening Maggie had to break away early from Jackie's because a major snowstorm had already begun. She would have liked to bring the paper mache cat home and keep working on it, but its damp form was too fragile to transport. At home she decided to try drawing instead, expecting the whimsy of the winged cat.

Letting the drawing pencil move wherever it wanted to go, Maggie allowed shapes to form themselves. Much to her surprise, a woman's face emerged. Continuing to draw, shade, and shape, she watched the face develop. Darkness around the eyes set them deep; they looked tired. The face was narrow, eyes close together under definite brows, a long, strong nose, high cheekbones, small mouth, and slender jaw. Maggie was amazed. She did not usually draw faces this well. Staring at the finished drawing, she knew this must be Mary Magdalene. With the drawing taped to the wall above her desk, it felt like Mary was right there, looking at her.

"I bought the posters!" declared Tory two weeks later, just back from San Francisco.

Maggie's heart sank. Should she say something now? The writing was not finished.

"Except, they are not here," added Tory.

Maggie couldn't help but smile.

"I had them shipped because I didn't want them to get ruined in my overloaded luggage. It may take several weeks to get them."

Maggie wondered if that meant she would be done with Mary's writing by then.

"But!" Tory exclaimed, "I have a postcard of it, and you can have that now."

Maggie held her breath as Tory dug into her oversized bag. Tory searched and searched, but no postcard turned up.

Maggie laughed and said, "That's okay. I can wait."

For the next month and a half the posters did not come, Tory could not find the postcard, and Maggie knew she would not see that image until the writing was done. She was, however, very curious how it would compare to the face in her drawing.

Chapter Twelve: Finding Her Feathers

On a Sunday morning in January Michael caught Maggie's glance and held it as he stepped up to the pulpit. At the same time, she heard his other-level voice say, "Maggie, connect with me here on these other levels, support me here."

She could hardly believe he was talking to her on the other levels this way, right in the middle of church with all these people and complex commotion around them. On top of that, he was asking her to stay open and keep a conscious connection there while he led the service. She looked around the sanctuary. Faces and pews and candles and sounds were faint, muted background to what was going on between Michael and her right now. The two of them seemed the only live beings in the room.

He settled his books and papers at the pulpit, then looked at her again.

Well, thought Maggie, didn't I say I would be here and support him? That's what he is asking for now. This isn't a romance thing, it is about our souls caring for and supporting each other. Okay, yes, I will do this.

Maggie opened to the other levels and Michael was waiting for her. Their connection was as clear and strong as it had ever been. She watched him at the pulpit and saw him visibly relax.

"This is good," his other voice said. "Thank you. Now, while we're doing this I need to devote my outward attention to the work and to the rest of the congregation. Let me do that."

With a jolt she realized how much she sought his attention during the services. She wanted him to look at her and be aware of her as he led the service and delivered the sermon. He must have felt that and been distracted by it.

He's trying to find a way to make this relationship work, she thought, so that we can have the soul connection, with its deep understanding and caring, and at the same time in the physical world he can focus passionately on his work.

Maggie tried releasing her need for his focus. Michael turned from looking at her and sent his attention out all around the sanctuary. She watched him give more of himself to the congregation and to his speaking, and he clearly loved it. He blossomed, and his gratitude flooded back to her.

❧

Later Lydia pointed out, "Assigning most of your relationship to other levels of consciousness doesn't leave you with much that is very tangible. How are you with that?"

"It does take away a lot of the outward validation that we have any relationship at all. There's not much left, is there? And Lydia, what if all that other level stuff is only a delusion in my mind? What if it's crazy?"

Lydia laughed. "Yeah, right! Maggie, you are the most careful, skeptical, foot-dragging, questioning lightworker I've ever come across. Do you really think you made all this up? You wish! If you did, it would be easy to get out of it. No, this is about as real as it gets. And you, you do-not-wannabe-far-out-crazy-delusional-wild-woman, you are still standing here carefully wondering if you should take one step forward."

Maggie laughed, too, then got quiet and said, "Today when I released him during the service, it was pretty easy to let go of wanting a lot of eye contact and direct attention. I have to say, he did great at his preaching today. The congregation loved it."

"That makes sense, Maggie."

"The truth is that it worked better for me this way, too. Today I felt free to focus more on the message and more deeply experience the spiritual. The service was extra powerful for me, too."

"This is always the case, you know," said Lydia. "Whatever happens is for both of you."

❧

The next time Maggie worked on a client, she felt Michael's energetic presence standing in the doorway of the room, watching her. She sensed him there as easily as she felt his energy field when she worked on him. She knew he was impressed to see her work so effectively and powerfully, and he was interested in what she was doing, yet he stayed back in the doorway, out of the way, rather than come closer. As she focused on the client and the work, Maggie forgot he was there.

After the client left, she turned to Michael. "Now I understand what you want from me at church," she said. "When I work I have to be completely focused; I cannot be distracted. I could not have done my job today if you had been pulling at me for attention. And the same is true for you. You have to be focused on what you are doing and keenly open to spirit and guidance, as well as to the congregation. My wanting your attention distracts you from doing your job as well as you want to do it."

Tears welled up in Maggie's eyes. "Oh, Michael!" she exclaimed. "That's what happened at Christmas! I wanted more and more attention, and you had to close me off so you could do your work. I would have had to do the same thing. But why didn't you tell me? Why didn't you talk to me, even later, when you must have seen that I was hurting?"

"How could he?" asked Nu. "It would have become impossibly complicated."

"He couldn't have done anything to make it easier for me?"

"He truly did the best he could, Maggie. Let go of judging it."

"How can I let it go when I am still so affected by it?" protested Maggie.

"I'm not saying don't learn from it."

"You want me to see that he did what he had to do, and that it wasn't his intention to hurt me."

"It was never his intention to hurt you," said Nu.

"But he did hurt me," Maggie retorted. "I don't think I should forget that."

"Let it hurt, but let go of judging it."

She took a deep breath. "I've been drawing conclusions based on judgment of what happened. You're saying let that judgment part go. He did what he needed to do, and that hurt me deeply, period. No judgment, no conclusion. Okay, I'll work on that."

Michael's energetic being came to watch her work often after that. She could tell that he was intrigued by what she did and he wanted to understand it. Sometimes when she was tired she felt him come close behind her and lay a hand on the middle of her back, boosting her power. During a pause in one intense session, his touch released tight muscles in her shoulders and upper back. Then he gently rocked her head back and forth, working his way down her neck vertebrae, releasing them. It was wonderful.

"Thank you, Michael," she said. "I appreciate your being here to support me like this."

"I want to be here," he replied.

❧

One morning Maggie interrupted before Mary Magdalene could begin dictating. "Mary, why am I the one writing with you?" she asked.

"Because we are of the same patterns."

"Are these patterns about Michael, too? And Jesus?"

"Michael and you share some of the same patterns Jesus and I do."

"Is that why you're so interested in us?"

"Yes."

Maggie took a breath, trying to grasp what she was hearing, then asked, "Are there others sharing these patterns?"

"There have been, but not at this time and place."

"Am I in these patterns so I can write your book?"

"There are many reasons," said Mary. "This is only a part of it."

"Will the patterns end when we finish the book?" Maggie felt herself sinking fast at the thought.

"Michael will not leave your life when the book is finished. Did you really think so? These are far deeper patterns than that."

"As you say that I feel the truth of it in my heart. It feels..." Maggie could find no words to describe the fullness in her heart.

"Touched by God?" asked Mary, and Maggie nodded, her eyes welling up. "The sacred truth of this does touch your heart, Maggie. When deep, sacred truth comes into your awareness you know a fullness, a fittingness, and you feel it in your heart. Then you know your place, your home, in the vastness and completeness of God's love."

"Michael brings me to this."

"Yes, he does. And you bring him to it, too."

"Mary, did you help Jesus?" asked Maggie.

"I did. When he felt confused or discouraged, or just plain tired, I always knew who he was. Always."

"Knew who he was? That's what I keep coming to with Michael, that he can count on me to know who he is."

"It's pattern," said Mary. "It is strong in you two."

"Is my part in the pattern to know who he is?"

"That is a portion of it. Another part is to allow truth and clarity to pass through you to Michael and through him to you, and on into the hearts of others."

"Michael's words speak so directly to me every Sunday. I always get important messages. I know God speaks to me through him."

"And Michael gets important messages through you, too. Be open to pass those along to him."

"I need to be more open to such things," sighed Maggie.

"You need to know that such things are real."

"Mary, I still don't understand how the pieces of my relationship with Michael fit together. It deeply confuses me. But for now I just want to continue to focus on the writing with you. Can we do that?"

"You cannot avoid the patterns, Maggie."

"What does that mean?"

"You and Michael can fulfill these patterns. You can do what Yeshua and I could not. You can live out your lives and grow old together."

"That's what you are hoping for? That we will finish what you couldn't? What if we can't? What if I don't want to?"

"Maggie, you know that these patterns are deep within who you are, as well as in what is to be. Some things are set in us long before we get to them."

"All I know is that for now I need to put my focus on just about anything else. Let's write your story, then after that's done we'll see about mine."

Mary's Words

I left Eli and his father to head out into the mysteries. Laborers planted the last of spring crops, birds called out in nesting ritual, the river ran full to its banks, the sun rode high in the sky, afternoon rains replenished the soil and embraced newly sprouting seeds. Soon there would be many new mouths to feed off the rich produce of spring's fertility. New growth of every kind would recreate the world around us.

What a perfect time to resume spreading inner fertility and replenishment. A time to soften people's hearts like spring rain softens soil. A time to stimulate new growth like spring's warmth touches off each seed's sprouting, to awaken budding possibilities, to renew the rich experience of life, and bring forth life's exuberant potential.

All of life is thick with seeds waiting to germinate and burst forth in extravagant growth. Let any garden return to its natural cycle and it will grow the most impressive, spontaneous massing of wild specimens we can imagine. Turn the soil and a whole new population gets its chance. In any patch of earth there are more and more and more seeds waiting for the right conditions to awaken, to send themselves hurtling into full, colorful expression.

We are God's soil full of seeds, full of potential eager to flourish given the opportunity. Our rain and sunlight are God's grace and love, there to awaken in us those seeds of possibility, of expression, of expanded being, seeds carried in us waiting for the right circumstances, waiting for spring.

It is as simple as allowing spring rain and sunshine. When we open ourselves to life, to the miracle of renewal, to the mysteries of pattern and form, to the fullness of being, we allow all of life's abundance. Allowing beauty along with pain, sweetness and sorrow, disappointment, joy, hope, and despair. Allowing the child's smile, the cat's hard-edged calling in the night, the brilliance of a ripe fruit against green leaves, the fermenting decay in deep woods, the crisp air of winter, the wonder of a flock of birds flying as one shifting, fluid form. Allowing the miracle of life and aliveness and being in every creature, in every perception, in every moment, the miracle of springtime, of sprouting seeds, of awakening possibility, of the human spirit within each person's heart.

"Yeshua!" I gasped. "You have held my possibilities; you held my understanding."

"I held your beauty," he said.

"Then you reminded me of it so I could find my way back to its fullness."

"Yes."

"Thank you," I said.

I walked on until evening, rediscovering the wonders of being out in the land all day, walking the earth, feeling it pass beneath my feet with the sky overhead. Rediscovering home in my heart, in my perception, in my knowing what is and where I fit in it all. Rediscovering Mary Magdalene.

That night I stayed at a modest inn, treating myself to a first night's soft bed and morning meal with some of the money Reuben insisted I take with me. After this I would stay where I found myself and eat what was provided.

At breakfast I was the only woman not serving the tables. Some of the other customers eyed me curiously, some with hostility. I'd forgotten how it was to be a woman traveling alone. For more than a year it had been easy to sink into what passed for normalcy, being a member of a household headed by a man. I had quickly forgotten how foreign that was to me, and instead adjusted to protected ease.

Now I remembered that it was the women who were far more mistrustful of a woman alone than were the men. Some asked me questions, but most made up their own explanations, often dark ones full of judgment and resentment. When I encountered much of that, I kept to myself and moved on quickly.

Usually the men looked me over, then ignored me. Occasionally one would try to catch my eye, or even take a seat at my table. It was easy to tell what he had in mind, and usually easy to discourage him. Every so often his persistence and my resistance drew attention so that someone else stepped in to send him on his way. I was careful leaving the building after such an encounter, usually mixing in with a group and watching for trouble.

How complacent I had become! How used to assuming innocence. I'd have to reawaken my recognition now, or I'd close off meaningful encounters, too.

This morning there was nothing disturbing, only brief, polite greetings, and conversation with one gentleman sitting nearby. We spoke about my traveling north on the road on which he had come south. Three years of drought to the north was far past where I was headed, but the many moving to the south filled available beds along the way. He suggested detouring to the west.

"I cannot do that, my things are already sent ahead," I said.

"If you are determined to continue, do you at least have a confirmed place to stay?"

"I shall see," I replied.

He looked into my face, then shook his head and said, "You are a stubborn woman."

I held the gaze, replying, "I am a woman who knows what she is about."

He nodded. "Then God be with you," he said. He gathered his things, tipped his hat my way, and left.

I smiled, "Yes, God is with me. Yes, indeed." I soon followed him out the door, and turned north.

"Mary Magdalene! I have been trying to find you!" The woman's voice grabbed me from behind as I finished paying for a small bag of fruit at a busy market booth this early morning. Vendors brought foods and wares from all over the region to sell in open stalls. Shoppers filled the aisles, ladened with baskets and bags to carry home.

"Here, Abrile, take this home to your mother," I said to the child at my side before looking to see who had spoken to me. "Shana, how are you? How is your father?"

"Oh, Mary, he is not at all well. That's why I've searched for you. You must come to see him." Her face filled with anguish and she clasped my arm.

It was happening now like it used to. I was led to one person or one place, then to another and another. Everywhere I went they were waiting for me. It did not matter what town or what season, how many days, or who I knew, they found me and brought me to where I needed to be.

"Let's go now," I told her, and we left the market through the far side filled with colorful fabrics and piles of kitchenware, rows of new, bright clay jugs, and noisy cages full with small animals and birds. We walked through quiet streets of shops just beginning to open, then past closed gates and doors of prosperous homes. Shana turned in at the modest entrance to a compound built around an open courtyard.

"Will you have some tea and breakfast while I tell you what has happened?" she asked.

I nodded and we entered a low doorway into a cozy kitchen with fire on the hearth and the smell of baking bread filled the room. Shana spoke to the dark woman there, then led me into a comfortable sitting room.

"Father had been doing so well! Ever since we last saw you, there had been no reoccurrence of that pain, or the nausea either. His vigor and enthusiasm returned. He seemed like his younger self again. But then one day he fell. And another I found him confused, not sure where he was. He was frightened. I was, too. Since then we never know, sometimes he is fine, other times he stumbles or drifts off. I haven't known what to do, Mary. Praises be that you are here! You are such a comfort to him. You must help him!"

"Where is he now?" I asked.

"Sleeping still. He stays up late at night carving wood by lamplight, and rises mid-morning. I hate to rouse him. Can you stay? Have something to eat and we'll catch up. Tell me what you have been doing, and how you have been."

We chatted as the sun rose, brightening the sky. It would be a hot day; already this early sun baked dry soil and parched foliage. It burned the browned skin of those who spent their days out in it. This was a dry, hot season in a place accustomed to it. Water was precious here, and the whole community cooperated in preserving it.

Firewood clattered into the wooden box by the kitchen hearth. "Ah, he's up," said Shana. "Let me go tell him you are here."

I'd forgotten how tall Avi was. His slender frame stooped to come through the doorway. That smile was as bright as ever, and we greeted each other warmly, then shared tea as he ate and talked. I looked to Shana and she nodded. He seemed fine this morning.

He suddenly changed topics. "I had a conversation with God last night."

"So did I," I said, smiling.

"No, I mean really," he insisted.

"Tell me about it."

"It wasn't a long one. He never says a lot. He gets right to the point."

"What was the point last night?" I asked.

"I was telling him about how I used to know how to select just the right tree to cut for the wood I needed. I'd go out in the mountains and be with the trees till I knew. Now I have to go to a yard here in town where the lumber is already cut and stacked. I pick out a piece someone else has already begun to shape." Tears filled his eyes.

"It's not the same, is it?" I said, putting my hand on his arm.

"No. The heart has gone out of it. And then I have to work so hard to get it back in again."

"The heart, yes," I said, and as I waited for Avi to continue I looked at his heart and saw that it was stiffened and protected.

"So, I asked God this," he went on, "I said, 'What is this? This isn't wood I'm working with. This is something else, some artificial material I have to pretend is wood.'

"And God said, 'Avi, what are you saying? It's just cut up a bit.'

"'The life's gone out of it,' I told him.

"'You are a stubborn old man,' he said, 'who won't have it any way but your own.' And I laughed."

I felt myself reach out to lay my hand on Avi's heart.

"That feels good, Mary," he said.

"Go on, Avi," I replied.

"So I said, 'What's your point?' I always get to that, you know. He sort of waits for me to ask that."

I smiled.

"God smiled, just like you're doing. He does that, too," Avi said, nodding his head, and I smiled some more as he continued. "Then God said, 'Okay, listen up.' He always says that, 'Listen up.' Then he said, 'You are boxing yourself into a corner where you have no space to move.

Focus on what really matters and let go of the rest.' Well, of course he's right. He's always right."

I nodded.

"I've been making these silly little carvings that I take down to Amin and he sells them for me. I haven't seen any more than that in the wood. But you know what? I'm going to have a talk with Amin and I am going to explain to him what I want in a piece of wood, and he can find it for me. He's got a decent eye for wood. He just needs a little encouragement, now doesn't he? And I'm just the one to do it."

"Avi," I said, "talk to me about your head. What's going on in your head that makes you lose your way?"

"There's a pressure there, Mary, like a finger is pushing sometimes, inside, right here." And he pointed to a spot a few inches behind his right temple.

Shana's eyes widened. "He's never told me this," she said. I nodded.

"Can we see if we can take care of that, Avi?" I asked.

"Sure, Mary. I'd just as soon not have this," he said.

I took a deep breath and opened to God's presence. I felt Jesus at my right shoulder. My left hand went to the spot Avi had pointed to, and the right one went low behind his head. I felt his body relax and my hands seemed to sink into his head until they held the pressure spot. It lay heavy and dense in my palms.

"Please, God," I said, "through Jesus and through me, please bring your blessings upon this good man who always listens to what you say to him. Let your love fill his heart and overflow to heal this thickness in his head and ease his way. I ask for healing here, if it is to be, and I rejoice in your glorious light in the world."

My hands stayed there for a long time, until I realized they were empty and able to move. I felt like shaking out some minimal, dry residue. Avi stirred at the same time. As my hands released he rolled his head this way and that, and exclaimed, "Hey! That's amazing! It's gone! It's not there, for the first time in months. Mary! You're an angel from God!"

"I'm just a simple wood carver like yourself," I said, and we both smiled. Then I thanked God. "On behalf of this patient man and my humble self, we thank you for your love and your blessings. Thank you for bringing life and grace to everything that is." I placed a hand on top of Avi's head and said, "You are blessed, Avi. Do not hesitate, do not hold back. Listen with your spirit, see with your heart." I placed my other hand on his heart. "You will find the way. God blesses you."

Tears ran down Avi's cheeks. His hands reached out for his daughter, and Shana took them in hers. "I hear you, Lord, I hear you!" he exclaimed.

I slipped away unnoticed. The sun was bright in the courtyard. I took a cup of water to go sit in the shade of a tree with the gratitude and peace that filled my heart.

A man and a mule-drawn cart soon entered the courtyard. "Good day, missus," he said. "I've brought this wood for one called Avi. A stranger on the mountain told me it is for him and paid me to deliver it.

"Thank you, sweet Yeshua!" I exclaimed under my breath. Walking toward the man I said, "I will find out where to stack it. Please come in out of the sun and have a drink of water."

I looked up into the mountains and remembered the peace I had found there. Sometimes it was not so easy to be alone. Yes, now people surrounded me; yes, I was loved and generously cared for; and yes, I knew God. But it was not family, not steady and predictable and constant. Not get up in the morning and bump the same shoulder you have bumped for twenty years. Not anticipating someone's likes and dislikes, expecting that same scowl or twinkle or groan. I missed companionship, be it family or lover or close friend. I missed familiar, physical-presence companionship.

I went down into the city and there I found a man who reminded me a little of Jesus. Aaron was a caring man, reaching out to those in need or in trouble. He searched out places they could escape the cold or the heat, eat, sleep, bathe, or rest, and he brought people there, even carried them himself. He wasn't afraid to look them in the eyes or to touch them. He wasn't afraid to share his own bounty. He wasn't afraid to recognize the humanity, and the God, in every one.

I stayed and helped him for a while. There was much to be done. It is harder in the city to just get by. Somehow on a mountain all you need is a small shelter, a stream, and what little you can carry. The city complicates all that. So, one thing we taught them was how to live on the mountain, how to come back to simplicity. Some of them were clever, then, at translating that to their city life, and they, in turn, taught others.

We could see their faces ease. There is so much fear when people do not know what is happening. They have not learned to trust God to provide for them. They do not know, or they have forgotten, that there is a natural way with things, that life works. For the most part, a tree receives the rain and sunlight it needs. It grows, it weathers storm and season, it sets seeds and yields fruit, it reproduces itself, it matures, and it lives a full life. So does a person, if only they can let the process unfold.

If we can be like the tree and open ourselves to the sun and rain, flex in the wind, adapt ourselves to the seasons, and trust the life processes, we find a natural current carries us through, guiding and supporting us. We can let go of those burdens and worries and fears we've collected up and now clutch so determinedly to our chests, and let the current take them.

That current is what God offers us. Opening our hearts to allow that current to carry us changes everything, and makes life possible.

Aaron and I spoke for long hours into the night about faith and God and life. I told him many stories of my experiences traveling the land, touching people's hearts. I told him about Jesus and his messages and the followers who intend to carry on his mission. I told him about Sanctuary Farm and its women, about studying after hours, about living on the dark side of life.

He came from privilege. Aaron's family had wealth and he had access to it. He spent what he could on those in need, bridging two worlds, trying to narrow the chasm. It challenged his family. They wanted him to be a scholar, but he could not stay with books when he knew there were others with no food and no safe care.

When I spoke about seeing people's hearts open, his eyes lit up. He wanted to know more. He wanted to understand. I had to laugh, because as he did that I saw his own heart open more, though I would not have thought it could open any farther.

Then I understood that as long as we have any fears at all, as long as we hang on to any distrust, any caution, any expectation, we do not give ourselves over to faith and wholeness and knowing and peace. It does not take much to hold ourselves back. In doing so we close down our hearts. We do not allow our spirit to receive God's love and transform us. Even this kind, generous, humble man, who clearly did God's work, still clung to fear that stopped him from being truly alive.

I prayed with him, kneeling in the tiny dark room where six people had spent the last night. We asked to open his heart, and then we asked to open the hearts of those who had resources to help, as well as those who needed them. We asked that a way be shown for bringing people up out of despair, bringing them into the light of day and into hopefulness and faith.

It wasn't long before a friend of Aaron's parents, one who owned many buildings in the city, came forward with the idea of using one of his empty buildings for Aaron's work. This became "The House of Light." Aaron and others did much good work there for many years.

—~—

"I have to go," I said one day.

"Why?" he insisted.

I looked deep in his eyes and found such comfort there, as always. "This is your work, not mine," I said.

Aaron dropped his eyes to the floor, then nodded.

I took his shoulders in my hands. "You know I will always hold you in my heart."

"I wish you would stay," he said, his eyes pleading.

"I have to go," I said.

He sighed. "Yes, of course you do. I see you gazing into the distance, clasping your hands in your lap. You have work to do, and it is out there, not here"

We hugged, then he turned away. I gathered my things and left.

Body and Blood

Cloud crawls around trees and steeples,
hiding mountains and sun,
raining since yesterday morning,
roofs slick with wet, puddling in yards and street,
streaming, filling, overflowing.
Why isn't rain salty like my tears?
Like ocean? Like blood?
It gathers me, as it surrounds me, back
into womb and sea and primordial origins,
with its close clouds and muted light
and thick moistness.

You lift up the goblet of wine and the loaf of bread,
body and blood, you say, and I feel it
in my bones and flesh, in my cells, in my soul,
Jesus' message, God's message,
origins, primordial and sacred.
Spirit come into physical being, to be here, to be this,
soul come into person,
into life, awareness, and moment.

Body and blood, spirit into flesh, soul into tangible form,
with bread and wine you lift up my vision
from everyday concerns to what we really are,
carriers, holders, bringers, touchers, lovers,
God's love here in the world,
God's presence, God's wonder,
wandering, trying to find our feet,
God's soul-children, trying to find our feet
in the rain.

Body and blood, spirit into flesh,
God into Jesus, God into me.
Be God's hands, be God's eyes, be God's heart,
be God's touch, be God's smile, be God's peace,
be God's love in this world
of tears and rain and ocean and
cloud and tree and mountain.
Spirit come into this world,
spirit come into body and blood,
spirit come into bread and wine,
spirit come into me.

And the rain keeps falling.

Chapter Thirteen: Body and Blood

Mary's Words

Often it was a child who found me and brought me to where I needed to be. They more clearly recognized possibilities and connected the lines. So it was this time. The girl followed me all through the morning and all over town. She would not approach, even when I smiled, just lagged behind, watching. Maybe she had not made up her mind yet. I was patient.

I ate and left food on a ledge, gestured to it, then walked on. She eagerly ate some of it, then stuffed the rest inside her clothes. Ah, I thought, she is caring for someone.

I stopped and sat in the shade as if to rest, drew out a cloth with pretty stones from the mountains, and spread them before me. Then leaning against the wall, I pretended to nod off. It worked. The girl crept close, eyeing the array, then closer, until she touched one, intrigued. Slowly I half opened one eye. She looked at the eye, and kept looking at it, sizing me up. Then she sat down, wrapping her arms around herself.

"What's your name?" I asked.

"Mary," she said.

"Ah," I replied. "Me too. Mary." We smiled at each other. She was nearly as tall as me, with the long, loose arms and legs of a young one still growing. Her wide, black eyes watched every movement. She had tied her thick, dark hair back with a plain scarf, but lively tendrils escaped at every edge.

"What are these rocks for?" she asked, touching another one.

"Sometimes I do something with them, like this right now. But mostly they remind me of places I like to remember."

"What are you doing right now with them?"

"Meeting you, Mary," I said with a smile.

She smiled again, too, letting her face loosen, the full mouth expanding into rounded cheeks. "You're a healer, aren't you? Can you heal Olefre?"

"I don't know. Who is Olefre?"

"Does that matter? Does that decide if you can or not?"

"No," I said, "I just wondered why you are the one asking."

"I'm asking because there isn't anyone else to do the asking."

"Let's go see Olefre," I said, gathering the stones and standing up.

Mary led the way through narrow alleys and passageways behind and under the life of the town. If I had needed to know where I was, it would have been impossible to keep track, but I had released that need a long time ago. I knew I was where I needed to be. We entered a low doorway and came into a smoke-filled room.

"Oh, no!" Mary yelled. "I told you not to start a fire till I got back!" She threw open the door and the only window at the rear of the room, grabbed a tool, and set about adjusting the flue. I stooped low just inside the doorway, under the smoke, and searched for another person in the room.

Someone tapped me on the shoulder from behind. "Looking for me?"

"Olefre?" I asked, unable to tell if this wrinkled, stooped, ancient person was man or woman.

"Come out of there, Mary!" Olefre yelled at the child. "You'll pass out from the smoke."

Mary burst past us into the alleyway, gasping for breath. "It'll be okay in a few minutes," she said.

"I knew you'd fix it," said Olefre.

"Good thing I came when I did."

"Whenever would have been fine," the old one responded, turning to me. "And you are?"

"I am Mary," I said, nodding my head in respect.

"Another Mary? Good. That is good."

"Are you a relative of this girl's? Or a friend?" I asked.

"All of the above and more. I would be grandmother, were I able to care for her, but she cares for me and I am the granddaughter."

I nodded.

"Here, I have food, eat!" said Mary, shoving a handful of food toward Olefre.

"See? What did I tell you?" Olefre said, shrugging her shoulders. She carefully chewed on one side of her mouth, grimacing with each bite. Watching her eat, I saw how very thin she was beneath loose clothing.

"Look how hard it is for her to eat," said Mary. "She needs soft fruit and well-cooked grains. Her teeth are bad, and then her belly does not hold the food anyway. It spews it out as fast as she puts it in."

"Olefre," I asked, "when you finish eating may I examine you? Perhaps I can help."

"She's a healer, Olefre!" blurted Mary. "I found you a healer."

"We can't pay anything," protested the old woman.

"I am well taken care of," I replied.

"Oh? Some rich benefactor sends you out into the slums?"

"Not that. Let me have a look."

"Sure, but you're not going to see anything, because there's nothing there," she said, defiantly.

In a way she was right. It was as if she weren't there in her body, but instead hovering around it, here and there, darting out of reach. Within the abandoned body, especially through her lower torso, I sensed globs of dark heaviness. I had seen this before. I looked into her eyes, placing my hand on her upper chest. "Come back and talk to me, Olefre."

"Is there a point?" she asked.

"There is always something to do to ease the way," I said.

"Is she going to die?" insisted the child.

"Yes, I am," said Olefre. "I told you that. This healer, she won't change that."

"Are you ready for it?" I asked.

"I'm resigned to it. There is one thing you could do for me, though. Take this child to my niece in the city."

"No!" protested Mary. "I won't leave you!"

"Not now, you silly child," said Olefre. "Afterward. After I go."

"Not before?" I asked.

"You think you could get her to leave before? Be my guest, and good if you can. Save her the knowing."

"Maybe I'm supposed to know, huh?" declared Mary. "Maybe I'm supposed to know it all."

"Are you in pain, Olefre?" I asked. "There are herbs that can help."

"Expensive ones."

"I have some in my bag."

"I could try that, if you insist."

Young Mary replied, "I insist!"

—w—

I moved into their little room with them and together the three of us walked Olefre's path. We spent time out in sunshine and basked in the phases of the moon, we told stories and played games, we laughed, we loved, and we felt blessed each day. I found benefactors with food and bedding, the herbs to make Olefre comfortable, and kind visitors to stay with her while Mary came with me to help attend to others and to explore being a child. For Olefre life eased, for Mary it blossomed.

"You've got to find Etta a husband!" insisted the old woman one evening about that afternoon's caretaker. "She fusses and fusses over me. I can hardly take a breath without her jumping up to check on me. She needs babies!"

"Maybe I'll take her with me down to Ruth's. She can help with the babies there."

"There you go. That'll do it. Find me one who is more worn out so I can get some rest."

"Are you tired, Olefre? Is it progressing?"

"Oh, my dear, it will come along in its own time. I don't evaluate it. I just see what this moment brings."

"Is there anything you would like to do that we have not taken care of?" I asked.

"Well, I haven't mentioned this, Mary, but I had thought that some time in my life I would get up to the mountains."

"What would you do there, Olefre?"

"I've heard you can get close to God there," she said with twinkling eyes.

"Oh, you sly one, that was me told you that!"

"Well, do you think we could?"

"You know you'll be with God soon anyway."

"Yes, but I've got some talking to do first, some things to straighten out here before I go."

"That sounds important. And you need to do it on the mountain?"

"That would be a good place."

"I will see what we can do."

"You work miracles, Mary. I know you will find a way."

—w—

One week later, a young carpenter named Benjamin came with his wagon and we began our journey. Olefre sat in the back on cushions with most of our little household around her. Mary stayed with her while I rode on the seat up front.

"You are so kind to do this, Benjamin," shouted Olefre from the back. "Thank you!"

"Yes, ma'am. And if you say that one more time I'm quitting right here."

"Oh, I better shut up, then. Mary, pass me that bundle and I'll show you my mother's jade piece."

"You brought that?" exclaimed young Mary. "Did you bring everything?"

"Yep."

"Well, let's leave it safely bundled for now."

"Okay, grandma," said Olefre, laughing. She had been lively like this ever since we had decided to go.

Benjamin was the son of a carpenter who was the son of a carpenter, so he knew the mountain forests well. He would leave us in a spot with good shelter, then go do some tree felling. Ordinarily he would have loaded his wagon for the return trip with wood cut on previous trips and left to dry, but this time he had agreed to carry us back home instead.

The trip was difficult for Olefre. No amount of cushioning could protect her from the rough ride. But this was the only way we could get her up into the mountains. She could not walk it.

Late in the day Benjamin stopped the wagon and said, "I'm going to take Olefre on the mule for this last part. It will be easier. You two can walk along if you like, or wait till I bring the wagon up."

"Benjamin, I've never ridden a mule," Olefre said, eyeing the creature suspiciously.

"You're not too tired?" Mary asked. "You won't fall off?"

"She'll be fine. I'll see to it," said Benjamin.

So we walked the last two hours up the mountain. It was a good way to arrive there, touching the earth, single file in the silence, sounding only footsteps, each delving into our own sense of place and purpose.

The shelter was an open lean-to in a clearing near a bright mountain stream. Mary gathered firewood while we waited for Benjamin to bring our things. Then we set up camp and Olefre slept. She never complained, but the trip had exhausted her.

I prayed that evening, "Dear God, please open a path for this precious, aged child of your heart to complete what she has undertaken. And guide me to know how to support her in every way I can. And thank you for the reminders to pay attention."

Animals called out all night long. It was comforting. It brought me back to essential living, unburdening me of the complexities of human life. Eat, sleep, mate, survive, live, die. Here on the mountain, spirit was so ingrained in every aspect of nature that there didn't ever need to be mention of God. Every movement, every breath, every leaf, every pebble, every drop, every spark of life was pure God in its very existence. So there was no "God" on the mountain or in nature because it was all God.

Here there was no such thing as hesitation, no questioning, no doubt, no discouragement, no blame, no decisions to be made. There was simply being, in its purest, clearest, most complete sense. With absolute trust and faith and knowing that what is is.

We humans sometimes have to come to the mountains or the desert or the water to remember this way of being. To remind ourselves how simple it is to live as holy being surrounded by holy being, knowing holiness, being holiness, simply, wholly, being.

I woke early, before dawn, in that breathless chill between inhale and exhale. The last of the night creatures scurried across our clearing. An early bird called as the barest tinge of light entered the eastern sky. Olefre had said, "Take me to the mountains," but it had been what I needed, too.

The sun would not come onto the campsite until late in the morning because it had to clear the ridge first. I left Olefre and Mary to sleep late and climbed up and around to meet the dawn on a high flat rock that overlooked distant land below. I spent the early morning in quiet solitude there, and returned each dawn to sit alone in silent awe at the sun's rising on another day.

I needed that way to begin, for the days with Olefre's decline drove me to depths I had not known before. All three of us wandered in our own labyrinths, alone with our thoughts and fears and doubts. Some days we barely spoke to one another, silently performing whatever tasks were needed, grateful for a touch or a look, but unable to tolerate more. Along with Olefre, Mary and I journeyed into those realms close to God, where truth and self and faith demanded perfect awareness, and nothing else existed.

I sat on the rock in the first light of each day and my heart ached. Sometimes impressions came of events or situations passed and I sobbed for that younger me who lived such desperate times. Sometimes there was nothing to which to attach the sorrow, and I cried out in anguish to the colors of the sunrise, so absent from grief, so impossible in pain.

There on that ledge I found perfect honesty with myself, clear down to my core. I faced my missteps and my frailties. I sat as alone as I had ever been. If God was around me in the mountains and in the sunrise, soon I could no longer sense any presence or support. All I knew was myself facing myself, completely, and alone.

I walked back down the trail, leaving fully expressed morning on the ledge, returning to prolonged dawn on the shadow side of the mountain. Meditation felt incomplete lately; I could not touch that sacred place where all things meet. I could not reach my hand out far enough because I had slipped too far from it. So all the webs and filmy coverings held their ground among my thoughts and there was no clarity.

Olefre's condition quickly worsened. Unless she recovered, she could not make the trip back out of the mountains. She would finish life here and be buried here. We would not risk having to bury her next to the road. But she knew all this from the first.

I had not seen her so peaceful and happy as she was now. And I had never seen her in such pain either, or so in need of comfort and reassurance.

I tried to reach out to her, tried to connect, but the gestures seemed hollow, the touches ineffective. Perhaps each of the three of us needed to do this alone, Olefre most of all. Mary and I did what we could to care for her physical needs, and we hoped our presence was enough. It was all we could do.

Mary spent her days exploring the forest and mountains alone. I was grateful when she returned each time after many hours away. She was easy with being out there. She quickly learned to gather food and herbs on her way.

Olefre found her own spot on the edge of a nearby meadow. She sat there most of each day, in sun or light rain, watching wild life happen around and before her. As she grew weaker she seemed to grow stronger. There was a peace about her. Perhaps I could no longer find God on the mountain, but she had.

I went sometimes in the afternoon to sit near her, to share in her peacefulness. I knew, sitting there, that she sat with God, and angels surrounded her. She knew the grace of complete acceptance and she sank deeply into God's love. I saw it, I felt it, but I could not get to it myself. I sat outside of it, alone, waiting.

Waiting? Was I back to that?

Yes, I realized with a start. I had forgotten to look for Jesus. I had accepted the loneliness and separation, walked in it, lived in it, resigned myself to it. I hadn't even thought to look to see if he was here. And now I looked and saw that he was not here. I was entirely alone. All I could do was hope that it was true that God's existence still came to me through the mountain, even if I could not sense it.

I could not remember ever feeling so alone. Then bits and pieces came to me from that previous time, when Jesus died and I could not reach God and my heart closed. I remembered sitting, then, looking out at the land, feeling the emptiness in the land, knowing the land waited, empty, like I did.

So I returned to the rock ledge and sat again, looking out over the land, waiting. Day after day I waited. At first I felt so lost. I was more question than knowing. Then gradually, over the empty days, I began to let go of the questions. And then I let go of the need to know where I was. Gradually I came back to just being. I was Mary, on the rock, within existence. And that was enough.

Then one day I knew that the existence surrounding me, and my awareness of it, was God. And then I knew that the rock I sat upon, that held me and supported me, was God. And then I knew Jesus was right here, and had been here all along, waiting with me, patient and true, just as he always said he would. I felt his presence, I felt his hand on my heart, I felt the love between us. I looked in his eyes, deep and clear and fully open to the depths of all he is, and I knew, with no question or doubt or hesitation, that I am a bright, clear, perfect being, and this being that is me is a repository for God's love and blessing in this world. As are we all, if we can only make room for knowing it, if we can only open, even slightly, to awareness of it. If we can only allow ourselves to be any small part of the beauty that we are.

"You did it again, Yeshua. You held my beauty until I could get back to it."

"Yes, I did. And I always will."

"You are such a blessing to me. There is such love."

"Ah, there your heart is opening again. You were so lost for a while."

"I feel it opening. I feel love pouring into it and out of it, multiplying itself as it heals the pains of these past weeks, as it embraces the loneliness."

"Release yourself into it, Mary. Allow yourself total trust and faith in the love. Let it hold you, like this mountain ledge holds you, like the dawn holds you, like existence holds you. Let it fill you and expand, let it expand your heart and expand you, until love and consciousness of that love are all there is, are everything as far as far goes, filling all being. Let all that is be love."

We sat together in silence on the rock ledge as the sun rose and the sky blossomed with colors and light. We sat together and I knew I was never alone, even in the deepest despair. He had always been with me, right here, waiting even as I waited. Even though, for whatever reason in what I was going through, I blinded and numbed myself to him and then sat here not at all aware of his presence. Even though I did not allow myself to know the connection that would always be between us.

I looked at him now and he smiled. He had such trust in me. He waited, always, knowing I would come back to him, knowing it much better than I did. Thank God! I wanted to exclaim, "Don't ever leave me!" But I smiled instead, because he never would.

My heart knew that, deep within. And the knowledge was safe there, even when I needed to close myself off, even when I found myself painfully alone, even when I waited, not knowing why or what for. My heart's deep places knew that he was always here, and that I would find my way back to him.

I came down the mountain path slowly this time, cherishing every step as sacred journey, feeling the miracle in everything I touched and saw and heard and felt. The sun filtered through a canopy of fresh new leaves, casting brightness into the world below. Birds sang out their extravagant spring enthusiasm for life. New shoots began adventuring from cool earth toward the light. Delicate blossoms scattered color across the floor of the forest, adding exotic highlights of scent to the underlying smells of earth and green and renewal.

I entered the campsite clearing wondering what changes I would discover there, coming from this fullness of awareness. If Jesus was here all along, what else had I closed myself off from? Mary sat on the ground by the fire circle, a long stick in her hand, absently poking at the coals. She glanced up as I came to sit next to her.

"She's gone," Mary said, shoving her stick into the coals again.

"Gone? You mean she wandered off again?" I asked. A couple of times Olefre had forgotten how to get to her meadow spot and headed off in the wrong direction. "Why are you sitting here instead of finding her?" I asked. Then I knew. Gone. Olefre was gone. Now I sighed and asked quietly, "Where is she?"

"At the meadow," answered Mary.

I began to speak, but she interrupted me.

"I already started digging there. She should be there," Mary said.

I nodded, and we sat for a while in silence, staring at the sparks released by Mary's jabbing stick. We did not talk or touch each other, but we felt each other's presence, finally. We sat together, no longer separately. We allowed the comfort of that to wrap around us in the shelter of the forest.

—

Benjamin soon arrived. "Thought I'd check on you today," he said, not knowing until we told him. Then he sat with us by the fire. When he offered to dig the grave, Mary said no, she wanted to do it. He gave her a good shovel from his wagon, and she returned to digging. Benjamin gathered firewood and tended to the campsite while I began to prepare the body for burial. As I worked I remembered not being able to do that for Jesus. Remembering, again, that time of loss and emptiness.

Jesus' hand settled onto my shoulder as he said, "I am sorry to have put you through that. I tried to warn you but it was too much to hear."

"I could do it now," I said. "This time I would understand." He laughed. "Tell me," I asked, "is it the same now for Olefre? Will she rise up out of her grave and still be with us?"

"I have said that I will walk among the people to show that our spirits continue after death, but I am a bit of a special case." He hesitated.

"You are still so unassuming that you hate to even say that!"

He smiled. "Mary, you say I am a blessing in your life. You have been such a blessing for me. You have truly known me, in all I have been, from dirty feet and bad moods and self-doubt and all the way to the sublimely sacred. And through it all you have cherished my whole being, all of it. That is such a gift! You open my heart."

"Yeshua, my dear! I could do no less. It simply is what is."

"That is what I mean. You do not hesitate. You do not falter. There is no room for doubt or questioning or reservation. You are right here," he said, and he laid his hand on his own heart. Then he reached across to lay the other on mine.

I took a deep breath and let myself fully be in that moment, in that connection, in that touch. Around us spread the burial preparations and the bright meadow and the mountain forest and the brilliance of a sunlit afternoon in late spring. And around and through all that, was God's loving embrace.

Mary stopped digging, walked out into the wildflowers, and lay down among them, face up to the deep blue of the sky. Benjamin appeared at the edge of the woods and he watched a hawk soar high and wide on warming mountain air currents.

Later we finished burying Olefre. I laid her hands upon her heart and wrapped her in the blanket she slept under every night. Benjamin sang prayers I recognized from long ago. Mary gathered flowers.

"Thank you, God, for the life of this wonderful woman," I said. "She has been a joy, as well as a challenge, for those who were fortunate to spend time with her. She showed us how to be real, how to hold to what we know to be true, and how to continue to do what needs doing, no matter the cost. She has been an inspiration and a blessing.

"And now, her spirit walks with you," I continued, feeling Jesus' hand on my shoulder. "Forever. In everlasting life and love. May she be in the peace she so deserves."

"Good-bye, Olefre," said Mary. "Good-bye, Grandmother."

Mary scattered her blossoms over the grave. Benjamin placed a stone on it and chanted an ancient prayer. We stood in silence and left as we each completed our good-byes. Then we stayed one more night, together, on the mountain.

Early the next morning I returned to the ledge and sat in that familiar spot where the stone fits my body, waiting for the sun to rise one more time to reach my face with its light.

"I'm back, God," I said. "I'm really here. Do you think I am a fool with my wanderings and confusion? Do you know that I will return knowing more than I did? Do you watch over me to make sure I do not go too far astray?"

I gazed out at the land just beginning to distinguish itself from sky. I could see as far as two days walk from here, at least. And the land spoke to me, calling to me to come down from the mountain again and walk among its people. I would begin by taking Mary to the city to find her cousins.

Chapter Fourteen: Spirit into Flesh

Mary's Words

We rode toward home in silence at first, Mary and I together in the back of the wagon, sharing the bedding as cushion. We bumped and jostled each other, and grabbed on as the wagon lurched. Touch assured us that we were alive and here and not alone.

"I miss her," said Mary, welling up with tears.

I nodded, put my arm around her, and replied, "Life changes. This is a big one."

Mary nodded and leaned into my body. "She was very peaceful at the end. She did what she needed to do."

"That's important. We should all pay more attention to what we need to do."

"What do you need to do, Mary?" asked the child.

"I need to keep my heart open. That is the most important thing. When I do that I feel the love flow through me. My hands do God's work, my touch is God's touch, and my words are God's words. Then I am at peace. Then I am where I need to be, doing what I need to do."

"How do you know that? How did you figure all that out?" she asked.

"I figured it out by stopping trying to figure it out. I let go of wanting to know how and why. The first step was when I woke up at the women's farm. I saw that I hadn't died, that I was going to spend more time in this life. I saw that another day would happen whether I wanted it to or not. So I watched that new day, I watched its footsteps and sounds and passing light. I watched with no desire or need and let it happen."

"That's what I did on the mountain!" exclaimed young Mary. "Just be there and watch it all, as if I were invisible. Almost as if I could pass right through a tree without any resistance. I even tried that a couple of times, it seemed so real. But I wasn't quite able to."

I smiled. Such a wise one already, and still so young.

"Do you ever feel like that?" she asked me.

"Oh, yes, Sometimes I melt right into all that is, and there are no edges and no separation at all. It is all pure being."

"I like that."

"In that sense of oneness, that total immersion in being, where all there is is is, I realize that all of being is saturated with such enveloping love! Total, absolute love, with no conditions, no judgments, no holding back. And that love is God."

"So that's God. I've seen that love in Olefre's eyes and in the deep forest and on a rock ledge in sunshine."

"You have been on my rock ledge, eh?"

"Oh, is it yours?" she asked.

This child grew wiser by the minute. "Well, no," I replied with a smile, "I only borrowed it, as did you."

We rode a while in silence again, until Mary spoke.

"You said yesterday that Olefre is with God now. But today you're saying that everything is full of God. So, she was always with God."

"Both are true. There is more to us than this body and our thoughts and feelings. There is that whole, vast, spirit-self that always knows and experiences the oneness. Olefre has returned to her wholeness."

"Nobody but you says these things, Mary," she said. "The God I hear about is a powerful being who decides what is right and wrong, like a judge or a king. Why do you talk about love and wholeness, and call that God? Why don't you call it something else?"

An answer took some thought. "I started with that other impression of God, too, a powerful judge watching over and deciding our fate. And I thought, when bad things happened to me, that I had done wrong and God had decided to punish me."

She nodded.

"But the more I saw of life, the less sense that made. There are very good people suffering terrible experiences. And not so good people living easy, comfortable lives. So I was confused. And then something happened..." I hesitated, caught as old waves of mourning claimed the next moments.

"Mary? Are you okay?" she asked, peering into my face.

"I had a child...and she was taken from me. I could not care for her, and there was a woman who had the means and so wanted a child. My child. I watched her go."

"You have a daughter?" Mary stared at me as I nodded. "Taken from you? Where is she? Do you know where she is?"

I shook my head.

"Can't you find her?"

"She is grown. She could be anywhere."

Again we rode in silence.

"There was another baby, too," I eventually continued, "a son. This one died inside my womb. He was stillborn."

"Oh," she said, and she put her hand on my heart.

Breathless, I asked, "How did you know to do that?"

"I don't know. I guess because you said the most important thing is to keep your heart open. And it just closed."

"You could tell that?"

"Yes," said this amazing child. "Go on, tell me about it, because this leads to God and love, and we both need to get there."

I sighed, then began again. "When there is a child out there in the world, where ever she is, growing and living life, there is possibility. But this other one, to die already? Before even taking a breath? Where was the just God in that? Where was right and wrong? Where was anything but blind grief? I was disgusted by a God who could be so heartless. So I turned my back on God. I walked on with no faith."

"That's why you don't observe the holy days and religious laws," she said.

"When you have no regular home, there is no foundation for that. And eventually I barely remembered."

Mary nodded. "Go on."

"Then at Sanctuary Farm I found goodness and generosity and complete acceptance and limitless love. It renewed me. It fed those places in me that yearned for meaning and richness of spirit. This was worth getting up to in the morning.

"I watched people from then on, and saw that in some there was a fundamental trust. They seemed to expect things to work out. Not that everything would be perfect, but that life would continue in some form and be worth living. They believed in hope and possibility. They saw the pure being and potential in a person, underneath the obvious. Those people knew something, whether they realized it or not.

"Still, I was skeptical. I was too caught up in my own losses and disappointments to really open to whatever it was that carried those people. I continued on, trying to touch that gentle trust, even if I could not fully grasp it.

"I found that, even without understanding it, without any idea how to truly be it, if I wanted to become something I could live it anyway, as if it were true, and before long it would gradually, naturally begin to happen. After a while it would begin to come from deep inside me, as if it were mine all along.

"When I treated people with respect and kindness, soon respect and kindness truly came from within me and I began to feel a deep love for each person, no matter what the circumstances. I listened to the land, heard its whispers and its exuberance, watched its colors and patterns and forms, felt its generosity, and accepted its offerings. Before I knew it I opened to its ancient wisdom, became part of its patterns, and knew where I belonged.

"I lived as if there was goodness underneath and supporting all that is. As if everything naturally, inevitably goes toward healing and wholeness. As if everyone desires to live a life of mutual caring and open generosity. As if we are all doing the best we can, and yearning to be the best person we can be. As if all life is precious and holy and beautiful and ours. As if we are only a tiny portion of all we see, and we do what we can for the good of the whole. I lived this way and I became this. For all this truly is who I am and who I have always been.

"As I did all this, I felt a new understanding of holiness coming through me from deep inside me, a holiness that is open-hearted loving for all that is, a holiness that sustains all existence, that is essential for our being who we can be. And then I knew this is the source of peace, of grace, of faith. This is that underlying, overlying, all encompassing caring, that endless, accepting, allowing love that is always with us. Oh, child, these words are so inadequate! They only limit our perception."

"You mean God, this is God," she said.

"Thank you for understanding." I smiled into her young, bright face.

"Mary," she asked, "what about the God who judges? The one who has all those laws? What happened to that God?"

"All that seems to have faded away for me," I said. "It is no longer relevant. I think it is like having one impression of someone for a while, and then you learn some more about her or him and your impression changes. Maybe the person changed, but maybe she didn't. Maybe it's just my impression that changed."

"Different people can have different impressions of the same person," she added.

"Yes, depending on their own perceptions and interpretations."

"So, some see the judge and some see unlimited love."

"Some see parent, some see friend," I continued. "Some see a remote God, some see God within."

"I like this. It explains a lot."

I looked at her eager face, and said, "I want to tell you about a man named Jesus. I met him later, after I had walked this way for a while, after I learned to let it come from within me and began to see it reflected all around me. He had such a gentleness about him. I saw that he knew. Not only did he know, but it was as if it came from so deep within him that its origins were there. I was drawn to that, and listened to his teachings. Now, Mary, Jesus was good at putting words to these things. He could capture an audience to the point that they barely breathed. His words were poetry that spoke to people's hearts and souls. He reached deep within them, touched them there, and awakened them there."

"You speak of the past. Is he gone?" she asked.

I smiled. Gone? How could I answer that? "Yeshua,?" I called to that other space where he and I meet. "What do I say to this child? Can she talk to you as I do? Are you always there for her, too?"

"Tell her I am here as that love you spoke of is here," he said, "always and everywhere for everyone. Tell her to look for me in the sunrise as well as in your words. She will know how to do that. And when she sees me she will see God and know God's love."

I conveyed his answer to Mary, and she curled against me to be with all she had heard. I wandered off in memories of conversations Jesus and I had in many places and times. We had shared our stories and what we understood, then went on from there, dancing with the images and impressions that grew out of all that and out of us.

"What happened to him, Mary?" asked my young friend as the wagon turned from one road to another. So I told her the stories of his last days, of the imprisonment and trial, of that dark, hellish day at the end, of my despair and the emptiness and waiting for something of life to reappear. I told her of the remarkable day when he returned, transformed into this other presence, and the message it brought. I told her that he was always with me now, if only I opened to knowing it. And that through that opening I came to knowing God within everything and within myself. I told her that because of the form he is in now he can be that for everyone. For her, too.

"There is a special relationship with you, though." She smiled and touched my heart again. "He fills your heart in a special way."

"Yes, he does." I smiled, too.

We rode for a while in silence, then Mary said, "Tell me why life is so hard if everything is love."

I laughed. "You have a lot of confidence in my ability to answer your questions. Well, I can tell you what I have found. That is all I know."

She nodded.

"I have seen many hardships in this world," I said. "I've experienced them myself and witnessed the suffering of many others. And I've asked myself, why would a God who is capable of healing allow suffering? Jesus and I spoke of this many times. He suffered so much himself, not just at the end but all the time I knew him.

"He wanted people to understand and take into themselves the message of God's complete and perfect love, and to know God's support for our journey in life. People followed him and they were comforted by his words, but most did not really get it. This grieved him terribly. Here he was, fully giving himself, living the message he brought to them, so that they could see it right there in front of them. He hoped they would recognize this as a precious opportunity, grasp the challenge, and relish it. He hoped they would jump into it with all they were and discover that they, too, could be heaven and earth together as one. Yet for the most part they looked mainly for reassurance, not challenge.

"It isn't easy to respond to challenge the way Jesus wants us to. It takes trust and faith to allow a new understanding. There's nothing to do but jump in with all you are and see if it works, like I did when I started living as if everything comes from love. That's how I discovered that it does."

"But what about the bad things that happen?" Mary asked. "How does that come from love?"

"This may sound outrageous at first, but I will give you a good example after I answer your question. My experience has been that when a challenge comes into my life, along with the hardship and anguish there is something to be gained from it, some understanding, some strength, some skill, some empowerment, or some change I need to make. When I examine the challenge, whether it is life-altering or minor, painful or merely bothersome, I see that it is pointing me to something that I need to pay attention to, something that I need to deal with. If I can open to what there is to learn, I find that I emerge with new wisdom. In that sense, the challenge bears gifts.

"What is your example?" she asked. "Help me to see this."

"My example is you, Mary. Your grandmother has died, leaving you with no family but cousins you have never met. Life as you have known it is over. Everything ahead is unknown. And look at you. You have grieved, and you will continue to grieve. But you discover new strength and wisdom and maturity with every step you take. It began with her illness. You took on responsibilities and choices you never would have faced if you had an easier life. You have accepted the challenges, every one of them, and through them grown and become an impressive young woman.

"Tell me, my dear, before all this, if you had been at the burial of Olefre, and you had gathered all those wildflowers, what would you have done with them?"

"I would have held onto them," she said, "wanting their reassurance, fleeting as it would have been."

"Instead you scattered them over her grave. Why did you do that?"

"Because they were for Olefre, in honor of her beautiful spirit. The spreading was a celebration of her."

"Yes," I agreed. "Now, look how you have opened yourself to know and experience life. In that way Olefre's illness and death gave you many gifts."

Benjamin called back to us, "We're nearly there. I need to make one stop, then I'll get you home."

Mary and I drew close to each other, beginning to think about what lay ahead. Her voice broke the silence with words I never expected.

"I want to go find your daughter," she said.

"'Before I formed you in the womb,' says God to Jeremiah, 'I knew you, and made you holy.' Hear this!" Michael insisted from the pulpit. "Before God formed you in the womb, you and you and you and you, God knew you and made you holy. God knew you. And made you holy. That's who you are. No matter what you do or feel or think, no matter what has happened or may yet happen, nothing can take that away.

"In this passage the Hebrew word for knowing is one of deep, rich, intimate knowledge and understanding. God knows you. God knows you and loves you so completely, so intimately, so deeply that God declares you holy."

Maggie could scarcely breathe. Minutes later, as Michael merely lifted up the bread and wine, she felt everything rush together. She felt God pour into her, into the depths of who she is, into thought and perception and vision, into promise and possibility and purpose. She felt God come into her body, into organs and tissues and cells, into muscle and bone, into heartbeat and strength and determination and endurance, into the deepest meaning of her tangible presence here in this physical world.

And in that she experienced communion. As bread and wine would come into her as body and blood, bringing Jesus, bringing holiness into her, bringing spirit into manifest being, as communion, so God came into her body and into her being as communion, entered her and knew her with understanding so deep and complete and intimate that she felt profound and unlimited love and she knew the sacred, worldly presence of divine holiness and love in her. She was spirit come into being in flesh, and she was flesh taken into spirit.

Michael's voice dropped low and gentle. "God comes through you, you, holy one. Allow God's love to flow through you. Be God's love in the world."

After the service, Maggie went to Michael for a long hug. "Thank you," she said, her eyes moist with emotion. "You're listening to this one, right?"

"Yes," he said with a smile.

"God, please, can't I bring healing into Amy?" Maggie was at the hospital bedside again, watching Amy sleep.

Jesus answered, "You do bring healing into Amy."

"Not into her body," replied Maggie.

"No, not into her body," he said. "Remember this? 'I would not let anybody else ever see me like this,' she told you as you helped her get back into the hospital bed, straightening all the tubes and cords and bags and monitors.

"'Oh, Amy, it's fine,' you replied.

"'I mean it,' she said. 'I always want to look good.'

"'You're beautiful,' you told her.

"'Oh, right, this is beautiful,' she grimaced.

"'Listen to me, Amy. Listen to me,' you insisted. 'You are beautiful, every day, always.'

"Amy stopped fussing and she focused on you. 'Even when I'm sometimes crazy from the drugs?' she asked.

"'Yes,' you said, and your eyes filled with tears.

"'Even when I'm crabby and impatient?' she asked.

"'Yes,' you insisted without hesitation.

"'Even when…?' She couldn't say it, but you knew, 'Even when I'm dying?'

"'Always, Amy,' you said. 'Always. Hey, you're making me cry,' you said.

"'You're making *me* cry,' she replied.

"Your eyes never left her, Maggie. 'I love you, Amy,' you said.

"'And I love you, Maggie,' she said. 'Come here and figure out how to give me a hug with all this paraphernalia in the way.'

"Do you see, Maggie?" said Jesus. "You bring other kinds of healing into Amy."

Maggie shook her head, broke into tears, and begged, "God, please let me bring healing into her body!"

"You will have to let her go, Maggie," Jesus tenderly urged.

After several minutes Maggie managed to say, "I don't know if I can do this. I care too much."

"You're doing fine," he said.

"How come I'm the one surviving, when she is such a beautiful person?"

"Maggie!" Jesus exclaimed, "don't you see your own beauty?"

"Not really, but Michael may be holding it for me. I hope so."

"Look in the mirror, see the beauty he sees."

"Oh!" she gasped, collapsing into her heart. "That's what that is? I see that sometimes, catch my reflection, and the beauty in it stuns me. I never understood it."

"Now you know."

"That is how Michael sees me?" Maggie whispered, astonished.

"Yes," Jesus answered softly.

Maggie sat with that for a while, holding it, letting her tears flow. Then she asked, "Jesus, Mary Magdalene loved you so much. How could you leave her?"

"You know the answer to that, Maggie. Just as you have to be with Amy now, just as you have to do this work you do, it is all deeply sacred journeying. You know that."

"And Michael has to do his," she said.

"Yes, and I had to do mine."

"And Amy has to do hers," Maggie added, sighing. "Even though you touched her, she still has to do her work."

"There is more going on than is apparent to you."

"Okay, I give up trying to try. Please, God, take care of all this. And whatever I am supposed to do, I'm here. I am yours. I am ready."

"You are already exactly where you need to be, Maggie," said Jesus, touching her heart. "You have been all along."

Dawn

Winter morning peeks at life through sleepy eyes
barely willing to open,
quiet and still, save far-off furnace rumblings.
A throat-clearing cough echoes too loud
under kitchen lights, too bright,
a spoon clinks into a coffee mug,
a sigh spreads to the wall and back.
Beyond still-dark windows, day hesitates,
reluctant to throw off sheltered sleep.

Spring day starts way before sunrise, too,
in early, early morning when
birds begin to sing the sun out to shine,
enticing it to spawn a mystical dawn dance
of shadow and light and life.
Spring morning rouses outdoors,
green and damp and fertile.
Moist air caresses leaf and skin and petal.
Flowers, in their extravagant, erotic abundance,
insist on ripening seed and rebirth.
Color and scent and song and brilliance
impassion senses and yearnings and dreams.
The warming sun and breeze and bright sky
play on skin and body,
tease, entice, insist.

Spring morning grabs us up in its ecstasy,
claims us, takes us,
and we are reborn with all the rest,
set out into the new day
with new eyes,
to reinvent ourselves.

Chapter Fifteen: Dawn

Mary's Words

"I will call, and you will come." The voice startled me awake. I looked around in the stark light and shadow of full moon and the room was empty. Where was Mary? I found her sitting in the moonlight on the ground outside our door and sat down next to her.

"You didn't say anything just now, did you?" I asked. She shook her head and I shook mine, too. "I didn't think so."

"I'm feeling restless," she said. "The moon is making me restless. I need to go find something. Is it your daughter? Is it myself?"

"I don't know, dear. Sometimes when I want to go, the thing I need to do is to stay."

She shook her head again. "No, it's not here. Whatever it is, it is south."

I nodded. That would be the way to go looking for my daughter, and the city, and Mary's cousin. Neither of us had much to arrange or pack, so we left the next day. We both fell easily into traveling. The time on the mountain had prepared us for simple living and since Olefre's death we flowed easily with and around each other, almost of one mind.

The people who had adopted my daughter were long gone from the town where we first asked, but a neighbor had heard that she was, for a time at least, in a town farther south. There was little else to learn, except that her name was Leal and she had been a smallish child with wide-open eyes and quick hands.

We followed the road south, beyond where Mary had ever been, where they spoke languages she'd never heard and ate foods she'd never tasted. During the day everything intrigued her. At night she clung to me for comfort and allowed herself to grieve. She was at that age between child and adult when one overlapped the other, catching both of us off guard.

We went to the house where Leal had lived in the next town. "No, there is no one named Leal here," said the woman, already beginning to close the door.

"Wait, please," Mary called out. "How long have you lived here?"

"Four years," said the woman.

"Is there someone, a neighbor perhaps, who has been here longer?"

"My mother-in-law has lived in this town all her life."

"May we speak with her?" asked Mary.

Eva remembered Leal as a smart young woman who wouldn't easily follow what others designed for her. Eva called her headstrong and stubborn. I laughed, recognizing myself in that. Like me, Leal refused the marriage her parents arranged and instead went to the city to work in the house of a wealthy businessman who had local ties back here. We were able to get a location.

Before leaving this town we stopped in a shop to buy supplies. "I've been here before," declared Mary, suddenly alert, her eyes darting this way and that.

"I thought you had never been this far south."

"I've been here before. I know this place," she insisted.

"Very well, what do you want to do?"

"Stay a few days and look around."

We found a room in exchange for work and settled into rhythms as the days grew into weeks. Mary kept discovering things and places that felt familiar. And finally we determined that this had been Olefre's hometown and Mary's mother was a child here. Mary had been here herself when she was only three or four, come with her grandmother for a visit. We found the street Olefre had lived on, and then the house. We found an elderly neighbor who knew Olefre in her youth, and we all cried and laughed together telling Olefre's stories.

It was a healing time for Mary. In a way, she brought Olefre home. Now Olefre would forever be both on the mountain and here. Finally Mary said, "I have done what I needed to do here. It's time to go to the city."

We arrived at the city in the autumn, just before harvest celebrations, when preparations were at their peak and rooms scarce. The first night we slept outside the walls and kept to ourselves. The crowded streets were too congested and hectic for two who still cherished mountain simplicity. We went very early the next morning, hoping to find fewer crowds, and arrived at the house of Mary's mother's cousin before anyone stirred inside.

As we waited nearby for signs of activity in the house, Mary asked me, "What do you think of this?"

"Meeting your cousin? Or looking for family in general?"

"That last part. This whole thing."

"I admit, I don't know what to expect," I said. "We show up at their door and declare ourselves relatives they've never met. What would you do if someone appeared like that?"

"I'd be curious," she said. "I'd want to get to know them."

"And if it was awkward? Or what if you didn't like them?"

"Why Mary," she said, "what happened to love in everything and everyone?"

"I guess this is one of those challenges for me, pointing out something I need to change in myself. I meet new people all the time, and I do it with heart and hands open. And yet now that I am so close to meeting my daughter I feel reluctant and doubtful. Unfortunately, I am letting it spill over onto your situation, too. I apologize."

Do you need to open your heart?" she asked.

"Yes," I said, "but I am not ready for that yet. Do you mind if I go off by myself for a while? You can either go ahead with this yourself or wait for me to return. I need to talk with someone."

"You go," she replied. "I don't know what I'll do, but don't worry about me."

I walked back out of the city and up onto a high hill. The sun had risen by then and there wasn't a cloud to be seen. I stood up there in the blue sky, looking out over the land.

"Yeshua," I said, "please help me do this with God in my heart. I am so full of questions and fears instead. Will she want me? Will she hate me? Will she care at all? Will she be the bitter product of pain, of fear, of abandonment? Or will she be peaceful? Will she be kind? Will she be more than I could ever hope?"

"All that can only be answered by meeting her," he said. "What about you? What is your part in this?"

I burst into tears. "I feel such a failure to her! I have done nothing for all these years, offered no comfort, no care, no presence, no support, no love."

"Oh, Mary, that last is not true. You have loved her."

"But none of this love was set before her," I said.

"So that is necessary to make love valid?" he asked. "Tell me, Mary, what is love?"

"It is seeing the beauty in another, holding the beauty."

"And what does love do?" he asked.

"It fills the empty places in us, and it brings us, and everything around us, to life. It wakes up life."

"I notice you put no conditions on any of that."

"There are no conditions on love," I said.

"And no conditions on your love for your daughter," he declared. "Be in that open-hearted love, Mary." He touched my heart and I felt myself expand into my love for her. The worries and guilt slipped away, irrelevant in the face of now bringing Leal my love.

"All that really matters at any time, Mary, is to open your heart to love in the present, no matter what has happened, no matter what is happening, no matter what may happen. Open your heart."

"Yeshua, I want to know I am doing the right thing. What if it is better to leave her as she is?"

"Better to never know you?" he asked. "How can that ever be better for anyone?" He smiled at her, then continued, "This is not only about you, Mary. You bring God's love. Through your love God will touch her heart in ways you won't see, and she will be blessed by it and through it. If she is hurting she needs it all the more. Go to her, Mary. Go see your daughter."

I walked slowly down the hill toward the gate. Had he said this is not only about me? Was I so self-absorbed that I thought it was? Suddenly I saw more of Leal than that baby taken from me. I saw a whole person, with history and a life going on. She would have needs and challenges like any other person I met. She would have burdens on her heart and questions entangling her mind. She would have today's chores to complete and the future's possibilities to wonder about. Suddenly I knew how to do this. With the same open heart with which I met any new person or situation.

"Thank you, Yeshua," I said, and re-entered the gate. I found the house Leal had gone to years ago, and spoke with a servant there. Yes, Leal was still in the city. She had married a number of years ago and gone to live not far away. In my eagerness to find her I left without asking more than directions. The streets were full of people finishing shopping for their holiday meals. I threaded my way through until there it was with the letters painted plainly on the wall.

"Please, God, keep my purpose clear," I said, "and my heart in your hands. And please let her be happy. I know, Yeshua, I should let go and accept whatever is, but I can't help asking for that."

He chuckled and said, "It is who you are, Mary, part of your loving nature."

I pulled the bell cord. A young servant girl half opened the thick wooden door. "I am looking for a woman named Leal," I said. "Is she here?" Without saying a word, the girl opened the door more and beckoned me into a wide courtyard. She led the way to a small sitting room and left me there.

The person who came through the door next took my breath away. She looked as much like me as anyone could. Sharp eyes a little close together over a straight nose, hollowed cheeks—I'd thought my hollows were from hard living and now I hoped I was wrong. Her mouth was wider than mine and so was her jaw. This eased her face into a little softness. Her dark brown hair tied back and braided up onto her head escaped in soft wisps.

Her hand stayed on the doorframe as she looked at me. "Ma?" she said. "Are you my ma?" I nodded. "Oh, my!" she said, sinking onto a chair next to the door. "Oh, my!" She looked at the floor, she looked at me, she turned her wedding band around and round on her finger. She looked at me again. "Oh, my."

"Leal?" I said. "That is your name?" She nodded. "I am Mary. Mary Magdalene." What else was there to say in such a moment? Where to start on all the years of life not shared? Where to start on beginning anew?

We looked at each other and, without intending to, took a breath together. As we exhaled and settled into a comfortable place, we both smiled. Upon seeing our own smile on each other's face we laughed and I knew we would be all right. What a relief that she could smile and laugh that easily. I said a silent prayer of thanks.

"You've come," she said.

I nodded, and looked at her some more. She wore a plain brown dress, not fitted to her body, and a gray apron over it. Now I saw that she was slender, with long fingers and narrow feet. She had collapsed into an open position, her body revealing that she was one who dealt with whatever came up, holding her ground until she knew what to do.

"You knew about me," I said. "What did they tell you?"

"That you were unable to take care of me, and no family to help."

"My family was already over-burdened with too many mouths to feed. That was why they sent me away. I could not have taken both of us back there."

"And my mother—I mean, the woman who—"

"She is your mother, Leal. Call her that," I said.

"My mother wanted a child so much! I was the light of her life. She was so grateful to you. Did you know that?"

"Enough to always hope you were well taken care of."

"She died when I was eight."

"Oh no."

"My father was a steady man. He kept on. His sister came to live with us. She took care of me, but she did not fill Mother's place." Leal sighed. "It has been a long time since I spoke of her."

"You loved her very much."

She nodded.

"And now you are married?" I asked. "Do you have children?"

Her hands moved to her belly and she looked at me. "One right here, if it makes it this time. And one running around the house somewhere."

I was a grandmother. I had grandchildren.

"I lost a child, too," I said. "He would have been your younger brother. It was very difficult to accept." Leal nodded again, her face cast down. "There are things you can do," I said, "to help keep this one. I can teach you."

She brightened and sat up. "Oh yes! Wonderful! But I've forgotten my manners. Can I get you some food, some drink? Have you come far?" Leal stood and moved into the doorway again.

"Not far. I spent the night nearby."

"You must stay here," she said. "I'll prepare a room."

I nodded and asked, "Is this your house?"

"It is my husband's family home. Joshua's mother lives here. She is ailing. I care for her, but it is difficult." She sighed again.

"Perhaps I can help with that while I am here."

"Anything you could do would be most welcome." Her hand went to her belly in an unconsciously protective gesture.

"I do have a girl traveling with me," I said. "She is seeking relatives here in the city also, and I do not know how that will turn out."

"We will find room for her, too," said Leal.

"She can stay in the room with me, if that is all right," I said.

"Oh, good. That will be easy then." Leal stopped and looked at me, then let go of another deep breath and her face softened. "We will be a family."

I nodded, and we shared another smile.

"Your husband, Joshua, what does he do?" I asked.

"He is a merchant," she said. "He travels a lot. He is away now and won't be back until early spring."

"In time for the baby to be born?"

"No. This baby is farther along than it seems," she said.

"Oh?" Concern crept into my voice.

"We can talk about that later," she sighed. "I need to go check on Ester."

"Ester is your daughter?"

"No," she laughed. "Ester is my mother-in-law. I have a four-year-old son, Micah. Come with me and I will show you your room."

In the meantime, young Mary had not had the good fortune I did. Her mother's cousin was not at home, and the friend who was staying there didn't believe Mary's claim to be a relative. I found her later, tending courtyard plants at an inn where she had arranged to do a few hours of chores in exchange for food for both of us.

"You would not believe how rude that friend was to me," she said. "If this cousin is anything like him, this is not going to work at all."

"I met my daughter Leal," I said.

"You did! Oh, my!" Mary exclaimed.

"That's exactly what she said, 'Oh, my!' She's married, has a son, lives with her husband's mother who is ill, and her husband is gone a lot. Mary, she looks almost just like me, except younger, of course."

"What's she like?" asked Mary.

"We laughed. I was so relieved when it happened. She seems stable and strong. She handles things."

"That's good. So she was okay with meeting you?"

"She wants us to stay there with her. She has a room all ready for us."

"Me, too? She must be a kind woman then."

"She wants us to be a family, Mary," I said, still amazed at that myself.

Mary's face clouded, "But I'm not your family. All I've got is this mysterious cousin," she said.

"Oh, Mary, you truly are my family. You are a daughter to me." I put my arms around her and she let herself cry.

Chapter Sixteen: New Day

Mary's Words

We brought our meager possessions to Leal's house and began to learn who these people were and what life was there.

Ester must have been formidable when she ran the household. Now confined for the most part to her bedroom, she had plenty to say to Leal about how to do things. She sat propped up in her bed or in an armchair by the window looking onto the courtyard. From the window she had seen me first arrive that morning and insisted that we be introduced as soon as I returned. This was her first chance to welcome any mother of Leal's to her home.

I found her dressed in an elaborate bed coat, her white hair done up, and color on her pale cheeks. She was graciousness personified, with not a flicker of hesitation. She was very earnest and proper in the hostess role. With her there would be no intimate sharing of breaths or touch. And, I suspected, no sense of our coming together to love Leal through her pregnancy.

As we spoke I saw that her heart was cold. Her husband had died many years before, and her only son, Joshua, was away from home so much that he seemed all but gone, too. She felt abandoned, and she did not like being dependent on this strange young woman who seemed more like a servant than a daughter.

Ester never had a daughter, so she had looked forward to sharing with a daughter-in-law in the planning and carrying out of household responsibilities. She had thought they would entertain a lot. But she hadn't expected Joshua to be away so much, and it was not proper to entertain with no man in the house. Ester looked at Leal and sighed. Things just hadn't turned out the way she thought they would.

"Why don't you get our guests some tea, dear. And some of those little cakes to go with it." she said to Leal.

Leal sighed too, perfectly aware of the first sigh, nodded, and left without saying anything.

"And now, Mary," said Ester, looking first at me and then at my companion. "Oh, dear, you are both Mary. This won't do." Turning to the younger Mary she declared, "We shall call you Lily, like the lily flower embroidered on that chair on which you are sitting."

And so it was from then on, for everyone in the household and coming through it, Mary was Lily. She even began to introduce herself as Lily. I resisted, wanting to feel sure it was what Mary wanted, and reluctant to let go of sharing our name.

Changing Mary's name was typical of Ester, giving unilateral orders that addressed something she saw, no matter what effect it had on others. Her solutions did seem to work, so we could hardly complain. Except they carried a sense of personal unimportance, of one's merely being an accessory in the room décor, moved this way and that for effect. It sometimes felt as if Ester and her theoretical guests were the only people of any substance in the house.

~

Micah crashed into me in a narrow corridor and that was how we met. He smashed into my body, collapsed onto the floor in a flurry of arms and legs, and sat there staring up at me, his dark eyes wide with questions. I decided to join him on the floor.

"Hi, Micah," I said, "I'm Mary." I pulled out of my pocket a carved wooden boat I'd found in my room and held it out to him. "This must be yours."

"Oh, that. You can have that," he replied, shrugging his shoulders.

"Okay," I said, putting it back in my pocket, "if you need it, I'll have it."

"You're staying in the end room, aren't you? If you ever find my clay whistle in there, I do want that. I've been looking for that," he said, his little round face as serious as could be.

"Sure, I'll watch for it. How old are you, Micah?"

"Four. No, five. Or is it four? One of those," he said.

Either way he was small for his age. As I watched, his eyes wandered, looking for something to capture his attention. He was ready to go back to his own world at any moment, not counting on my continuing to be there. I could tell this child was alone a lot and he had already learned to make his own way. He had no siblings and a father scarcely here. His mother was too harried by other responsibilities to do more than be relieved to periodically notice that he was taking care of himself.

"What are you playing at, Micah? Who was chasing you?" I asked. He eagerly told me the story of his adventurous play, which included far away places and thieves and heroes.

"Do you miss your father?" I asked.

"Father? Oh, I guess. Want to be the rich, old Chinaman and I come to buy jewels and swords and stuff?" he asked.

"Sure," I said. "Where is my palace? How about the end room?" We spent the rest of the afternoon playing and became fast friends.

"Micah, this is your grandmother," said Leal later in the day.

He looked at me, shrugged, and said, "I thought she was an old Chinaman," then giggled as he ran out of the room.

She shook her head. "He's off in his own world," she said.

I searched her face and all I saw was weariness. "Do you have any time to yourself, Leal? To wonder who you are?" I asked. "To watch your son grow and to feel this next child within you? To pray? To thank God for all these blessings?"

She shook her head no and sank into a chair. She didn't say a word, just went limp with her limbs splayed loose like an abandoned puppet, staring at the floor. A bell rang in the distance and she began to slowly pull her body back together to get up.

"It's Ester, wanting something," she explained.

"Can't someone else go?"

"She likes me to come," she said, sighing.

"What do you like, Leal?"

"I don't know, Mary," She sighed again.

"Well, that's a good place to start. Let me go check on Ester, and you can sit here and think about that." I left her there, sunk again to the depths of the chair with her head leaning back against the wall. But when I returned she had gone to the kitchen to complete preparations for dinner.

~

Mary left early the next morning to try to catch her mother's cousin at home this time. She hadn't given up on making a connection. As soon as I could, I followed her across town. When I knocked at the door, Mary answered.

"You're here!" she exclaimed to me, reaching for my arm. "Come in! I'm so glad you have come. It turns out my cousin is a man, at least that's all that is left, and he was here all along. That other man just wouldn't tell me. Come inside. We are having some breakfast. Please join us!"

"You're okay then? Maybe I should go."

"No, come in!" she insisted.

She brought me to a somber room with close-drawn drapes and a small fire in the hearth. A gray-faced man with a long beard sat wrapped in a blanket by the fire. He looked up and motioned me to sit opposite. "Come, come, sit," he said.

"Anuf and I were just talking about you," said Mary after introductions. "He wanted to meet you, and here you are."

"I'm happy to meet you, Anuf. So, you are nephew to Olefre?"

"I am that. And I am sorry to hear of her passing. Yet I am not far behind her. I am not well," he said. "You were with her, both of you? That is comforting.

"I always enjoyed my aunt," he went on. "She often surprised everyone, one way or another. Once she brought a live bird in a cage to a holiday meal and made all of us look at it while we ate. She wanted us to stop eating birds. And it has never been easy since then to do so. She saved quite a few birds as a result of that day.

"Another time she declared that she was going to travel to the Far East. She wanted to see it for herself. So she set out and she was gone for two years. It turned out that she never made it farther than a week's walk. She had broken her leg and then stayed on after it healed. Why she never sent word is beyond me."

"Because she was still off on her adventure," said Mary, "even if it was not as far away as she'd expected."

"She had her own way of looking at things," he said, then peered at Mary. "Maybe you do, too. This is a choice one," he said to me, pointing to Mary. "She brightens a room."

"Yes, she is special, like her grandmother," I said.

"And she tells me the two of you are staying with your daughter?" he continued. Mary, out of his sight, anxiously gestured to get my attention, and nodded vigorously.

"Yes, we are," I replied. "Leal lives across the city in the house of her mother-in-law Ester."

"Good, good, good," he said. "Though, we could certainly use her help here," he trailed off, suggestively.

"I think we'll be fine there," I said, and Mary let out a great breath of relief. We conversed with Anuf for a while more, and then Mary and I excused ourselves to leave, promising to visit again.

"Come back soon," Anuf called after us.

Outside the door Mary exclaimed, "Oh, thank you for catching my meaning! Mary, I do not want to live here. I want to be with you!" As we walked back across the city, she told me more about this cousin and his household. The unpleasant man of the other morning lived there with him, and continued to be suspicious of her and pessimistic in general. He prowled around the edges of their conversation, listening in. "It's a gloomy place," she said. "And it smells like the windows are never open to allow fresh air inside."

"You could make a difference there," I said.

"I can make a difference somewhere else," she replied. "I get to choose where to make my difference, and it's not there."

"We are drawn to where we need to be," I said. "You are clearly not drawn there."

"What is clear," she said, "is that I want to be with you."

I smiled at her and put my arm around her shoulders. "This is fine, my dear. Then here is what we must do." We talked the rest of the way back about how the two of us could take some of Leal's load, in particular with Ester, and free her to attend to her children and herself.

Outside Leal's gate I stopped Mary before entering. "Now, you tell me, do you sincerely want me to call you Lily? Because if you do I will make myself learn to do it." I searched her face for her answer.

She smiled in my eyes, then said, "I will be Lily to everyone else, but you call me Mary. It will remind me of Olefre. She so liked that you were another Mary. And it will keep alive and present the bond between you and me. I want that."

"I do, too," I said. "Very well, I will call you Mary, except with other people, for they would be confused." We hugged a good long hug. "Welcome home, Mary," I said, and we went inside.

*

Later I asked, "Yeshua, did I do right with the child? Am I being selfish keeping her with me?"

"Are you following your love for her?" he asked. "If you are, and it is ever best to let her go, you will let her go. Trust the love."

"This feels right, and the other felt very wrong. Did you see her face when she was signaling me?" I laughed. "It can't get much clearer than that." I paused, then continued, "I have two daughters now, Yeshua."

He smiled and took my hands in his. "And this brings you great happiness."

"And I have a grandson, too!" I added. "With another grandbaby on the way!"

"That one needs great care." His voice grew solemn.

"Mary and I have a plan," I declared.

"It will take more than what you and Mary have planned," he said. "You must help Leal connect her heart to the child's."

"She needs to connect to Micah's heart, too," I said.

"This is more pressing, Mary. If this child is to be born and live."

"Oh, Yeshua!" I exclaimed, now frightened.

He took me in his arms and held me while I cried for all of the lost babies. Then I said, "Thank you, God, for these children who now fill my life. I did not know how much I missed them. Or how much I needed them."

—∾—

We settled into making a life together, Mary and Leal and Ester and Micah and me. Ester adjusted to new hands helping her, and even loosened her hold on what we did and how we did it. Leal took Micah for walks and spent time every day with him. She relaxed her desperate grip on the new child in her belly and allowed love to blossom. Laughter burst forth from all corners of the house. Ester softened to her daughter-in-law and began to enjoy getting to know her. All of us were new to being this family. We learned to trust that rough spots turned again toward peace and love stayed steady.

One evening at dinner, with all of us gathered around the table, Ester suddenly clutched her throat, wide-eyed, as she choked on a bite of meat. Leal ran to her, pulled the chair from the table and knelt before her. She drew Ester forward to lie across her shoulder, and slapped her soundly and repeatedly on the back until Ester began to cough and gasp.

When it was over, Leal looked sheepishly at the rest of us. "Like a baby, you know, helping the baby clear an air bubble." She smiled, laying her hands on her expansive belly, then turned back to Ester. "Are you all right?" she asked.

Ester nodded, took hold of Leal's hand and gripped it hard. "Come here, my dear, come close. You have saved my life, and it is not the first time. Bless you, child. I am grateful. I will not forget this." Looking around at us, she said, "I want you all to hear this. I will do whatever I can to make sure Leal has everything she needs or wants." She looked back at Leal. "I mean that," she said as earnestly as she had ever said any words.

Leal leaned over and hugged her, not something either of them usually did. Ester looked startled at first, but then softened into it, smiled, and patted Leal's back.

—∾—

One early morning at a market across the City, I turned a corner and came face to face with my old friend Aaron. I was as surprised to see him as he was to see me. My life had changed so much that this didn't seem to be the same city in which I'd met him before.

We found a quiet spot to sit and talk. He looked well, and his work was going well, too. Many volunteers now came regularly to help. I told him about my daughters, our family, the changes in my days, and the rightness of it all. He could see it, too, and he did not ask me to come back. He was too kind to force me to say the no we both knew I'd have to say. We parted with much affection, shared good wishes, and good-byes.

—∾—

As the time for Leal's birthing came close, I saw a darkening in her. Fear grew, fed by memories of her last attempt. Leal's previous baby had been fully-grown, but he was dead at birth. Now she feared the same again. My experiencing a similar tragedy with her brother reinforced Leal's fears and brought up my own, too.

It was Mary who helped us both. She spoke softly to each of us about life and God and faith. Her words, as well as her love and her gentle hands, touched our hearts and opened them. It was as if she took us to sit in the sun on that rock ledge, surrounded by all the beauty of existence. She told us that we could stay in that love or stay shackled and crazed by the fear. It was our choice. She said if there was anything we could do to help this baby it was to let the fear go and wrap all of us and the entire process in positive anticipation. So we all busied ourselves with preparations for a new baby in the house.

"Maybe it will be a boy," said Micah, brightening. "I'd like that." He looked around at all these women he lived with.

"You could think of ideas for a name, in case it is a boy," said his mother.

"Stefan," Mikah immediately answered.

"No others to consider?" she asked.

"No, Stefan is his name," stated Mikah.

"Stefan Michael," Leal said with finality. She spread her hands across her belly and declared, "Well, child, we seem to be ready for you."

"Unless it is a girl," said Mary. "We could name her Lily and then I'd change my name again." She laughed and winked at me.

"How about Stefany?" said Leal.

"Stefany Michaela!" exclaimed Ester. "And we shall call her Michaela. Michaela and Micah. Doesn't that sound wonderful together?"

"Now I don't know which to hope for. I like both names," said Leal.

"That is as it should be," said Mary. "Let be whatever is."

~

Stefan came into this world in a time of storms, with hard rain that flooded nearby fields. Leal's cries filled the house between thunderclaps. Ester and Micah went to stay with a friend of hers, while Mary and I attended to Leal. It was a long, hard birth. Leal would not let go of the baby. She had allowed herself to feel the life in him, to know his presence, to believe in his heartbeat. She had allowed her heart to open to him. Now she could not bear the thought of losing him. She could not risk it.

Mary and I stayed with her through two days of labor. We bathed her, we fed her broth, we wrapped her in our arms, we walked her around the courtyard, we made special teas and compresses, we prayed, with her and separately, and we waited. Neighbors and friends came quietly, bringing food and other offerings, to sit with us and to pray as the wait continued. If they began to whisper concerns, I gently asked them to leave. We stayed focused on a joyous outcome.

Late in the second day Leal decided she was going to die. The weariness was impossibly heavy and the pain unbearably bad. Indeed she might have. "Mary, tell me again what you told me yesterday," she asked, "about the way to get to believing all is love, even the bad things. Maybe I can hear it now."

She had been so tight, so clenched, all through the labor. Now, since midday and with her growing resignation, I had felt her begin to give up her desperate hold on the strands of her life. No matter why she was releasing, there would come a time of opportunity, of opening. Was this it? Could she release the baby now?

I took her with me in our minds to the rock ledge in the mountains and to the meadow where Olefre sat and then died and was buried. I took her to catch butterflies with Eli and then to walk by the river with the grief of his father Reuben after his wife's death. I took her back with me to the emptiness of the land and life and deep into my anguish that horrible day Jesus died. And then I brought her back, through resurrection and the presence and opening hearts. Through love, and love, and more love. Through learning and stretching and becoming and being. I brought her again to sit on the ledge in the bright light of creation. And then Leal's husband Joshua entered this vision, and together he and I placed this new baby in her arms and sat with her as the sun rose.

With that the birthing truly began. Stefan came easily then. Soon he was flesh in his mother's arms, squeals of life rang throughout the house, and fresh, new love was born.

"Welcome to this life, Stefan," I said. "Welcome to this family. You will be loved here. You will be a joyful light in our lives. May you walk in the footsteps of those who walk before you, and beyond. May you know peace and happiness and a multitude of blessings." I smiled at Leal and took her hand. "What a glorious day this is!"

Ester and Micah had arrived just before Stefan was born. Now Micah ran all through the house and out into the street, waving a flag and yelling, "It's a brother! It's a brother!"

Ester came quietly to the bedside and placed her hand first on Leal's head, smiling into her eyes, and said, "Good job, Leal. Mary is right, you are a good mother, given the chance. I pledge that I will do better at giving you that chance. And you, little one, little Stefan, named by your brother," she said, moving her hand to the baby's head, "Welcome to our family. I am your other grandmother, but we will get to that later. Now you just be with your mama."

Ester turned to look at me and nodded her head, acknowledging her appreciation for my help with the birth. She patted Mary's arm on her way out of the room. "I'll see to the neighbors and friends who will want news," she said.

—∾—

After rest and food, I walked the streets of the city in predawn stillness, wandering through silent neighborhoods, market places readying for the day's business, through alleyways and boulevards, past sleeping families and early morning prayers and the first smells of breakfast. I found my way through the gate and onto the hill as first light came into the new day.

"Yeshua," I said, "your stories are like water to a parched heart. Did you see how they eased Leal's path?"

"And so are yours," he replied.

"We must keep telling them," I said. "The stories bring God's presence to those who need it."

"As do you, my dear," he said. "You bring God's love into people's hearts and show them how steady and real it is."

After a long pause I said, "Yeshua, I'm going to stay here. I need to be here."

"Yes, you do," he said.

"Is that okay? I was so certain I need to keep moving."

"Of course it is okay. Things change. We come into new circumstances that change everything. Look at me," he said with a smile.

"You'll be here? You'll stay here, too?" I asked.

"I am always with you, Mary."

I felt his presence fill my heart, my being, my deepest knowing, as it always did, and also now settle into the land there beneath and surrounding me, and enter into the heart and life of the city. I would feel his presence with each step on cobblestone street, with each sound of merchant's cry or prayerful call or child's delight or wagon wheel clatter or women's passing conversation. I would see his presence in faces and gatherings and rain-wet walls and busy marketplaces and sacred celebrations. I would know his presence in the hours of each day, each moment pregnant with possibility, giving birth to love and life.

"And it is all in you, too, Mary. All that I am, you are. See that, too," he said.

I allowed him to take me, as I had taken Leal to the rock ledge, to experience and know all that I had just seen, but this time it was in me. I was sunrise and bird's call, traveler and merchant, maid and midwife, mother and friend. I was clattering hooves and sacred song and written words and waving flag and water spilling from pitcher to soup pan and child's smile. I was fear and anger and lament, I was prayerful and brazen and hungry and dying, I was infant and soldier and sage, I was liar and thief, victim and defeat, ripe and rotten, sold and cherished, potent and twisted and courage and confession.

I was everything. I was the life force within all that is. Deeper even than that. I was the creation of all that is. I was the thought behind that creation. I was the impulse behind the thought. I was the desire behind the impulse. I was the love behind the desire. I was sacred beyond and encompassing love. Leaving words behind, I continued on into the deep places within sacred being. And there I knew God like Yeshua knows God. I knew. And that knowing became all that is.

"I'm not dead, am I?" I asked all of a sudden, as my toes grasped for soil at my feet.

Jesus laughed. "No, you are incredibly alive."

"Good. Because I have work to do. I have family. And home."

"Yes, you do."

"This is the end, isn't it, Mary?" asked Maggie.

"Yes, it is," she said, gently. "You are released from this now to continue on your path. As God and Jesus and circumstances set me on my path, empowering me with understanding of who I am, you have been brought to this same understanding, Maggie, and now you have work to do."

"Mary, thank you for trusting me with your words."

PART THREE

CALLING

A Hundred Crows

A hundred crows came in the evening,
flying from all directions, converging,
cawing as they came, calling as they came.
They filled three trees
and gathered our rapt attention,
pulling it along with them.
They spread a net of wonder and expectation,
their spell cast far through the emerging dusk
and tensed the air for what might come
behind them or with them or through them,
as the sun sank low and shadows played with our senses
and mystery claimed the opening between day and night.

"God sounds pretty insecure here,
like he's trying to convince everybody to pay attention to him,"
said my companion from across the porch in the last of the light.
We were reading Hosea, Bible verses from last Sunday,
trying to relate them to our own lives.
"In this other part God is downright brutal," I replied.
"What are we supposed to do with this?"

We watched more crows fly in.

The messenger in my dream struck an authoritative pose.
"The number one problem in health care today,"
he declared,
"is the use of stones;
the use of stones
resets the pattern of illness."
I woke, caught up in his urgency.
Stones? I asked. Stones?
Set in stone?
Calcification?
Calcified perspectives?
Assumptions?

Assumptions distort patterns,
in health care or otherwise.
Assumptions obstruct our lives,
like scattered stones stop us in our tracks.
Assumptions confine vision,
like a stone wall surrounds and blocks sight.
Assumptions destroy possibilities,
like falling stones crush breath.
Assumptions deny life,
like stones that weigh us down
to wait for the assumptions to come true.

Hosea's God was, in his jealousy and threats,
assumption's deadly repression of vitality,
and stone's severe, unrelenting hard hand.
I will condemn every alternate path, God said.
You will come to me because you have no other choice.
    Like stones that stop us in our tracks and destroy possibilities.
Your life will be hell without me, God said.
You will turn to me and submit to loving me.
Only then will I be good to you.
    Like stones that crush breath and stop life,
    and weigh us down to wait for the assumptions to come true.

In the morning a collection of stones across the room comforts me,
holders of earth's wisdom, of our stories, of our mysteries.
And one crow flies by the window, silent.

I will not give up stones' beauty to cruel metaphor.
I will not give up healing to any calcified perspective.
I will not give up mystery to assumptions or threats.
I will not give up living each moment of life as it comes,
in its fullness, its magic, and its calling to me.

In the morning I wonder,
will a hundred crows come again today?

Chapter Seventeen: A Hundred Crows

"Come with me," said the magnificent woman in Maggie's dream. She was tall and brilliant, radiating strength and confidence and reassurance. Her face was familiar; everything about her was familiar. Who was she? Maggie didn't know why, but she absolutely trusted her. This powerful woman would bring Maggie to where she needed to be.

They stepped out onto the floor of a vast, open desert valley of bronze and red and gold, with an endless, empty expanse before them and massive, fantastic rock formations in the near distance to either side.

"I've been here," said Maggie.

"Of course you have," answered the woman.

"I want to fly! I want to soar down through this wide valley and on into that boundless path ahead."

"Of course you do."

"I am where I belong," said Maggie, settling into being there. "I have worked all my life to get here."

Then it was Mary Magdalene who stood with Maggie, holding her hand and looking in her eyes, and she said, "Everything we have written is for you, Maggie. Everything I learned, you have learned. Everything I became, you have become. You have everything you need."

Mary let go of Maggie's hand, and Maggie looked around. She realized this was not just a physical place but a new way of being. She no longer stood in the old ways, peering into what she wished life would be. She had gone through a passage and come out into the new.

"I know things now," Maggie exclaimed in the dream. "There *is* spiritual wholeness and truth. There *is* guidance. It's real. There *is* connection at many levels and relationship in many realms. There is active soul's intention and path, and the need to be all I can be.

"It's not just inner wondering. It's not just an ideal or a possibility or an illusion cast out ahead of me. All I have sought and all I have learned about being and meaning and truth and God and love and wholeness is real. Everything that exists and everything that happens is amazing. It is miraculous. It is holy. The presence of the sacred forms and enlivens all that is. A tree, an afternoon, a bird's cry, a hug, a look, all are expressions of spirit and all are holy. And one moment, one experience, one touch in the heart can change everything. There is true healing!"

Maggie woke, exclaiming, "I knew it! Miracles and healing and holiness—it's all real! It's all true! Thank you, Mary. Thank you…who was that? I want to thank her, too."

"You know who she is," said Mary Magdalene.

"She is God! She is God in one of the many woman-forms we've called Diana, Shakti, Isis, Inanna, Tiamat—was that Tiamat?"

"Names and images do not matter, the essence is the same. God is God."

"Wow, that was God." Maggie sank back into the pillow.

"God showed you where you are and who you are."

"I am where I always wanted to be, where I am meant to be. And I want to fly!"

"Not just fly, Maggie, you want to fly into the boundless unknown."

"Hmm, right, I said that, didn't I. And I meant it. Except now God knows it, and I know God knows, and God knows I know, so I guess I'll really have to do it. I'm feeling nervous about that."

Mary laughed and said, "You'll get used to it."

The next morning Maggie spoke with Lydia. "Wonderful things are happening, but I miss writing Mary's words. I loved getting up each morning with such a definite, clear sense of purpose. Get up and get to work. Now what am I doing? Who am I? What am I about? I'm back to having to find my own value for what I do."

"This is another gift from Mary to you."

"What do you mean?"

"She showed you how valuable you are, and now, with that example to guide you, she has set you out there to find it for yourself. What do you wake up to now each morning?" asked Lydia.

"I used to wake up to Mary's story, now I wake up to my own life."

"Then your own life is what you need to feel purposeful about. Didn't Mary say you have everything you need?"

"Everything is changing. I've finished writing down Mary's words, and now I'm pulling it all together, which is very different work. My experiences with Michael, and with Amy, and with other people are, as always, in continual transition and discovery. I'm quitting the Montford Center to set up my own clinic because I need to get out from under Teresa's personality dramas and let the work be the focus. And the Energy Circle is taking off in its own direction without me, too."

"I'm not surprised by any of this, Maggie. You're going through a major shift. Stephen must be excited for you. He loves this kind of stuff, doesn't he?"

"I haven't spoken with Stephen for a couple of months."

"Now that is surprising. Well, when you talk to him, say hi for me."

"Don't hang up, Lydia! I'm not done!" Maggie exclaimed.

"I know, you still want to know what is happening. So, tell me, Maggie, what do you know?"

"Okay, I know that I need to quit the Montford Center and set my healing work free to become whatever it becomes without any outside constraints. That feels very good. I know that I need to put Mary's book together and follow it as it goes out into the world. I know that I need to be here in Western North Carolina, in these mountains, in Asheville. I find my center here, I connect to my soul here, and that is precious."

"What else do you know?" asked Lydia.

"I know that I'm supposed to be open to Michael, trust the connection between us, hear his words every Sunday, and pass along messages to him that come through me.

"Anything else?"

"My list is upside down, as usual," said Maggie, laughing. "Last, but really first, I know I need to be spiritually open and aware. I need to feel and see and know the sacred in everything. I need to live in holiness. And if I am this, all the rest will follow."

"Sounds like a plan, Maggie," said Lydia. "Turns out you know a lot about what is happening."

An email from Tory went out to everyone on the church's prayer chain saying that Amy was in deep trouble and considering stopping all interventions. Tory wrote that Amy and David had a lot of decisions to make and they did not want any visitors, just prayers.

Maggie grabbed the phone and called their house. It had been less than a week since she saw Amy. What could have gone so wrong? No visitors? Did that mean her, too? No one answered. Maggie called the hospital and yes, Amy was there. The call transferred to her room.

"What's going on?" Maggie asked, relieved to hear Amy's voice.

"Oh, it's my kidneys, the stents are clogging up again." She sounded tired and discouraged, but Amy's voice was strong, she was thinking clearly, and she was keeping up with things, all good signs. "They want to put in bigger ones so this won't keep happening."

"The stents have clogged before and they fixed it," said Maggie.

"Well, the extra complication this time is that I should have come in as soon as I realized, but I waited till the next morning. The toxins built up too much. They're trying to clear all that out now. It's getting better. They've already flushed the stents, and we're hoping they won't just clog back up again."

"How are you doing?"

"I'm really tired of all this, Maggie. And I want to be home. If they put in new stents it'll mean another week or ten days in the hospital."

Maggie took a deep breath and relaxed a bit more. This was unfortunate, but it did not sound or feel like a terminal crisis. What was Tory thinking? "Can I come over now?" she asked.

"Sure! I'm just lying here."

"I'll be right there."

Amy did look exhausted when Maggie arrived. "Have you been able to sleep?" she asked.

"Not much, but now that you're here I will."

"You could call me, you know."

"But you always show up at exactly the right time."

Maggie smiled at the trust contained in that thought as she sat down. "What are they going to do about the stents?"

"First I go for an ultrasound in the morning. I hate going down there for any more tests." Amy sighed and sank deeper into the bed.

Maggie began to see that Tory must have collected up all of Amy's meager, out-of-the-ordinary complaining and drawn her own conclusions.

"David will be at work tomorrow, so I'll go with you," she said. "What time?"

"Maggie, you are such a godsend, but I can do this by myself. You need to work with Mary on the book."

"Good news! Mary's part is done. Now I just need to put it all together."

"That's wonderful, Maggie!" exclaimed Amy with a big grin. "And I haven't forgotten my promise to help you with the editing."

"I'm counting on it, Amy. I need a good editor, so let's get you well."

"I'm trying, Maggie. I really want to get well."

Maggie leaned closer and her voice dropped low, "Amy, if you ever want to stop working so hard at all this, and let go, I'll understand. And I'll be here."

Amy's eyes filled. "I know that, Maggie. I really do. But I'm not going there yet, okay? I want more life. I love life. There's so much I want to do. If I can just get stabilized, spring is here and I can get on with some things. I'm really looking forward to it."

They smiled into each other's faces for a few long moments until Maggie spoke. "So, for right now let's get you relaxed, and then I'll see what else I can do. Close your eyes, and take a couple of deep breaths."

Maggie drew her hands slowly through Amy's energy field, collecting and removing the heavy load of stress and fear built up there, along with toxins and anything else ready to release. In less than thirty seconds Amy was sleeping peacefully.

"I don't understand what Tory is doing," Maggie said to Lydia later. "We've been through this with the stents before. The doctors can take care of this. Every time anything happens Tory is sure this is it, this is the one. And it's not. Amy is not finished yet."

"It's pretty obvious that Tory is going through her own stuff and she's reacting to that," said Lydia. "She must also be serving some purpose with Amy. And she certainly is with you. I can see right off that she gets you to know what you know. Whether she realizes or not, I think Tory constantly makes sure you do the work you're supposed to do with Amy. She's always calling you back to it, one way or another."

"I wish she didn't do it in such a panic."

"Would you pay attention otherwise? Maybe you need to wonder why you need her to do it so dramatically."

"But it's not all me, is it? I really like Tory. I respect and admire her, she is a wise and caring person, she knows a lot, and she's very good at teaching and leading groups. I learn from her, and usually we get along just fine. I don't understand why we are so dissonant on this."

"Do you need to see it as dissonant? Can you just let it be different? She's in her role and you are in yours."

"Okay, yes, I can see that," Maggie sighed. "And Amy needs both of us. I have to allow for Amy to have both of us. Hey, wise one, you're on quite a roll! This is all good stuff."

"Oh, don't say that! You'll break the spell."

"Lydia, am I keeping Amy from dealing with death? I want to support her, not hold her back or put my own attitudes onto her."

"From what you said about today, it sounds like she is reaching for life."

"The times I see her sink into despair are when others bring that to her and she gets lost in it. She always seems relieved to get back to faith and optimism. I really believe she still wants to live."

"Trust that, Maggie. Your instincts are good."

"There's something else I'm concerned about. Lydia, I'm getting too emotionally involved with Amy. I care too much. I'm breaking Rule Number One: always keep it totally professional, with a solid boundary line and impeccable objectivity."

"This is bigger than standard rules, Maggie. It's exceptional. Hear that? Exception. Don't try to put it into a pre-fab box you were handed in some generic class or lecture. Let it be what it is."

"It's true that there is more going on here than my just working with a regular client. I don't even seem to have a choice. This is where I'm supposed to be. It's my own soul work, too."

"Right."

"So, you're saying then it's okay to let it be personal? You're sure?"

"Just let it be."

"Thanks, Lydia."

"You're doing fine, Maggie."

"Amy constantly amazes me. Nothing brings her down for long. A couple of days ago they put on another tube and bag, and she just straightened out all the cords and lines and bags and carried on to wash her face and put on some makeup. Give her a few minutes, or sometimes a bit longer, at most a day, and she handles whatever comes."

"She's a gutsy woman. She reminds me a lot of you."

"No wonder I like her so much," said Maggie, laughing.

Maggie called Stephen to order a small grid for a client, and he invited her to come out to the mountain for a visit. "I'm fixing breakfast on Saturday for my neighbor Margaret over at her house. Come join us. I'm making my famous sour milk pancakes."

"How can I pass that up?" Maggie replied with a smile.

Margaret was a bright, fascinating woman well up in her eighties. She used a cane, moving slowly and carefully, but there was nothing slow or careful about her sharp mind and clear, blue eyes. As they ate Stephen's delicious pancakes, they spoke about energy work. Maggie told them about the bad results that she'd had recently when she let a local woman work on her in exchange for a treatment. Margaret looked firmly at her, and declared, "You don't need to have anybody work on you."

"I'm so glad you're saying this!" exclaimed Maggie.

"See? You know it's true."

"I have been told many, many times that energy workers need regular treatments, as if it's an absolute, and never heard anybody but me question it before. The fact is that since I moved here I only get occasional, long-distance treatments from my friend Lydia, and I'm fine."

"Of course," said Margaret.

"Lydia is supremely respectful of my energy and path. She usually just holds the space, invites in the guides to work on me, and she doesn't even know what happens."

"You don't need that from your friend, either," insisted Margaret. "Think about it. Whoever is doing the work on you doesn't need her help."

"Right! Thank you, Margaret. This validation is wonderful."

"You don't need validation, either, Maggie. Trust what you know. You know plenty."

Maggie was amazed. They had met a couple of times before, but this was the most they had ever spoken with each other. Margaret saw right into Maggie's strength and said exactly what she needed to hear.

"Thank you, Margaret. This feels very good."

Margaret looked sharply at Maggie, then she nodded again. "See how strong you feel? This is who you are."

When a physical therapist arrived, Margaret excused herself for a session. Maggie was then able to concentrate on Stephen and reconnect with him. They were as easy with each other as ever. She talked about writing with Mary and about how difficult it was now to be done with that.

"Writing with Mary was so clear and compelling," she said. "Doing the layout and editing of her manuscript is not at all the same. I wander through my rooms looking for some focus, not knowing what to do with myself."

Stephen laughed and said, "I'm sure that won't last for long."

Maggie also told him about Amy and about learning to be humble and to trust.

Stephen nodded. "Good stuff, Maggie. As always, you're doing your work. Good for you."

"What about you, Stephen? What's been going on for you?"

"I've been sitting up in the grid for twenty minutes every day all this time. It's awesome. I'm learning to know more. And, I've been handing out bottles of elixir and getting some feedback. It's powerful stuff. I'm not sure the average person can handle it. We're going to have to learn more about using it. And, a guy's developing a website for me to sell the small grids. That's exciting." He hesitated, suddenly shy and awkward, then added, "And, I'm in love."

"Oh, Stephen! With that woman you told me about before?"

"No, that didn't work out. I really thought it was going to, and I was disappointed. I should never anticipate, you know. I'm always wrong. Its failure was, of course, all for the best, because then I met Tanya. We're absolute soulmates," he declared, beaming with joy.

"That's wonderful, Stephen." She saw the delight in his face and felt a momentary twinge of envy. "I'm really happy for you," she said, returning the grin.

"It's not easy," he said. "It brings up all your stuff."

"Is it worth it? That's the important thing."

"Oh, yes! Definitely! The connection between the two of us is phenomenal. I've never experienced this. It is so powerful! I don't feel like I have any choice but to do this. She keys into everything about me, pushes all my buttons, good and bad." He laughed. "The good times are really good, and the bad times are really bad, so I'm clearing all my stuff. I know I'm doing what I need to do, Maggie. As long as Tanya wants to be with me, I'll be with her."

"I wish you the best, Stephen." She smiled and added, "I feel a little like I should have a talk with her and tell her to be good to you and appreciate you." They both laughed.

"I'm okay, Maggie. Don't worry."

"Yes, I know."

Margaret returned and drew Maggie aside before she left. "You come back and see me, Maggie Blume," she said. "I like you."

"I'd enjoy that. I like being here, and I like you, too. Very much."

"It was good to see you, Maggie," said Stephen.

As he bent down to hug her Maggie said, "I hope Tanya is tall so you can have good hugs."

Stephen laughed and said "Yes, we do have good hugs."

They smiled at each other and Maggie realized that this changed things. Stephen would always be glad to see her, but he wouldn't miss her now. He'd be occupied with this new relationship.

❧

Maggie wrote in her journal a week later, *"I complain that Michael ranges all over the place in how he relates to me, but I've been noticing how erratic I am. Sometimes I'm supportive and available, sometimes I'm closed off. Sometimes I think I want more, but then at the slightest suggestion of it I run the other way."*

"You don't need to be consistent," said Nu. "You just need to be fully present. That means feel what you feel and be who you are."

"I guess that means I'm supposed to be a bold, go-for-it woman who eagerly flies into the unknown." Maggie laughed.

"You are that woman. And you also are the woman who pulls back when she feels the ground shift under her."

"I am paradox personified," declared Maggie.

"Yes, it's all you."

"And that's okay?"

"What was it Michael quoted recently from the Bible? 'Before God formed you in the womb, God knew you and declared you holy.' Is being holy 'okay' enough?"

"Nu, did I ask for a relationship that stays only in the realms where daily grunge can't hurt it? One that stays where it will remain amazing and mystical and magical and never touch the ground? But I can't talk to him! I can't touch him! I can't share planting peas or sitting on the grass or laughing at the dog or crying about bad news or surprising him with fresh strawberries. There's no physicality."

"Physicality?" asked Nu. "You mean sex?"

"I'm not even going that far. There's no physical presence, sharing space, sharing happenings. No togetherness. I want to be together. When I imagine it, every shared moment seems incredibly alive, incredibly vibrant. The idea of washing vegetables at the sink together to make a salad is magical. The sun comes out and lights up all the colors and textures and sensations. I want to play together! I want to find joy in small gestures and the sacred in a look. I want it all, Nu. And this is miles away from giving me that."

"For now."

"But it sure doesn't seem likely there is ever going to be any more than this to look forward to. If I thought there was a real possibility, that would make a difference, but I don't, so all I can deal with is what is."

"What are you saying, Maggie?"

"I accept that we will always have the soul connection, but I need to be honest with myself about the rest of this. The simple truth is that we are not doing an in-this-world relationship. What we have is not a whole relationship. And it's not enough. Nu, I think I need to stop doing this dance along the line."

"What does that mean?"

"I need to let go of Michael."

"Are you scared again? Is that what's going on?"

"I'm tired of cycling between trust and disappointment."

"But Maggie, both are true."

"So what? I'm tired of it all."

"Then take a break. But don't throw it all away."

"Nu, why can't I just have a simple, ordinary romance?"

"You can, Maggie. There are three other men just waiting for your smile, and you know it."

Maggie groaned.

"See? You don't want them. You don't want simple and ordinary. You want paradox and extraordinary. You want Michael. And that's what you've got."

"Damn it, Nu, this is not what I want to hear."

Nu laughed. "You know I'm right."

❧

At church the next morning Michael sang the old Shaker song, "'Tis a gift to be simple, 'tis a gift to be free, 'tis a gift to come down where we ought to be. And when we find ourselves in the place just right, we will be in the valley of love and delight."

Maggie couldn't help but laugh, even as she shook her head in dismay. How could he possibly have known what she had said yesterday?

Michael preached about gifts from God that come in many forms, sometimes subtle, sometimes obvious, and about letting them change our lives. "Watch for the gift today," he said, and Maggie felt a gesture in the energy between them. It reminded her of when Michael lined up with the guru and Jesus to shake his penis at her. Now Michael turned to look straight at her and said, "When you recognize that gift, grab it and hold onto it." Her eyes, wide with amazement, held steady, looking right back at him. She took a deep breath, and she felt totally exasperated.

"Here I am," Maggie complained at Jackie's kitchen table an hour later, "trying to find a workable way with this whole thing, and then he goes and does stuff like this. And I don't think he even realizes he is doing it!"

Jackie laughed.

"Oh, don't laugh," Maggie moaned. "This is serious. I'm trying to get myself out of this and let the whole thing go."

"Okay, serious. You want out, but the spiritual connection is still there, right? It's like a mountain, solid as a mountain, that's what you said before."

"I don't want to even look for it right now."

"Okay, but I know it's there," said Jackie, "no matter what you say."

"Okay, yes, it is. I admit that. But what is it, Jackie? I know it is soul-connection and it is undeniable, but what is it in this physical existence level of being? No, I have to stop this love stuff."

"You're just cycling again, Maggie, and it's okay. Do what you need to do."

"But I don't want to cycle. I just…I just want…" Maggie stopped and stared at Jackie through eyes filling with tears.

"Yes? What do you want, Maggie?" asked Jackie.

"Damn. I just want him to stand right here and insist on loving me." And the tears burst loose in a flood.

Chapter Eighteen: Calling

Tory finally gave Maggie the poster of the Mary Magdalene painting well after the last of Mary's story was written down. "They lost my order," Tory explained. "We had to start the process all over again."

Of course, thought Maggie, chuckling to herself.

Apart from a slightly different angle, the resemblance between the face in Maggie's drawing and the one in the poster was stunning. They shared the same long, narrow nose, pouty lips, high cheekbones, tapered jaw, and tired, deep-set eyes. Maggie realized that if she had been looking at this poster image while she drew, she could not have created a better likeness. But as far as she knew, she had never seen it before. And Maggie had certainly not set out to draw Mary Magdalene.

She put the drawing and the poster side-by-side on the wall, and every so often during the day stopped to study them again. How was this possible? Yet here they were, two renderings of the same face.

"Mary, these pictures of you are very similar."

"Of course they are."

"But how did this happen?"

"You're not really so surprised," said Mary. "Let go of trying to make it logical."

"Okay, I'm taking a couple of deep breaths, and letting go of my concern that this is too weird."

"And now?"

"Now it's simply delightful. It's magical and mystical and wonderful."

"Even though you don't understand it?"

"Yes," said Maggie, then she added, laughing at herself, " but I do still want to know how it can be."

Maggie finished fitting all the pieces of Mary's story together. "*I spent the day reading the entire Mary book out loud to myself,*" she wrote in her journal.

"It was an awesome experience. Through a lot of it I had to keep one hand on my heart to support it in its fullness. Tears came often, for the beauty of it and for the miracle that it is. This is the first time I have experienced it from outside of it, having been so close all along. Now I understand Lydia's unhesitating awe."

The next morning at church, when Michael held up the bread and wine, Maggie felt that Mary's words were raised up, too. Mary's words were communion, spirit come into this world, bringing holiness into what is commonplace, bringing God into the world, bringing divine love into all that is.

Later at home Maggie wrote, *"I haven't said anything about this, but I've been shaking, off and on, for three days. I've tried clearing my energy, but that just makes it worse. I must be going through another big change."*

She went to the kitchen to get a glass of water, and ended up leaning against the sink, crying.

"Everything is so real," she exclaimed out loud. "Mary's book is real, Mary Magdalene is real, Jesus is real, and God is real. You are all real! And you are all right here. Right here!" She felt she could reach out and touch Mary and touch Jesus and touch God. She was living right in their midst, holding this book.

"Look at me!" she wrote back at her desk. *"I am a person who writes Mary Magdalene's book, and I am a person who lives with God right here, who can reach out and touch God. It is my resistance to knowing this that makes me shake. I need to allow this to be what it is.*

"I wonder, does a person get so used to having God right here that she says, 'Excuse me, could you move so I can get to the refrigerator?' Or, 'Can we please take a break from clarity and mindfulness and just be dense and foolish for a while?' Does a person get so used to having God right here that she knows, really knows, that if she ever forgets it she can easily get back to it?"

Later that week, at a concert at the church, Maggie sat with one of those three men Nu had mentioned were waiting for her to smile, and they had a very nice time together. She saw Michael watching them. Was that Mary next to him, watching, too? Nan had told her, "Go ahead and be friendly with other men and let Michael see what he is missing. Let him realize he could lose you." But when Maggie saw the concern and helplessness in Michael's face she felt awful.

Later at home Michael spoke to her on the other levels of consciousness.

"I saw you tonight with Charles," he said.

Maggie looked at him, waiting for more, and when nothing came she said, "Say it, Michael. Go on, say it. Do something," she insisted. "This is one of those gifts from God you spoke about."

"What is the gift in this?" he asked.

She blurted out, "Me! I'm the gift!"

That's not what she meant to say. She meant to say the gift is this chance to face the truth, but these other words pushed past.

They stared at each other. Finally he said, "Tell me what I am to you, Maggie."

She looked straight in his eyes and saw that he was as real as the book and Mary Magdalene and Jesus and God. "Okay," she said. "Because you asked me to, I have tried to get out of this, deny it, change it. I've done everything I know to do, and it just gets clearer and stronger. I love you, Michael. I can't imagine life without you in it.

"What about you, Michael? You stand up there on Sundays and talk about surprises, and you look at me. You sing about love and you look at me. You watch me with someone else and I feel your fears. Your eyes light up when I approach you, and you often are very flirtatious with me. What is going on, Michael? What are you doing?"

Maggie pushed away without waiting for an answer and instead phoned Lydia.

"Help! I'm going crazy here!"

"You're trying to get what you want," said Lydia.

"I swear I can accept any possibility, from nothing to everything, and make it work. I just want to know which one is actually happening so I can adjust to it."

"And that's what you want!" Lydia exclaimed.

"Okay, yes, I want to get it under control. So, you're suggesting that I need to not even hope to know what's happening? I get it. Okay, I'm working at letting go."

"Try breathing, too," Lydia said, laughing.

Maggie breathed consciously for a while, till everything settled.

Then Lydia said, "Maggie, I want to talk to you about your anger. It really is not okay to be getting angry at Michael like this. Tell me, what is it doing energetically?"

"Oh, Lydia!" she exclaimed. "I've been so self-absorbed I didn't even consider that. You're right. I've been angry at him and the anger projects energetically."

"I'm glad you are seeing that."

"His eyes are scared, vulnerable, afraid of hurting and of being hurt. Behind them I see the pain he has gone through in his life, the losses, the people who have said they will be there and then weren't. I've been throwing anger and frustration at him and pushing him away, all mixed in with saying trust me and I love you. He has been affected by all that, consciously or not."

"You better think about this, Maggie. And make some choices."

After the next couple of hours of facing hard truths and taking responsibility for them, Maggie opened to the inner levels and spoke to Michael there. "Okay, I've made some decisions, Michael. You're real for me, and I'll be real for you. I've told you that our souls are deeply connected, that I know you, that you can trust me, and that whatever happens between us these things are always true. I need to take responsibility for those statements."

She stopped to take a breath and get a good grasp on what she was saying. "I need to be trustworthy. I need to commit, as they did at Sanctuary Farm, to no further hurting here, only loving and caring and truth and support. Michael, I will do my best to be your friend, to honor and hold precious your trust and your true self. And I will do my best to deal with my feelings within myself, and not project them onto you."

The next morning as Maggie watched Michael at the pulpit, she saw him stand within the holiness of all life and do the sacred work he does, and she felt a new clarity and sureness of intention and commitment toward him. She knew she could support him in this and be a trusted friend.

As soon as she reached that realization Maggie felt her whole life path shift, as if one of those massive railway switching levers swung from one track over to another. It was that definite and that powerful. She did not know any more about it than that, and that it was done, and that it was good. And that there was no going back, only forward.

Michael went on to preach about savoring blessings. He told the congregation how much he loves being here in his life now. He related an earlier, hard and dark time, and finished by saying, "but it got me to here and I'm immensely grateful for that." He urged them all to open to the many and varied blessings in their lives. Then he shared a handful of big, fresh, ripe strawberries with a few people in the front row, and he walked up the aisle to hand one to Maggie.

"Come inside," said Nu when Maggie sat down later to write. "Come into your heart."

Maggie took some deep breaths and let herself sink within. Her heart was still bruised from Christmas. Tears welled up. She moved her hand to her heart to support it and felt Jesus' hand already there. After a few deep, releasing breaths she said, "His hand on my heart brings a deep peace. I feel calm. It reminds me who I am, and helps me open my heart."

"Your job, always, Maggie, is simply to open your heart," said Nu. "That's all. Answers will come when they do, if they do. Don't search. Just stay in your heart."

Maggie felt her heart spread wide open, and the rest of her settled into place around it. "I'm getting a message to speak from my open heart," she said.

"Yes, always."

"Even when making a clever little wisecrack at a gathering of friends."

"Always."

The next Sunday was Palm Sunday. Easter week. A whole year had passed since that Good Friday lunch Maggie had with Michael to talk about Jesus. On this Palm Sunday Michael again told the story of Jesus going to Jerusalem knowing what would happen there. This time he preached about betrayal and suffering and crucifixion, and Jesus' last words, "Father, into your hands I commend my spirit." Again Maggie felt it all profoundly.

How can I know this pain so well, she wondered.

"Don't search, remember?" said Nu. "Don't look for understanding or explanation or even for anything to make sense. Just stay in your heart and be open to what comes."

Maggie stayed for the next service, and when Michael went to the altar early in that service her heart was open and full. Was that Michael standing there? Or was it Jesus? She felt drawn to energetically reach out her hand to touch his heart. To Maggie's surprise, the energy of her hand went out open, palm up, instead of turned to lay flat against his chest. Then it was as if she reached inside his chest and held a living, beating heart in the palm of her hand. It was a heart full of pain. As she held it she knew Jesus' pain of walking into the week ahead. And she knew how full of pain Michael's heart was, too, as he entered his own Passion Week.

When the service ended, Tory came and wrapped her arms around Maggie there in the church's sanctuary, held her, and let her sob. Maggie cried for all the pain in those two hearts, she cried for Mary Magdalene, she cried for Amy, she cried for her own meandering way with faith, and she cried for how hard our life is on earth, adrift in this separation from spirit, struggling to grasp meaning and wholeness.

Maggie and Michael found each other at the front doors of the church after most people had left. His arms were full, so he held one door open for her by backing into it. They looked in each other's heavy eyes, with all that had been happening loaded into the space between them. Maggie knew, then, what it meant to have this line separating them. Despite their deep connection, there would be no holding, no comforting, no consoling, no resolution. They would part at this doorway and both leave alone, each with their own burdens and journey. She looked deeper into his eyes. This is what we are doing, she thought, this is what we are choosing, connection and separation, knowing and withdrawal.

"Bye," she said, and she was immediately sorry she had said it. It was too much. Their eyes bore the weight of the shattered silence between them.

Walking home, she could not escape that anguished leave-taking. It was only later that afternoon when she checked her email that she discovered through the prayer chain that Michael's favorite aunt, his last remaining elder relative, had died unexpectedly just the day before. Maggie wrote an email letter to Michael.

Dear Michael,

Now I understand why you spoke so strongly today about running into wall after wall, and why your face was so full of pain. I am so sorry for your loss. I wish you well as you find your way with what is clearly difficult for you. I wish I had offered you a hug before you left the church.

The following is an excerpt from the book I am working on. The words are from Mary Magdalene.

"I went to where I thought there was no way to be there with me, and there God was. I went to where no one has ever been there with me, and there God was. It seemed that no matter what, there God was. Out in places where nothing can touch, nothing can bear, nothing can exist, nothing can stay, nothing can hold. Just God and me. That was it. Just God and me, out there alone.

"So now I put one foot in front of the other foot and I keep on walking out there, even though nobody else can even see me, let alone be there with me. And I go and I go and there I am, out there, out there, out there, and there's God, keeping right with me. Even though nobody else will even look at me, nobody else will even acknowledge me, nobody else will even take a breath with me, nobody else will even imagine me out there where I really am. And then I know. I am me and I am there and I am who I always was and will be and it is what it is. It is what it is. It is what it is."

Love, Maggie

Several days later Maggie realized she still held Michael's heart. She felt the substantial, moist aliveness of a flesh and blood, living, beating heart in her hand. It was that intimate, that vulnerable, that trusting, that beautiful.

Maggie wrote in her journal, "*When the message came to open my heart, I thought it was about me, about how I see the world. It was that, but it was also so that Michael could get to me on Sunday and find the support he needed. I'm glad I could do that for him, except now my own heart is still spread wide open and I am not used to being this available and exposed. I don't know how to be this open. I don't know how to do this.*"

"Just do it," said Nu.

Early on Easter morning Maggie woke to thoughts of people all around the world paying attention today, listening to the words, opening their hearts. The sky had just begun to brighten and birds to sing as people gathered for the sunrise service out behind the church. As Michael began to speak Maggie realized he had found his strength and taken his heart back.

Michael spoke about life going on and love going on, no matter what happens, and he said, "God is always there, always, as far out there as you can go."

Maggie felt a cord, clear and bright, connecting his words to her letter, and connecting his heart to hers. And she sensed Mary Magdalene standing off to the side, nodding and smiling.

Michael always listens to me, she realized. He takes it in and lets it become part of him, and then he speaks from there. He never tells people that I said something. He keeps that between him and me.

Next Michael asked people to call out places in the world or situations needing prayer. He began it with the Middle East, others added Chiapas, hungry children, understanding between religions, and names of individuals. Tory called out, "Amy and David." Then at the end Maggie said, "Open hearts." As she said it she knew that opening hearts would be her work, passed on from Mary Magdalene. She felt her words touch hearts right there, and the hearts opening.

Then, as her words still hung in the air, Michael took hold of them. He began to sing them in a song and everyone joined in. "We open our hearts to find love in the world." The last line of the song was, "I open my heart to find love in you." Maggie and Michael looked at each other, and they sang it together.

Later, inside the church for the regular services, every seat was filled. The choir sang from Handel's "Messiah," and Michael shared his deep love for Jesus and Easter and God.

"The crucifixion is the easy part for us," he said. "We're used to that sort of thing. The good guy rubs the wrong people wrong and next thing we know, he's in big trouble. The people in power get rid of the upstart. We see it in the movies, we even experience versions of it ourselves. Good Friday, the crucifixion, that's believable. We can deal with that.

"But this Easter thing, what we're looking at today, well, it's pretty dramatic. We try not to think about it much. Jesus rising from the dead? He gets up and walks out of there? Shows up on the road and downtown? Come on. I don't know about that. That's just a story, right?

"It's quite a story. Look how much effect this strange story has had on the world over the past two thousand years. Look around this room. You all showed up here this morning, some of you before sunrise, because of this story. Whether or not you think Jesus actually walked out of there, you showed up here to hear about this story. Again.

"The story of Jesus' resurrection, dying and not dying but rising again, going on, is the foundation of why we live a life of compassion and peace and justice and forgiveness and love. Because it tells us that all of that is bigger than us, all of that transcends death, all of that goes on, no matter what. Jesus' resurrection shows us this.

"Resurrection means that nothing, not even death, can stop God's love.

Nothing, not Herod or Pilote, no horror or nightmare or anyone who turns on you, can stop God's love in the world. Nothing can stop God's love from going on, nothing can stop this essence of our faith. God's love transcends death. God goes on, no matter what. God is always there. God is always there. God is always there!"

"Our showing up here today to be part of the telling of this story, again, two thousand years later, shows us that. Our living lives of compassion and peace and justice and forgiveness and love shows us that. This, this right here, is the story. We are the story."

Maggie realized that when Mary Magdalene walked out where no one but God would go with her, she had seen the reality of herself and of everything around her. Mary said, "It is what it is." The message of Easter, thought Maggie, is that God, or holiness or love or source energy or whatever you want to call it, is always, always there, and that is what is. There is holiness in everything that is and in everything that ever happens. The sacred takes form, literally takes material form, in every breath, every word, every glance, every touch, every sound, every moment, every thought, every feeling, every hope, every pain. God is right here in us and with us.

After the last service ended and the organist stopped playing and everyone had greeted everyone else and moved on, Maggie went to Michael. She didn't try to talk. She just looked in his eyes before and after they hugged, held onto both his hands, and whispered, "Thank you." He smiled and hugged her again. They looked at each other once more, and then parted. Maggie went to visit Amy before Easter dinner with friends, and Michael went to be with family.

Howl

Wolves howl through the rain at dawn,
calling out another day of gray clouds,
dark and heavy, dragging across the sky.
It has been a week of gray rain and meager light
as the closely blanketed land
labors to birth spring without sunshine.
Daffodils and jonquils and forsythia
offer their brightness instead,
illumination from beneath the sky,
lit from within.

The wolves howl just up the river,
out of place, inside fences,
with feeding plans and curious crowds
that watch them live.
They call, they remind us,
treasure freedom,
run and dance and
listen and love and live.
Express the deep sacred,
and avoid enclosures.

Today we begin a war.
Today American bombs fall on a distant city
we have declared our enemy.
My friend has concluded that warring is our nature,
human nature.
We do this.
We keep doing it.

Her shoulders close around her
as she considers another mother,
much like herself,
in a far-off, but not so far-off, foreign place,
who, today or tomorrow,
will lose her child
or her husband
or everything she knows.

Caught up in our frustration,
my friend and I say,
let those men who want to live life this way
send their own children out in front of the guns.
And then we looked at ourselves in horror,
seeing our own violence.

It starts with me.
Who am I?
I hear the wolves howl and I know that
even though we may all be locked inside
whatever fences bind our lives,
there is in each of us
a sacred wholeness and grace
that is our true nature.
Dear God, be my light.
Keep my heart open and clear.
Remind me who I am.
Howl at me.

Chapter Nineteen: Howl

Someone had brought another healer to work on Amy, and afterward told Maggie to stay away for three weeks. It was not easy to stay away, and it hadn't even been two full weeks when Maggie felt strongly that she should go to Amy. She went against the other healer's request, and it was a very good thing that she did because the other healer was not following up at all. There was no presence with Amy, no one watching out for her or helping her energetically. She was abandoned.

Amy was in horrible pain when Maggie came back to her, and the nausea was unrelenting. New drugs caused hallucinations and confusion, and Amy was terrified. Any movement in the room frightened her, and whenever anyone touched her, her body clenched into a fetal position and she actually whimpered. It was appalling. There was a strong sense about her of having had way too much done to her. Amy desperately needed peace, and she was too far from it to even ask for it. Maggie had never seen her in such bad shape.

Maggie immediately set to work clearing pain and fear and whatever else would release. She calmed Amy's panic and relaxed her. She reestablished an energetic healing grid around her to provide on-going care. She asked that the angels and guides do what they could and that Amy be supported and held in love as she walks her path.

When she was done and Amy was asleep, Maggie sat down at the side of the bed and she cried.

"I'm so sorry, Amy," she said. "I should not have listened to someone else telling me to stay away. I should have been here. I'm so sorry."

Maggie placed one hand on Amy's heart, the other on her own. She willed herself to be more open to Amy, to the remarkable journey they were both on, to the mysterious connection between them, and to the multifaceted emotions now tugging at her. As Maggie prayed, Mother Mary was there, Jesus was, too, and God's sweet, bright light and love flooded through the room. Tears rolled freely down Maggie's face and finally her heart unfolded, filling with love.

Eventually Amy stirred and Maggie's hands released their touch.

Afterward, back at home, Maggie sobbed. "God," she begged, "Jesus, Mother Mary, anybody! Please can't I do something more to help this beautiful, precious woman? How can you let her suffer like this? How can I bear to watch it? I don't understand. What do I need to do? Tell me and I'll do it. Help me be enough to help her. Please!"

Nu responded, "It is what it is, Maggie."

David asked Maggie to stay with Amy for several hours the next day while he took care of some things. He didn't want to leave her alone while she was so scared and weak. Amy still couldn't think clearly because of the drugs and the build up of toxins. Maggie worked on her and Amy slept.

Amy had changed. She was not in control like she had been, and she knew it. She had to focus on herself now and stand face to face with her own journey. She didn't have the strength to take care of anybody else any more. She had become less gracious and more direct.

Amy's letting go of control gave Maggie more access. She was finally able to do some limited work on Amy's liver and stomach and intestines, though it still had to be done with the restrictive intention to only support Amy's path, relieve what could be relieved, and release the outcome.

Amy's organs were so damaged and compromised that even what little Maggie could do took very strong energy, and a lot of it. Maggie wouldn't usually be so aggressive, but with illness this serious it was no time to be timid. She went as far as Amy was able to go, and Amy took it all in, trying hard, as usual, to get back to life.

At the end of the day Maggie sat on the porch at home, breathed deeply, and sank into the mockingbird's songs. It had felt very good to do more powerful work today, but she had no idea if it would make any difference.

Maggie walked up from the bottom of the big grid to the bench in the center and lay down on it. Over the next hour she felt her energy clear and then a soft, fine, golden glow filled her. She noticed shift and change deep in the patterns that define her, and she trusted that they were necessary and right. When it was finished she got up to move to the Earth Portal, but first she stopped, feeling she should leave something of herself here at the center. Running fingers through her hair, she gathered a few loose strands and dropped them by the rocks marking the center. Now it was okay to move on.

At the Earth Portal Maggie sat on the ground and sifted through a pile of small quartz crystals Stephen had left there to charge in the energy of the portal. There were a few double-pointed ones mixed in, and she picked out one to bring home with her.

"This is still my spot," she wrote in her journal. "I love it here. I feel amazingly comfortable here. Being here, I realize how much I have to work at maintaining my patterns out in the world. Here I don't have to work at anything at all; the energy carries me."

Maggie could feel that now familiar connection with a far-off place and the presence of beings there. She let her mind wander for a while then asked, "Will someone answer a question for me? How am I doing?"

After a hesitation the answer came. "Excellent."

"What should I do differently?" she asked.

Another pause, then, "Whatever you do." These answers were awkward and stilted, and she wondered if this source was not used to verbalizing.

"But am I doing what I'm supposed to do?" she asked. "Am I doing what is needed?"

A small, golden-brown spider caught Maggie's eye as it ran up a strand of web from the journal notebook to her hair. Spider woman, weaving the web of life, weaving both Maggie and her writing into the web. The message became clear, "Continue to write. Don't stop after Mary's story." She sat for a few quiet minutes, first with that idea and then just being there.

"I have another question," she said. "Is this a sacred spot?"

"This is a place."

"That other place out there in the far distance, the one that feels like home, is that a sacred place?"

"It is home. It is source. It is familiar. You experience long-standing, deep recognition."

So, was there no such thing as a sacred place? Was every place as sacred as any other? Maggie let go of questioning and sank effortlessly into the inviting support of the grid, welcoming its comfort and ease as it opened to receive her, taking her in.

All at once, from every edge of the two-acre field, a chorus of birds burst into song, loud and full and strong. She'd never heard so many birds sing so loud. Something had happened. Then she realized that the entire grid had expanded and opened wide, and now a continuous stream of energy was coming through. The impression she got was of preparation to make major, positive, healing change in the world.

"Now I understand why I came here today," she wrote in her journal. "This needed to happen, and like the other times, for whatever reason, I had to be here to open the way. I think I should stay here in the Earth Portal until the flow completes." Maggie lay down on the ground. On an impulse she put the crystal on her heart, thinking it might help keep her heart open. She felt alert and excited; whatever was happening felt important. The flow into the grid continued for about half an hour, and then, abruptly, it stopped. Surprised, Maggie sat up to look around and saw that Stephen was walking up the field. That was why.

"You have activated the grid to the next level," Stephen called out to her, not realizing what had just happened. "It has expanded and it is much stronger."

Should she tell him he had interrupted? He'd be terribly disappointed. It felt okay to wait and finish later.

"You always show up here when it's time for it to advance," he said.

"Is it still true that nothing happens without my being here?"

"Nothing of significance."

"Yesterday I couldn't get this place off my mind. I felt I had to come whether I got hold of you or not."

"When you can't contact me, just come anyway, Maggie. Come whenever you want."

"Can I take this little crystal home?"

"Sure. Take anything you want, any time. Will you help me move these stones out to mark the new edges of the portal?" he asked, tugging at a large rock.

"You don't have to do that, Stephen. In fact, it's better to leave them to anchor the portal at its center."

"Great, save me some work. Thanks."

They walked up to the center and sat on the bench there. While Stephen spoke, Maggie brought herself back into the energy of the grid's earlier opening, and the flow resumed. It was not as full as it had been, but it was enough. She held it for a while, then gently pulled her attention away, only occasionally checking to make sure it continued.

"Romance is not relationship," Stephen was saying, his feet stretched out in front of the bench. "It's attraction. It's on the personality level, not soul. Romance is low vibration, and it's only going to hold you back. The real thing, the soul thing, now that's really nice. Yeah, really nice."

"But even soul relationships complicate life," replied Maggie, squinting toward the sun to look at him. "Take how it has been for both of us. We're so distracted. Maybe it's better to not be involved in any kind of intimacy while there is so much going on."

"It's tough, but it's good. It gets you to do your work."

Maggie sighed. "I have to admit that if Michael ever comes for me on this physical world level, I can't imagine saying no." He nodded when she looked at him again. "The trouble is," she said, "then I would still find it very difficult to keep doing all I'm doing, and I want to."

"That's one of the exciting challenges of relationship."

"You find it exciting, but to me it seems way too much. So, I may complain about keeping my relationship with Michael on the deeper levels, but I'm also grateful for it."

"Whatever happens will be the right thing at the right time, Maggie. You know that. Just remember, whatever happens, stay in your heart. Hey, as we sit here I think I'm receiving that clearing you got earlier. This is great!"

When she got home, Maggie called Tory to ask about spiders.

"The body of the spider is in the shape of the infinity symbol," said Tory. "Spider walks the infinity path, that thin line that weaves the web of fate between the worlds. She balances at the intersection between realities, and challenges us to walk those circles and maintain the balance."

After hanging up the phone, Maggie got out her journal and wrote, *"I cross over between realities all the time, between regular life and energy work, between the different levels of relationship, between physicality and spirit, and between this world and wherever that far away home place is. My challenge is to hold the balance at the intersections between those realities.*

"The grid is definitely an intersection between realities, and my energy seems to be a key that must be inserted in order for the crossover point to open. So how come I feel that it's still open and flowing right now? Oh, I remember. I left the strands of hair, DNA. That must be enough."

Maggie paused, marveling, then wrote more. *"Tory also said the spider teaches us how to weave words into written magic. I hadn't told her I was writing as the spider built me and my notebook into her web. Last week a wolf spider came straight down in front of me as I wrote. Both spiders brought the message to keep writing and to add my writings to the web of life, sending them out into the world."*

Later that night Maggie drew a spider web with an infinity-shaped spider hanging in the center. As she filled in layer after layer of pattern, looping around the infinity symbol design throughout the background, she thought about how varied people's experience of the world can be. Stephen, for instance, worked very hard at life, believing that he needed to spend a lot of time delving into old darkness in order to clear it. Maggie's path, on the other hand, seemed much more full of light. We weave our own perspective out of expectations and assumptions, thought Maggie. We create our experiences with our thoughts and feelings and actions. The hard thing to remember is that there are an infinite number of possible perspectives, and we can step from one to another. Changing perspectives changes everything.

"How are you doing with Mary's book?" asked Jackie once they settled for a break on rocks alongside the Mount Pisgah Summit Trail. "Have you written any letters to literary agents yet?"

"I've been trying," said Maggie. "I've been reading about query letters and strategies and contracts and I've been researching literary agents' track records. It becomes so overwhelming! I had made a list of possible agents, but as I've researched them I've crossed each one off for one reason or another. I've basically got to start a whole new list now."

Jackie scowled. "You were so sure about sending the book out into the world. I'm surprised it's so tangled."

"I get too much in my head, don't I," said Maggie, "trying to figure it all out and wanting to know what will happen before I even take a step."

"You get lost in all that mental complexity," agreed Jackie. "You forget to trust and use your intuition."

"Exactly! I wanted to do this by following intuition. How do I get back to that?"

"What if, when you see that you are stuck, you stop and back up a couple of steps, back to where you were more open and clear? Then simply, trustingly, consciously take the next step."

"That's good, Jackie. I like that."

As they continued talking, Jackie stopped several times when she saw Maggie's tangle taking over again, and she patiently brought Maggie back, saying, "Well now, okay, there you are in that tangle. But didn't you say you want to be over here?"

Each time Jackie did that Maggie took a deep breath, ceased struggling, sat still, and looked at it all. Then she said, "Oh, right, yes." It seemed simple then to leave the tangle and return to where things were clear.

At the end of the next day Maggie called Jackie. "I have spent all day continually getting stuck, stopping, and then backing up to where I had last been clear. One time I backed up to where I'd been five hours earlier, having spent all that time off in a head-tangle doing research again. I learned good stuff, but it kept me in place instead of moving forward. Jackie, I do this constantly!"

"Only when you're scared, Maggie. It's how you avoid going forward. It's not a bad thing, it's just a tactic. Now that you see it so clearly, you are already changing it."

The next afternoon Maggie stood at the mailbox holding the first thick envelope. "Here we go, Mary, heading off into the future, into adventure. This could be the one." She dropped the envelope into the slot.

"I spoke with one of Amy's nurses in the elevator," Tory confided a week later, "sort of off the record. She told me that Amy's nausea is caused by the cancer, and that's why they can't resolve it."

"Cancer?" asked Maggie, startled. "But David told me they got all the cancer in Texas."

Tory shook her head. "No, they didn't. And this nurse said the doctors never would have done what they did in Texas if they knew it would be like this. They never would have put Amy through this."

Maggie turned away. No, I'm not going there, she declared to herself. Tory is just doing it again, being pessimistic. She gathers every little hint that things could be going wrong. Who knows what that nurse actually said, or why. No. I'm not giving in to that. Nothing has changed.

As if to confirm Maggie's optimism, one of the local doctors suggested another surgery and Amy decided to go for it. When again it didn't work, the failure was devastating for everyone. And then there didn't seem to be anything else for the medical doctors to try. Tory spoke to Amy about letting go, and Amy asked Maggie to tell her more about healing miracles.

"Let's do it, Maggie," she said. "I want to get well!"

Maggie went very deep into the patterns this time, beyond pain and scar tissue and organs and disease, to the disturbances deep in Amy's energy field that allowed the cancer to take hold. This was the first time she could get to them. She tried to reach into the thickness to loosen it and work down through it, but she couldn't get into it. It seemed like it would all have to come out at once. Maggie reached even deeper to slip under and lift it out. Finally she had it all in her hands. There was so much! She carefully lifted but couldn't move it. She braced herself, used all her strength and did everything she could. Still it would not budge. Okay, if she couldn't lift it out, she would transform it from beneath. She ran a tremendous amount of energy, stretching herself, reaching farther than she knew how to reach. Nothing changed the dark, unrelenting density. In the end all she could do was leave it there.

Maggie sat for a long time, exhausted, her heart aching, desperately wanting to come up with something else to try, unable to do anything but watch Amy sleep. She called Lydia.

"I know that we can profoundly, absolutely change things. We can change the energetic pattern, and then the physical expression of that pattern will change. I am certain of this, Lydia. But our logical minds get in the way; they are so convinced otherwise. Our minds believe in the illness and hang onto it. So, we doubt the healing, and that blocks healing. The client and I both have to be wide open to the real possibility of miraculous healing. We both have to know it, be ready for it, and allow it. We have to stop calling it a miracle and know it is just how things are."

"I agree, usually, except when it isn't how things are," said Lydia.

"What do you mean?"

"Maybe Amy is supposed to die. Maybe her dying is teaching you and David, and me, too, and probably a lot of other people, something really important to learn."

"You're saying I can't make anything happen because it's not supposed to happen."

"Whatever is supposed to happen will happen."

"I want to help her! I have to help her!" Maggie choked on her words and burst into tears. "We're losing her, and this isn't just about healing any more. I can't let her go."

"Can you stop it? You can't, can you? You tried your best just now, and you can't."

"Oh, Lydia. This is impossibly hard and painful."

"Yes, it is."

"If this is how it is, then what's the point? What's the point of anything? What am I doing? What is all this for? Why try? Why try at all? The work, the book, Amy? What am I doing?"

"I'll tell you what you're doing, Maggie. You're hanging on to expectations and judgment. You've got to let things go. You've got to let them be what they are."

❧

"It's tempting," wrote Maggie late one night, *"to climb into someone else's problems and fears, trying to help, trying to be kind. Then you are being such a good person, there for them, giving and generous. But look what happens when we do that. Lydia is in a panic, right now, driving in the rain for six hours, alone, late at night, probably crying and scared and exhausted, putting her own safety at risk because she believes that she has to personally be right there for her father's early morning emergency surgery tomorrow, supporting and encouraging him. And another woman I know just told me today that she is actually going back, again, into an emotionally abusive relationship because she feels sorry for the man. Then there is me, still up at 2:30 in the morning, wearing myself out, jeopardizing all I need to do tomorrow, still trying to find answers so I can help Amy.*

"We're doing, giving, and being too much for the other person, while abandoning our own well-being. That doesn't work. I know from energy work that if I don't take care of myself first, whatever I try to do for the client is feeble and ineffective, and I just end up in trouble myself, too. Then I'm useless."

Maggie sighed and stared out at the city lights for a few minutes before continuing.

"The message in all this for me is to stay in my own experience of whatever is going on. I need to deal with my own impressions, responses, reactions, feelings, memories, triggers, fears, hopes, knowing, and being. I need to take responsibility for me first. Only after that can I even hope to effectively give anything useful to anyone else. Once I've done my own work, then what I have to offer to others rises up, naturally, exuberantly, out of who I am, filled with life and truth and grace.

"This means that with Amy my role is not to climb into her story, but to be in mine. Sit with her as if we are sitting together under the Buddha's bodhi tree.

Simply be there with her, experiencing whatever I experience, and only then do what becomes evident to me. So, I may sometimes work on her, sometimes simply watch her sleep, sometimes answer her questions about my day. I may do nothing but sit if that is all that becomes evident. It's all the same, in a way, under the bodhi tree. And it is all fine."

That sketch Maggie had done in the middle of the night a year and a half ago, the one of the cross that wouldn't let her sleep, turned up in a pile. She had forgotten all about it. Now it grabbed hold of her again and would not let go. As she looked at it she realized the circle around the center had to do with Mary Magdalene and life and earth and fertility and path. The cross part related to Jesus and spirit and faith. The whole, the circled cross, was the coming together of Mary Magdalene and Jesus in a beautiful, centered balance. It was also the coming together of God and life, of spirit and form, of grace and humility, of chaos and knowing, of choice and flow, of discovery and loss, of love and confusion, of trust and doubt, and of Maggie and Michael.

She took the sketch to her table and began a larger drawing. As she worked on it, as it became more defined and real and present, she was increasingly taken with it. And, she was very aware of Mary watching.

Maggie stared at the half-finished drawing, seeing it completed. She saw that the cross itself would be gold, while a multitude of brilliant colors filled the circular band and a fluid, foreign script covered the background. She couldn't pull herself away from the image. Gazing at it she felt complete, needing nothing more than this graceful, spiritual wholeness of coming together in balance and beauty.

What was that strange lettering in the background? Were those Mary's Words? Was that some sort of ancient Middle Eastern language? It was wonderful, of course, but how would she ever write or draw that? Couldn't they use some of Mary's Words in English instead?

Maggie called Lydia.

"You can do this," insisted Lydia. "Let go and see what comes. Try it on another piece of paper, then you can cut and paste it together."

"How am I going to write in a long gone, totally alien language I don't know anything about?"

"You don't have to know. This is Mary Magdalene we're talking about. Just allow."

"Okay, Lydia, I will try it, but if this works you are the amazing one for believing it will."

"Yeah, right. Call me after you do it."

Maggie grabbed a pad of lined paper and a pen, and she found her hand going to the right edge to begin. "Oh, it's right to left, like Hebrew," she said. "Okay, maybe that strangeness will make it easier to give way and do this."

She let herself relax and open and go deep. And then she let her hand begin to move. It worked. Her hand just did it, flowing along like regular writing, only not at all regular because it was backwards and totally foreign and unrecognizable. Actually, it was fascinating, and it was surprisingly easy. Shapes similar to scrawled letters formed into words, as if she knew what she was writing. Except nothing about it was known to her.

Maggie stopped abruptly. "I can't believe I'm doing this," she said out loud. "I better do it on the real thing before it gets used up on scrap paper." She quickly drew light pencil guide lines behind the cross, then got a drawing pen and began to lay in the script, well aware she was taking a chance on ruining the drawing. It worked. It was easy. In twenty minutes the background was filled. She laid down the pen and stared.

"I've got to find out more about this cross!" she said. She spent the rest of the day reading on the Internet and in books, and writing her own thoughts in her journal.

She learned that the circled cross, usually called a Celtic cross, had ancient and prehistoric origins way before Christian times. It only became a common symbol of Christianity in the fourth century. The Roman Catholic Church adopted it, along with many other symbols and holy days and stories from previously existing religious practices, taking advantage of their familiarity to reassure and more easily convert people. Earlier circled crosses were always equal-sided. The version in this drawing, with its extended base, was called a "high cross," and it was purely Christian.

It's interesting that Christians lifted the cross up, thought Maggie, like Christianity lifts spirituality up from its ancient, accessible earthiness to God-in-the-sky, out there not here, reachable only through priests and experts. Right here and now it's fascinating that this symbol, which is so insistently after my attention, is a combination of both Christian and ancient designs. Lately I've been very involved with church and Christianity. Is Tiamat reaching for me again?

She read that just about every indigenous culture on earth, from prehistoric to present day, has used circles and crosses and circled crosses in their sacred painting and decoration. The circle alone often represents the moon, and the cross or the cross inside a circle represents the sun. The earliest known examples, found in a cave in the French Pyrenees, were on small, flat stones engraved and painted with the design as early as 10,000 B.C.

She read that the circle and the cross are geometric opposites. A circle encloses and contains; a cross reaches out in all four directions. A circle never ends, in that its line is infinite; a cross marks one, finite point at its center.

Oh! she thought, looking up from the book. Bring it together and you have paradox! The circled cross is both enclosing and reaching out, both infinite and finite. Paradox.

Maggie read that the Druids and many others believed the sun was God, and they symbolized the sun with a circled cross. So, thought Maggie, they were saying that God is both infinite and finite and God both encloses and expands endlessly outward. With this symbol they were saying God is opposites together, God is paradox, God is impossibility, God is ultimate mystery.

She picked up her journal and wrote, "*Circle and cross, Goddess and Christ, ancient and new, earthy spirituality and lofty spirituality, all the opposites and paradoxes and impossibilities, all one, here in this circled cross. All this is in Mary Magdalene and Jesus. And in Michael and me.*

"I've known that the cross alone symbolizes the coming of the sacred into physical being. The vertical, representing spirit, intersects the horizontal, representing earth. Together they illustrate spirit coming into form, like Stephen's "Spirit into Form" grid at the heart of the "Tree of Life" does, bringing the sacred into material being. Now I'm realizing that at the very center of the cross, at that finite point marked by the cross, that would be the precise act and moment of creation itself. This crossing point is where the sacred expresses itself as incarnate form, where spirit becomes flesh. It is the Christ taking form as Jesus. It is that point deep in the core of each of us, our core star, where spirit comes into our own personal being and from which our energetic patterns generate."

What happens, Maggie wondered, when we draw the circle around that point of creation? The sexual imagery of penis and vagina, sperm and egg, seems obvious and meaningful, but there is a lot more to this than intercourse and conception. She looked at the shapes some more. The circle surrounds and embraces the cross's center, she thought. It holds that moment of creation, holds that mystical coming together of spirit and matter into manifest being.

Holds? Be-hold? Maggie remembered what the book had said, that we aren't truly, fully being unless we learn to hold the sacred beauty of another person.

Taking that idea back to the image, Maggie saw that here at this central point of the cross, held by the circle, is where we, and everything that is, come into being. We need both the circle and the cross, she thought. We need both the miracle of creation and the holding in order to allow and enable that dynamic creativity of spirit to come into physical form, in order to enable the sacred to come into being.

Maggie went back to study the shapes some more. She realized that the cross is both finite and infinite within itself: its lines mark and hold a single point, while its shape reaches out in all directions. The circle is also both finite and infinite within itself: its shape encloses and defines a limited space, and yet its line is never ending. Both cross and circle contain the same paradox, yet they express it oppositely. In line, the cross defines one point while the circle's line is infinite. In form, the circle's enclosure defines and limits, while the cross's form points to the infinity in all directions. They are the same, but opposites.

"Bring them together and their paradoxes play off each other," wrote Maggie, *"multiplying paradox upon paradox, creating new levels of paradox. The more I look at this, the more paradox I see. The paradoxes bubble forth in layer after layer, creating patterns in the essence of being."* Maggie watched the patterns grow outward from this circled cross, like minerals crystallizing into infinite complexity of form, extraordinary in its beauty.

"This is all of creation!" she wrote. *"Conceived in the 'beholding' at the center, and birthed through paradox! Fascinating! I love this! This circled cross represents the divine mystery expressing, manifesting, and realizing itself in all of life. All the layers of patterns I work in, deep into infinity, all the patterns of existence, grow out of this. The circled cross symbolizes container and source for all expression of the holy in this world. Everything that exists comes through this wholeness of being, this holding of being."*

Maggie put down her pen and sat with this for a while. When she looked back at the drawing once again, it was only a half-finished drawing, line and form on paper, with strange writing in the background. She called Lydia to tell her that the writing was done.

One day Michael's energy caught Maggie's attention as she carried a bowl of soup to her kitchen table for lunch. His field felt fractured, with cracks all through it. She went to work clearing a lot of jittery congestion and finally felt him ease. Again she was drawn to hold his heart until it accepted some healing energy. Then she cleared and balanced his thoughts and mind. When she finished he seemed much improved but still quite vulnerable.

When it happened again two days later she went into the other levels and asked, "Are you okay?"

"Sort of," he said.

"It doesn't feel like you're in danger, just burdened and vulnerable." She passed more energy through to him, then said, "I'm here, Michael. I'm holding the space for whatever you need."

Maggie gasped as she felt him climb into her heart as if he climbed into a tree house or a secret spot to be safe there. Quickly recovering from her surprise, she checked to make sure she could handle this, then said to him, "Okay, we can do this. I'll carry you here for now. I'll keep you safe."

"Yes, he is there," Lydia agreed. "It feels like part of his soul is seeking a loving place to take refuge and rest. He is nestled in on the left side of your heart."

Maggie nodded, "Yes, that's where I feel him."

"He's sure paying attention. It's like he's watching the opening of a cave to see what and who is coming, to see if he needs to retreat. He's wary of me, so I'm keeping my distance. I don't think I should work on you until he's ready to head back out."

"I agree. Thanks for the confirmation, Lydia."

Maggie wrote in her journal, *"Michael has sent a part of himself to seek refuge in my heart for safe keeping. I had said he should come for me. Now he has come for refuge in me. Again he has come but it is not what I expected. He hasn't come to get me, he has come for who I am."*

Michael stayed in Maggie's heart-refuge for two days, and then she simply noticed he was gone. She smiled when she realized he had left, glad she was able to do that for him, and that he trusted her enough for it.

"Don't you want to know what that was about?" asked Lydia.

"It really doesn't matter," Maggie answered, shaking her head. "It only matters that he trusted me, and that I was trustworthy."

Chapter Twenty: Howl at Me

"David is taking Amy home to die." Tory's words rushed out fast, piled in an appalling mound, and Maggie stared at them. It was the last Sunday of April and Michael was already up at the pulpit ready to begin the service. Maggie had stopped for a quick hug with Tory on the way to sit down.

"What?" she murmured in confusion.

"The cancer is all through her blood and there's nothing they can do," said Tory, still urgent, talking low and fast, shoving the words at her. "David is convinced now and he's crying all the time. He finally believes it."

Maggie stared at Tory, then turned and walked away. As she sat down and Michael began speaking, everything crashed in on her. Confusion, anguish, failure. She couldn't just sit there. She felt trapped and wanted to escape. She looked at Michael, desperately wanting to go to him, interrupt him, interrupt the service. No, she couldn't do that; she had to wait till afterward. She had to sit through the service first. It was just an hour. She tried really hard to listen, but just couldn't focus on what he was saying. She couldn't make any sense of it.

Then she saw Allen, another member of the prayer chain, at the far edge of the sanctuary. Maggie had spoken with him before about Amy's illness and Tory's intensity. There was an empty seat next to him. Without thinking, Maggie burst up out of the pew. Michael turned to look at her, his face puzzled. She froze and stared at him, knowing she should sit back down, but she couldn't. She crossed over to Allen, collapsed into his outstretched arms, and whispered what had happened. She felt Michael watching them, even as he continued the service. She heard the distraction in his voice as he skimmed the surface of his words.

"Do you know this is true?" Allen whispered. "Can you feel it yourself?"

"I don't know. I can't tell."

"That's okay, take some slow breaths."

Maggie moaned, "I let Amy down."

"Would you like me to pray with you?" asked Allen.

"Yes, please." She clung to him as he prayed in a whisper near her ear. She tried to listen to his words, tried to open to God, but all the time she heard Michael, too, speaking from his notes about love and life catching you off guard, and about passion and being bold. She wanted to listen to both of them, but all she could do was watch it all slip away.

Michael avoided looking at her through the rest of the service. At the end she was desperate to apologize and explain her disruptive behavior. When she got to him she blurted out, "Tory told me that Amy is dying," and her eyes filled again with tears.

Michael nodded and said Tory had talked to him about it, too. He seemed far away and cautious.

"Can you tell if it's true or not?" she asked.

He shook his head no, then said, "Tory is usually right about these things."

"But she has already been wrong about Amy several times." Maggie searched his face, silently pleading.

"Tory seems to know," he said, trailing off, held in place by her pain-filled eyes. "But she could be wrong," he added unconvincingly. Then he just waited, looking at her.

That was when she realized she was trying to get him to tell her that Amy would be okay, and he couldn't do that. He wouldn't do that. She took a deep breath.

"Good idea, breathe," he said, and he took a deep breath himself.

"I'm sorry. I'm really thrown by this," she said.

He nodded, but he still didn't reach out to touch her. He seemed at a loss what to do or say. "Are you going to be okay?" he finally asked, hopefully.

She sighed and nodded. "I always find my way through things," she said. He still looked so distraught that she touched him on the arm, reassuring him, releasing him. He seemed relieved by that and he nodded.

Maggie stayed for the second service. Michael skipped all the part about love this time, but he did look at her, and she was able to connect with him. At the end she went to him again, and as they hugged he asked, "How are you doing?"

"Better," she answered. "I'm going to the hospital now. I have to find out what's happening." Michael nodded and watched her leave.

Tory was finally right. Amy was dying. David told Maggie he was taking Amy home in the morning, stopping all interventions, and Hospice was stepping in.

Maggie stayed away for two whole days. She kept herself too busy, let her mind tangle in whatever it could get hold of, avoided thinking about Amy, and she did not deal with what was going on.

On the morning of the third day she wrote in her journal, "*I seem to think or feel that something is going to happen and then I will do all the right things and make all the right choices. I seem to want to be rescued, maybe have some cowboy hero rush in, take charge and make everything okay. Do I want Michael to do that? Surprisingly, no. Somebody else? Aha, it's God. I want God to come sweeping in and gather me up and make me feel safe. I want to feel and know and trust God's love without any doubts, really know it, absolutely. I want absolute faith. And I want it so much that I yearn for it. I ache for it.*

"*Every Sunday Michael says God's love is always right here and all we have to do is open to it. Can I manage a slight opening right now, a peek, a possibility? Yes? Is it working? There, don't I feel it? It seems impossible to feel it, but I think I do.*"

She stopped writing, put the pen down, and sat up straight in the chair. With slow, deep breaths she grounded her energy down into the earth, and opened her chakras to receive. After several more minutes continuing to breathe deeply, Maggie picked up the pen and wrote, "*Yes! God's love is here, all around me, holding me, ready to lift me up. Despite my anguish, I have managed to return to it. I'm so relieved. But then, I never left, did I?*"

Now Jesus stood right in front of her, bright and glowing in white robes and golden sunshine, his hand on her head. She let herself allow it and open more. He took her hand to lead her, and they stepped into somewhere different, changed.

Maggie's body shook. The shaking increased, growing until it was frighteningly strong. It shook her to her core, shaking loose anything in deep patterns that no longer worked. Finally it finished and she emerged into a soft, peaceful, graceful state of being. She picked up her journal again and wrote. "*I'm right here. This is who I am. This beautiful place of transformation is mine.*"

That day Maggie went to see Amy. It was Wednesday, May first.

❧

Late that night back at home, Maggie wrote, "*She's not talking. And she's not making eye contact, either. Everybody says she's not there, but David and I know she is, and that she hears and senses. She knows what is going on. It seems obvious to me that she reacts. I am very in tune with her, more than ever. I'm right there with her, feeling it all, knowing it all. This is way beyond being a healer. This is happening to me, too. It's my life, too.*

"My heart is beyond open. Mary, do you see this? It has no barriers. It has no boundaries. As if it encompasses all of existence. And yet it is very focused, too, focused on Amy and what's happening here. How is this possible? How am I doing this? Well, okay, all that matters is that I am.

"When I got there I could see that she was terrified. She hates not having control. And she hates being doped up on narcotics so she can't think clearly. It was very hard to see her like that again. I didn't know if we'd be able to connect while she is so heavily drugged for pain, but it was like I reached through a curtain and we were there together, as clear as could be.

"I managed to ease things for her, pulled out fear, cleared her field, and built up some energy she can use as she wants. And I talked with her about what is happening, from giving up on controlling things to what happens when we die. She relaxed quite a bit. Thank goodness. I'm so grateful I can help.

"I told her, 'Amy, you need to go to the light soon, and you can ask for help in the form of an angel.' Amy loves angels. She has angels all over her house. Immediately there was a big, brilliantly silver-white, gorgeous angel, and a few other slightly less bright ones with him. Then I remembered a child spirit I once helped release who had wanted a whole flock of angels. So I said to Amy, 'Or, you can have a whole flock of angels if you want.' I wouldn't have been surprised if she sat right up when I said that. Yes! She wanted the whole flock, though in the next moment she didn't really believe she could have them. Here they came, a whole flock of angels, maybe thirty of them, coming to escort her home. She was so joyful! That was great.

"David lit a large candle when he brought Amy home from the hospital, and he says it will go out when she dies. We both watch it. Sometimes it burns brightly and other times it flickers and appears about to go out. It definitely seems to correspond to how Amy is doing; strong when she clings to the world, weak when she lets go.

"Amy is very aware of David's presence and comforted by his love. She knows when he leaves the room and when he comes back. She absolutely trusts

him, and she knows he can take care of things, including himself, but she worries about him, too. I feel her react.

"With me, it is different. She doesn't have to worry about me. She knows I'll be okay. With me she can be purely selfish and honest. That is an amazing thing for one who has always taken care of everybody else. Especially now, when everything is so insistently real. It seems very important for her to have this kind of support right now.

"I'm there with her as she walks her path. I'm sitting with her under the bodhi tree, doing what becomes apparent while I have my own experience and do my own work. People expect me to be falling apart over this; they talk to me in funeral voices. They don't understand this is an extraordinary experience for me. I'm learning about how things work and about being me. I'm learning to be incredibly real, to see what I see and know what I know, hold true to it, and follow through on it. I'm learning to go with what becomes apparent, to trust that it is what is, even if everybody around me sees something different.

"When I started to leave earlier this evening, Amy became agitated, struggling to speak. I had told her months ago that there is a technique I can do to make it easier to leave her body. She remembered and she wanted me to do it now. As soon as I said I would do it, she relaxed again. This technique is a way to spread open the chakras, the energy centers, to allow release of the spirit. It is a sacred process and needs to be done very respectfully and carefully. As I began I found that a lot of pressure had built up. Her spirit was shoved up against the chakras, trying to move through, but the drugs made it very hard and confusing. She really needed this help.

"As I expanded her heart chakra she gasped and moaned and her eyes filled with tears. I stopped and held her heart and talked with her. 'Yes, Amy, there is grieving to do,' I said. 'And you are feeling anger, too. It is okay to feel any emotion you feel.' I stayed with her heart for a long time, holding it until it felt okay to move on. Then I completed the rest of the work.

"I sat with her for a while, then, and she tried in vain to talk again. 'Amy,' I said, 'you don't have to be able to speak out loud. You can send whatever you need to say from your mind to the other mind. It might not always work with everyone all the time, but try it.' Her face relaxed and I knew she was relieved. That was the last time I saw her struggle to physically speak.

"When I finally did leave tonight, I said I'd see her in the morning, one way or another. I didn't want to say anything that might tie her to her body in any way. David told me that Amy never liked the night, and he was sure she wouldn't

allow herself to die in the night. I insisted he call me at any time if there was any change or if there was anything I could help with.

"I feel like I am floating on a river, allowing the current to carry me. I'm just doing this. Nothing else matters. It is time out of time, reserved for doing this."

Maggie went back to Amy's house in the morning. It was Thursday, May second. Amy's parents were there again, and they gravitated to Maggie, wanting to know what she understood and what she knew from Amy. They asked Maggie questions, told her stories, and together they sat on the porch watching the day miraculously continue.

Amy's college-age son had come, too. He pretty much kept to himself. Maggie was very respectful of him, making sure he had easy access to his mother. Other than occasionally asking if he'd like to sit with Amy for a while, she did not try to take care of him, beyond being kind and gentle.

She did not take care of David, either. Maggie and David were very supportive of each other. They were a good team, flowing gracefully around each other. But they both focused on Amy, and they never forgot that. For them, for now, the center of the universe was upstairs in that bed.

Maggie easily tuned into Amy. She knew what was going on for her, her feelings, her fears, and her wants and needs. Maggie was able, then, to ease or explain or validate or clarify Amy's way.

She didn't just sit by the bed. Maggie was out there where the path was, walking with Amy. She didn't know how to do it; nobody had ever taught her about this and she had never read about it. She didn't know if anybody else ever did this, but it didn't matter if anyone did or not. All that mattered was that she be there, fully present, paying attention, open, and willing.

"Hey, Amy, where are all those angels?" Maggie asked, laughing. "Are you still passing them out to everybody else?" Amy loved having the angels, but she kept giving them away. Every time Maggie realized they were gone, she asked for more. A crowd of new ones appeared each time, and Amy lit up again.

On Thursday afternoon Maggie realized Amy had wandered off the path and was nowhere to be seen. Maggie had to go far out into other realms to look for her, and wasn't at all sure she could get to her. Fortunately this time she did, but what if she couldn't?

"Please don't do this, Amy," she begged. "I'm really afraid I won't be able to find you." But Amy kept disappearing, just heading off whenever Maggie wasn't paying attention. Out there Amy encountered lost souls and gathered them up, whatever their problems. She held onto them until Maggie came, and then of course Maggie helped these others get back on their own paths to move to the light. Together Amy and Maggie rescued many dozens of lost souls.

Every time Maggie brought Amy back to her own path she told her, "You need to be heading for the light yourself, Amy. That's how this works. I know you trust me to find you and bring you back, but you don't realize how little I know about this. I don't want to lose you out there."

It didn't matter. Before long Amy would take off again.

The Hospice nurse, Jeremy, visited in the afternoon, took care of Amy and then spoke with each person there. Maggie asked about Amy's wandering off. He nodded and said, "You're right, she gets lost. When you see that, explain to her, again, what is happening and how this works. Remind her." Jeremy saw Amy's last days as a vision quest, as a sacred time of learning and soul work. He said, "Everyone around Amy will learn from what Amy learns, including me. We are all here to share in the journey."

Jeremy explained what would happen over the next few days. Amy's breaths would become slower and farther apart. There already were occasional pauses, and these would become increasingly longer. Then, finally, she would simply not take another breath. Jeremy told them to breathe for her in the gaps. In the Native American tradition when someone goes on a vision quest the members of their community eat, drink, laugh, and take part in life for them. He told Amy's family and Maggie to do all that for Amy as she goes through this sacred journey.

Jeremy's advice was a great gift. Now, instead of holding her own breath along with Amy, Maggie could take the empty spaces as invitation to breathe deeply. And in that she learned about life going on.

That evening when David set about getting Amy ready for the night he said, "Go home, Maggie. You're exhausted. Get some sleep. Come back in the morning."

David went back to straightening the covers as Maggie gathered her things to leave, but something abruptly changed in the room and they both looked up.

"Look at the candle!" he said.

The candle's flame had flickered a lot since Jeremy showed Amy the light of the divine ahead and she began to move toward it. Now she reversed direction again, and both David and Maggie felt it. Amy was back, and the candle reflected it. The flame was strong and steady again. She was not ready to go yet.

They smiled at each other, and then Maggie said, "David, you have to promise me that you will tell me if I am ever in the way or intruding. Promise me."

"You are family, Maggie. It is not possible that you could intrude. Be here as much as you want. I want you here. You're good for her. You're good for all of us."

Maggie was so grateful for the acceptance that she could not respond more than to nod acknowledgment. Then just before she left she said, "Promise me another thing, David. That you will call me, any time, if anything changes or happens. I don't think I can leave if I don't know that you will."

"I promise," he said. He hugged her and then turned back to Amy.

At home that night Maggie wrote, "*Part of what this is for me is to learn about living love and putting it right out there. I watch David do that. He makes it so clear and simple. You do what needs doing, whatever it is, whatever it costs you. He never even hesitates. Whatever happens, he handles it. Always.*

"*Sometimes I wonder how I got into all this. If Amy and I had met when she was healthy, I would have liked her, I think, but I doubt I would have ever felt comfortable to get close. I would have felt awkward and unfinished compared to her. The cancer has exposed the heart of life for both of us. I have looked at her from a deeper part of me, and I see way beyond the pretty, gracious woman who lives an attractive life in a lovely house. I see real life in her. I see real life in this dying woman.*

"*I don't know what she sees in me, except that she feels calm with me around. She has from the beginning. And then I kept showing up, so she got used to me.*" Maggie smiled, thought about it, then wrote more. "*I don't know what this is with us, just that it feels absolutely right. It's one of those very clear things. To do it is right, and to turn away is not acceptable.*

"*Amy is such a southern woman. There is a great strength in her. There is a gracefulness and generosity that might seem to mean softness, but just underneath is formidable strength. I see that in other women I know now and I am in awe of it. I see in them how to be a real woman, to be able to be gracious and to love a man and be devoted, yet still be strong and proud and independent. Up north, women seem to have to emasculate and disempower men in order to maintain their own sense of self. But I don't see that here. The women I'm meeting here are able to let men be men. I see in these women that it is possible to love a man and still be a powerful, confident woman.*

"It's late, I need to sleep. Tomorrow I want to bring written words to songs. I sang to her a little bit today and she really liked it, but I couldn't think of words."

Early on Friday morning, May third, the candle still burned vigorously. Amy's parents and her son left. They had each said their good-byes. They knew David and Maggie would take good care of Amy, and they did not feel they needed or wanted to be present at the very end.

Maggie felt Amy panic about their leaving. "Feel their love," Maggie told her. "You're still connected to them. There are cords of connection between you and each of them. Feel the cords. There you go. Now let those cords stretch. It doesn't matter how far they stretch, they do not weaken. Yes, even after you're gone you will still have these connections. Forever."

The house was very quiet and peaceful after that. David and Maggie fell into a flow of care and mutual support, all done to the rhythmic sound of Amy's breathing. The minutes of each day strung out like beads on Amy's breath, and when her breath paused, they both listened to the silence, waiting.

"I'm not going to pressure you any more to stay on the path and go toward the light," Maggie told Amy after everyone left. "I talked with Lydia about it last night, and I want to honor your way of doing this, not try to get you to do it the way I think it should happen. I'll still help you when you want me to, and help with the lost ones. I'll help you get back when you are lost and you want to get back. Amy, I'll be here, and I'll hold the space for whatever you do."

"Of course," Maggie added, "that's all you have ever let me do!" She laughed and she felt Amy laugh, too. She also felt Amy's gratitude. Everything eased, from then on, into a beautiful, graceful procession, all exactly as it needed to be.

"That's when I got it," Maggie wrote in her journal when she took a break to sit on the stairs, *"how precious it is to be in this world. I understood what she is doing. Amy is in no hurry. She wants every minute she can have in the beauty of this life. I feel her paying attention to everything that happens, soaking it all in. She wants to experience every amazing wonder of life. Yes, there is awesome beauty in spirit, in soul, in God's light. But this, here, what we have here, is extraordinary. I'm seeing that, too, through her."*

Later when David started to leave the room, Maggie felt Amy panic and energetically reach for him. "Amy," she quickly said, "you will never lose David. Feel for the soul connection. That is forever. Forever." David stopped when he heard this, and Maggie felt them connect. "That's it. Feel how strong it is. That will be there forever."

Maggie felt Amy recognize this sacred, powerful connection she had with David. And then she felt Amy send the lesson right back to her, telling her to know and trust her own connection with Michael.

"You're teaching me now?" she mumbled. Tears welled up hard and fast. Maggie pushed past David to escape to the hall. Grabbing her notebook she wrote, *"Amy is doing this for me! She showing me and teaching me about life and passion. She's expanding my heart. She's doing dying this hard way in order to touch all of us. She's doing it for us."*

Now the tears flowed freely. *"She gives us so much love, and such abundant gifts. Now I sit here looking at my foolish resistance to trusting love and connection. This bond with Michael? How can I, knowing what I know today, waste one minute of this miracle of connection? No more than Amy can give up one minute of this precious day."*

❧

At about mid-afternoon on Friday David lay down next to Amy and fell asleep. Maggie sat in the armchair, watched the candle flicker continuously, and wrote, *"I don't think Amy is ever really asleep or awake any more. but she is very peaceful. Just a while ago she was confused again. I explained what's happening and she got back on track to the point where she is smiling now and looking happy. I know she sees God's light and feels it and she knows what is happening. Since this morning, whenever she gets clear about the light she brightens up and she just knows. The light is very compelling.*

"The wind is picking up this afternoon and it's getting cool. It's also darker with heavy clouds. It could rain. That's very good for the drought we've been in.

"I've been feeling strong energy movement around and within me. It makes me shake fairly often now. A lot is happening for me here under the bodhi tree. A lot is changing.

"Her dying is becoming more real. Her breaths are farther apart. This is what Jeremy said would happen. He was here a little while ago and said it is almost over. He said she will go when her work is done.

"She has been sending me messages. 'It's not just about honoring other people's paths and pace and choices, honor your own.' And, 'Time is irrelevant, what matters is what is.' That one came because I wanted to know if I should go home this afternoon for a break and then come back. Damn, tears again. I'm afraid if I go home it will be over. Now I'm shaking again.

"Every time she hesitates to breathe, I clench up. Next time I need to remember to breathe for her, like Jeremy said. There, it just happened and I breathed in the space. Now, did it again. And again.

"Yes, you will stop breathing, Amy, one of these breaths, and we will go on breathing. Now Dooley, lying on the floor at the foot of the bed, is audibly breathing, too. We will all take over the breathing. You can leave it to us.

"We will take over the living, too, the being in this physical world of sensory experience. Yes, Amy, the candle is going to go out. You are going to die."

Later Friday night, at 10:30 p.m., back at her own apartment, Maggie wrote down another message from Amy. "*You know that time is an illusion. What you don't know is how truly confusing it is.*"

"Are you going to explain that?" Maggie asked.

"It's hard to see it from where you are, inside of it... So much of what you struggle with is because of this notion of time."

"Linear time?"

"Yes," said Amy.

"So, I need to not let linear time confuse my perception of what is."

"Exactly."

The next morning, Saturday, May fourth, still at home at 7:00 a.m., Maggie again wrote a message from Amy. "*Believe in what comes to you, like you believe in this. You know what's true. You know what's real. Live your life from these truths.*"

"I know I keep diverting myself," responded Maggie, "denying, questioning, doubting. One reason is because I'm afraid people will think I'm crazy."

"What's more important? Truth or someone's quick judgment?" asked Amy.

"Truth, of course."

"Well, there."

"When I allow it, I already know that all these things you are saying are true," said Maggie.

"Yes, you do. I know you do. That's why I'm saying them."

"So that I admit they are true?"

"So you honor your knowing."

"I saw us change places yesterday, Amy. I used to be the wise one, knowing about going to the light and how to help you. Then you got about three-quarters of the way and you became the wise one. You started telling me things."

They both laughed.

"Now you sound like the guides who talk to me like this," said Maggie, "even though you haven't yet left your body, made the transition, and finished up. Yesterday it seemed important that you promise me that when you move so far that you're out of my reach you will do all those finishing up things, not go wandering around helping people instead and get lost. Today you know what to do. You don't need me for that any more."

Maggie just breathed for a while, then she put her hand on her heart and said, "Thank you, Amy, for letting me come along on this journey with you, for letting it be my journey, too. What a blessing you are in my life!"

Picking up her pen, Maggie wrote, "*I told David last night that nothing will ever be the same. Amy, you have gently, but firmly, drawn my attention to so much. You have placed things in front of me that got me to open my eyes, to free them from whatever veil covered them. You have touched my heart and gently charmed it open. You have shown me that every moment of this physical sojourn is precious and beautiful. What a miracle there is in every sight and sound, in senses, in consciousness, in being alive in this form. To be able to listen to the birds that woke me this morning. To write these words. To walk across the room with feet on carpet and fresh, cool, early morning air on my face. To feel with my skin and nerves, and know the richness, the sensuousness of body, to experience all the senses, what miracles! To see Georgia O'Keefe's 'Iris' poster on the wall, feel the weave of the cotton blanket on the bed, hear a dove call nearby and traffic in the distance, to know that people are going places, living their lives, noticing what they are noticing, taking their turn in this world. How extraordinarily full and wondrous life is!*

"This is another day of rain, bringing life to the dry land. A goodbye gift."

Maggie listened to the rain patter on the roof, then she wrote one more line, and she knew it was true. *"Today is the day."*

Before leaving for Amy's house, Maggie sent an email to the members of the prayer chain at church, with a copy to Michael.

Dear friends,

Amy is still with us. She is peaceful. She subtly reacts to things. She seems to be absorbing as much as she can before she goes. It can't be much longer. David is doing this very consciously. It's beautiful. We are all learning so much about life.

Please pray for David, for Amy's parents, her son, and her sister, who has not been able to be here.

I am so in awe of everything about this journey. There is so much love, and so much conscious connection. This is truly about life, in a very potent, rich way.

Love, Maggie

At 9:30 a.m. at Amy's house, Maggie sat in the bedroom armchair and wrote, *"Amy is handing over the living of life to us. I feel she has handed me a package full of gifts for living life. By being here to share in her death, in her life, in her journey, each of us who knows and loves her has already, without consciously knowing it, pledged to learn, and to let it change us."*

Another message came from Amy, "Life is about love."

"Everybody says that," said Maggie.

"Because it is true," answered Amy.

"I am loving this rain, Amy, and the cool breeze through the open windows, the soft piano music on the stereo. It is going to happen, isn't it."

"You know it is."

"Amy, how can you leave this?"

"I don't know."

"Is this like dying was for Jesus? Is it the hardest thing possible?"

"From here, within life, it seems like it," said Amy. "There is so much we don't know from here. But it could be that."

Maggie wrote, "*You so want every bit of this world you can get. I can feel that. A blue jay calls now, and I know you are listening. The music on the cd ended and the jay cries, the rain sounds on the house and leaves, candles burn around the room and shadows dance. You are keenly aware of it all.*

"*Your candle went out this morning before I got here. David lit another one by the bed, but we both know this is the day.*"

Maggie put down the pen and listened to Amy's breaths. Breathe in the spaces, she reminded herself. The spaces were longer now. She was already used to the slower rhythm. It felt good to breathe within the pauses. Maggie listened and breathed.

She went to the bedside and picked up Amy's hand. "Your hands are cold now. All along they have been so hot. I'm sure David knows this, but neither one of us has mentioned it. He is keeping himself busy today, distracted." Maggie sat for a while, holding Amy's hand and singing softly. Every time she came to the end of the song she felt Amy want more, so she sang it again.

❧

David came into the room and Maggie moved back to the armchair so he could sit by the side of the bed. She was hardly willing to leave the room now, at most just out in the hall to sit on the stairs where she could still follow the breathing.

"*That package Amy handed me,*" Maggie wrote in her journal, "*is handed to me as she goes, to be opened later, over time. It has many things in it, gifts, lessons, messages, reminders.*

"*I'm shaking again. I shook earlier this morning, too.*"

Maggie listened to the breaths for a while, breathing two of her own for each of Amy's.

"*You're asking an awful lot of us, Amy, asking us to really live life.*"

She wrote Amy's answer. "*It's only what you've already asked yourself to do, Maggie. It's only what you are there for.*"

"There? You said 'there.' Earlier you called this 'here.' You don't feel here any more, do you?"

"Maggie, did you hear what I said?"

"I don't know."

"Go back and read what you wrote down."

"Really living life is what I'm here for. Okay. I hear it. Michael says this, too, lots of different ways."

"Talking to himself, remember?"

"Amy, do you need me to do the chakra spread again now? Okay."

Later, at midday on Saturday, Maggie sat on the stairs to write while visitors spoke to Amy. *"Several friends and neighbors have stopped by today. They sit at her bedside and talk about their kitchens and yards like they are just visiting on a regular day, like we are back two months ago with plenty of time, like there will be next week, or even tomorrow. I want to take hold of them and shake them and say, 'This is it! This is the end! There won't be another time.' I also want to say, 'Don't talk to her about ordinary things, don't pull her back.' But today Amy isn't coming back.*

"Old friends drove from four hours away and stood in the doorway of the bedroom asking David to tell them the whole story of her illness. I felt Amy react to what he was saying, remembering how it was, becoming distraught, so I went to her instead of being sociable. I wanted to tell them to go out in the hall, but who am I here? So I talked to Amy instead, softly but out loud, to distract her. I told her they were just telling the story, and it didn't matter what the words were or what the story was, what they were doing was sharing the love. She relaxed. I kept talking, told her to just hear David's voice, not the words. She smiled that subtle smile around her eyes. I talked through the rough parts of David's telling, and then sat silent when he answered more pleasant questions. Amy was fine then.

"When they all went downstairs I sang to her and then talked about the light ahead. I stood with her, so close to God, in the dazzling light of the divine. It was incredibly bright and beautiful. I kept saying how beautiful it was and how good it felt, and she kept smiling. Then we just stood there, together, basking in it, feeling it, knowing it. To be there was not only to see the beauty and be in it, but to be a part of it, with a fullness of being we can only barely imagine from here. It is so much more than we can imagine.

"And yet, standing there, I also knew how much we yearn, from within that beauty, to be back here in physical, material experience and expression. I watch Amy still eagerly take in every bit of sensory experience and connection and recognition and knowing. She wants every bit of it she can get. She is hungry for it. We each want the precious, incredible, sacred experience of being in this life, even as we could instead be there in the awesome beauty of divine light. What a stunning thing to realize."

❧

At 1:00 p.m. on Saturday Maggie spread Amy's chakras open again, and as she worked she knew this was the last time. Tears ran down her cheeks and she let them fall. Amy was barely there. Then David brought out a whole carton of old photos and started going through them, telling Maggie the story behind each one.

The mountain breeze blew in open windows, carrying the smell of rain and wet leaves. Candle light danced on the ceiling and walls. David's voice drew vignettes of friends and family and homes and trips and pets and days. And Amy's breathing slowed more.

"The spaces are getting longer," Maggie interrupted. He just nodded and went determinedly back to the pictures. It was almost 2:00. Maggie tried to listen to him and answer his questions and all the time be with Amy's breathing. It was only a few minutes later when David suddenly jumped up and rushed over to the bed. Maggie was confused at first, then she realized. No more breaths. Later David talked about hearing the last breath, but for Maggie it was the emptiness. She heard the emptiness.

The Impossible

Crows come around to remind me
to look for the magic.
They call, they yell,
they insist that I open my vision and see
more possibility, more promise,
more potential, more mystery.
Crows enliven this morning;
they make me smile and laugh and wonder.
Crows are messengers;
they remind me all is mystical
and sacred
and more than it seems.
They point out grace and holiness and miracle.

Mockingbirds ask,
are you celebrating this morning?
Are you singing now?
Are you discovering fresh expression,
a new voice, fertile meaning, an imaginative way?
Are you paying attention? Are you getting
how magnificent this moment is?

Yesterday
I watched a crow ravage a mockingbird nest.
I did not see the details.
Not like last year, when I saw the crow
take the baby bird
up on the rain gutter
and tear it apart.

God!
Hey!
What am I supposed to do with this?

Let it be, comes the answer.
Make room for impossibility,
stretch to encompass it all.
Horror and mystery
death and laughter
destruction and magic
loss and miracle.

Today the mockingbirds build a new nest
in a different tree, with renewed determination.
Accepting the impossible,
life with crows
and magic.
Can I?

Chapter Twenty-one: The Impossible

Maggie drove up the Blue Ridge Parkway with Jackie into the mountains east of Asheville. They hiked through forests of wild rhododendrons to the top of Craggy Dome and looked out at Craggy Peak and Mount Mitchell and the Black Mountains, some of the highest peaks of the region. The sky was deep blue, the sun was warm, the breeze was cool, the earth spread into every distance. The only sounds were birds and breeze and breath.

Every breath brought another, rhythmically, like heart beat, with no gaps, no emptiness, there in the beauty of the mountains and the day, there in her body, there in her aliveness. Breath, giver and sustainer of life, precious breath. Breathe in, breathe out, breathe in, breathe out. Breathe in blue sky, breathe out peace. Breathe in mountain beauty, breathe out faith. Breath in sunshine, breathe out willingness. Breathe in life, breathe out gratitude. Breathe in God, breathe out self.

"Would you like to speak at the memorial service?" asked Michael. "When David and I were talking about it earlier today, your name came up. I wanted to offer it to you if you want to do it."

Maggie looked in his eyes and kept looking in his eyes, her heart full, her mind a swirl of the past months with Amy. She tried to figure out what to answer, then realized she needed to feel for the answer, not figure it out. She never took her eyes off his, and he kept talking, giving her time.

He came back around to it. "What do you think? Would you want to do it?"

Maggie nodded. She felt so over-full. Any release of words would let loose a flood of emotion and need and tears and grief. Michael spoke some more, he touched her arm, and then he was gone, and she stood in this new place, wondering what it would be.

She spoke softly, close in to the microphone as Michael had told her to do. "Amy was a teacher, in the classroom and out, and she still is. I've got her homework assignment for all of us, right here." Maggie heard her own voice come from the speakers around the sanctuary, clear and rich and full of feeling. It was a relief to be able to focus on the meaning and let the words project themselves.

"It was my profound honor to walk with Amy on her soul's path these last eight months. It was a long, hard path. More and more people thought she should let go, especially toward the end, when her body quit cooperating. But Amy stayed on, through nausea and pain and endless procedures and adaptations and losses, she stayed as long as she possibly could.

"On the next to last day I realized she did that for us, so that we would learn all we are learning from her living and her dying. What a gift to us!

"On the last day I realized she did that for herself, too, so that she could experience every possible minute of life. And then I realized what that means.

"I walked with Amy nearly all the way to God, and we stood in the radiance of the incredible beauty of what we are when in the full oneness of being. It is unimaginably beautiful, and it is absolute completion. I knew that she recognized home, and that she knew what it would be to be there. And yet she still held onto life.

"Because life in this world, on this physical plane, with sensory perception and relationship and the full range of emotion and response and expectation, life is so remarkable, so extraordinary, so stimulating, so satisfying, so precious, that as souls we choose to leave perfect beauty and oneness to come here and do this. We want it that much.

"Here was Amy, even that last morning, even that last hour, when she was right there at the passage through, when she was barely connected to her body, yet she was soaking up every minute she could get back here, cherishing every experience and sensation, gathering them like an armload of flowers or seashells or kittens or children. Precious minutes, not to be missed.

"Birds singing in the trees outside the open windows. Fresh, moist, richness of mountain-weather air blowing through. Spontaneous purring of the cats snuggled close and Dooley's constant vigil on the floor next to the bed. David's voice in the background telling Amy-and-David stories—she loved that most. Candlelight flickering on the ceiling and walls. Gentle music filling the room, soothing and reassuring. She stayed. She wanted all she could get.

"So what's our homework? To live life! Live this minute. Hear the bird, sing the song, hold a hand, open to that soul connection with a loved one, laugh, cry, reach out. Hold precious this minute. We came so far to have it. Cherish this minute.

"And in that willingness, in that bold opening, go for it! Live life! Do it! Be it! Take what matters as far as it can go. Never mind complications or busyness or fears. Experience the ecstasy of being alive in this minute. This is it. This is what we've come for. This minute.

"We're all wondering how can we go on with regular life after Amy has touched us so profoundly in her dying. Let's don't. Let's let Amy, teacher and soul friend, change that. Live this one minute, then sometime later, when you think of it, live another minute, and another, and another. If we will open to it, Amy will remind us. A slight whisper, a brushing touch, a bird's call, a turn in the music, reminding us to hold precious this minute.

"Thank you, Amy."

"That was beautiful, Maggie, absolutely beautiful," said Michael as he helped her step down from the pulpit. He had to have felt her shaking. She was shaking more now than she had been ahead of time. He gathered her into a hug.

"Thank you," she said, grateful for his presence and his embrace. Back in her seat she wondered what had made her think she could do this. Speak in the midst of all these waves of emotion, and all these people, and all the memories? A hundred people had gathered, some from far away, many she had never met before.

Maggie took a deep breath. She knew it had been beautiful. She had felt it, too. The microphone allowed the words to resonate with the feelings behind them. People told her afterward that it was amazing. Everything was amazing lately.

Mornings had been hard. Mornings without Amy in them. Birds sang and Amy didn't hear them. Misty, rich, moist mountain air poured in windows and Amy didn't feel it on her skin or draw it into her lungs. Amy's breaths no longer paced the day. Her smile no longer shaped it. Her being no longer deepened it.

For eight months Maggie had gone to Amy whenever she felt like it. In that going Maggie could rediscover that she was valuable and helpful just by being there, just by being herself. Talking, doing needlework, telling a story, singing a song, reading, writing, simply being in the room, her presence calmed Amy. What a gift it was to feel so unconditionally useful and appreciated.

All I had to do was be me and be there, thought Maggie. And now I look around the sanctuary at all these people gathered here to celebrate Amy's life, and the same is true. Be me and be here. That's all it took to write my remembrance and then read it this afternoon. Be me, be here. Maggie looked at Michael and he was watching her. He smiled. That's all I need with Michael, too, she realized, be me and be here. Let go of anything else.

She looked at David. He had said, "Well, you can go back to your life now." Go back? She didn't even know what that meant. There was no going back, only forward, into change, into new discoveries.

Michael led the singing of one of Amy's favorite songs, and when they got to the line, "I love you," Maggie glanced at Michael. He was already looking at her, and they sang "I love you" to each other. Don't look for answers, she reminded herself, just be me and be here, and let the rest happen.

Maggie went to Amy's house after the memorial service. It was the first time she had been back. The house was full of people and voices and activity. All the relatives and neighbors were there, but hardly anyone she knew from church. Lots of food, lots of wine, lots of stories. They said it was Amy who made them into a real neighborhood. Now they took Maggie into their extended family, insisting that she come often and join in. She wondered if she would. She wasn't sure of anything right now.

Dooley wandered in and out of the rooms, the porch, and the yard, his big paws heavy and slow. Maggie found herself following him, appreciating his gentle presence. These spaces and rooms had become so familiar to her, and yet now, with all the people here moving through them, filling them with talk and expectations and plans and the rest of life, Maggie felt confused. She went upstairs, finally, alone. She looked in the bedroom, saw the closed window, the still candle, the empty armchair, the empty bed, the empty silence. She sank into the chair and wept.

It was a tremendous release. So much had happened, so much had built up in her, so much had affected her. With the tears she let go of a deep tightness in her chest, she let go of Amy and David and death, she let go of expectation and tomorrow and questioning, she let go of Michael and whatever is to come. All that was left was a blanket of poignancy and the knowledge that she was changed. She faced out into the future, not knowing anything about it.

Maggie was barely through the front door at home when her daughter Rachel called. "Dad just told me you're writing a book about Jesus! Good grief, Mom, Jesus? Jewish people don't write about Jesus. We don't even think about Jesus. What's going on with you? First you get obsessed with this crazy 'energy' hocus pocus, and then more and more you turn your back on everything that ever meant anything to you, your religion, family, friends, home, all your beliefs and commitments, Dad, me! I'm really worried about you. I'm seriously considering doing some sort of intervention."

Maggie sighed deeply, then spoke. "I'm fine, Rachel. I'm perfectly sane. I'm finding my own answers to things. That's healthy."

"Your answers? Oh, that's fine; that's really nice! Does it ever occur to you to consider what havoc you are causing for other people? Do you ever think about anybody but yourself any more?"

Tears welled in Maggie's eyes, and she softly said, "Of course I think about other people." Then she added, "I'm not writing about Jesus, I'm writing about Mary Magdalene."

"That's Christian!" Rachel declared. "My whole life you went to Shabbat services every week, you were one of the regulars at Torah study every Saturday, you organized the community seder every year, you taught religious school, you were even president of the Sisterhood, and now, all of a sudden, unexpectedly, unexplainably, unbelievably, you're going to a Christian church, writing a Christian book, and turning into a Christian? How's that possible, Mom? Were you lying before? All the time I was growing up, being Jewish, you and Dad, being a family, being my mother, was it all lies?"

Maggie sighed again and kept her voice low and steady. "I'm still your mother, Rachel. I will always love you. And I will always be me. People learn and grow. It's what we do. I want to live life, see what's possible, and find out what more I can be."

"Mom, look in the mirror. You're not young any more. Your hair is turning gray. Get real. You should be settling down, moving into a condo, and playing Mah Jong at the Jewish Community Center."

"Oh, no, don't put me in a wheel chair yet. I've got plenty of living left to do."

"You're so selfish now, Mom. You never used to be this way. You're not even thinking of any of the rest of us or what you're doing to us!"

"What am I doing to you, Rachel? Tell me."

"Don't try to deflect this onto me. Just think about what I said. I have to go. Think about it!"

Maggie held the useless phone in her lap for a long time before she called Lydia.

"What should I do?" she asked her friend.

"I'm really sorry you told me this, Maggie. I thought my daughter Tina was going to grow out of this same behavior any minute now, but she's only twenty-two and Rachel is how old? Twenty-six, twenty-seven?"

"She'll be twenty-seven in two weeks."

"Two weeks? Oh, yes, her birthday is right after mine. Another bull-headed Taurus. We've got you surrounded. I wonder what that's about."

"Advice, Lydia, I need advice."

"Another reason I'm sorry you told me about this is that I recognize myself in this. I can see, as long as it's you doing it, not me, that you're not really listening to her. You're answering instead of listening. Of course this is no surprise, because lately you've needed to be in answer-seeking mode in order to look for your own answers. But Rachel doesn't want to hear about you. She's a child wanting her mama to look at her boo-boo, say 'uh oh,' and kiss it."

"Are you kidding? She'd eat me alive if I came across that way."

"I'm not saying this is on the surface. It's deep in. You've got to focus on her, Maggie, listen to her, make her feel heard. Don't even think about explaining or enlightening her. It's not the right time."

"I did ask her to tell me what's wrong. She got mad."

"Yeah, you wanted her to clue you in to what you need to explain away, right? So you could talk her out of it. That's not listening."

"Okay, I see that," said Maggie. "I can give this a try."

"I'm not saying it's going to work, mind you. Ultimately you are going to disappoint her, Maggie. It's inevitable. You'll never again be that attentive, faithful, ever-present, patient, accommodating, self-sacrificing mother she knew as a child."

"I can't do what she wants me to do."

"Right. So the question is, does she have to be resentful, complaining, whining, bitchy, and manipulative, and hang up on you every phone call? Or can she sigh, suck it up, and grow up?"

"And we're going to get to this by my listening to her? No explaining?"

"Uh oh, did I say that?" exclaimed Lydia. "Hey, what do I know? I'm hardly a model for successfully mothering an adult daughter."

"I'm going to try listening. I'll let you know how it goes."

"Or, maybe we should trade daughters. They always seem to do better with someone outside the family."

"I'm very fond of your Tina, but let's save that for a back-up plan," Maggie said, relieved to be laughing. Idly fingering through the stack of mail she'd picked up on the way in, she suddenly exclaimed, "Oh my God!"

"What?" demanded Lydia.

"It's one of my self-addressed return envelopes. It's from that first agent I sent sample pages to, Mary's first choice. He's responding, Lydia. I'm shaking."

"Well, open it!"

For one very brief moment Maggie considered looking for scissors or a sharp knife to neatly preserve the envelope, but she ripped it open instead.

"What's it say?" insisted Lydia.

"Hang on. I'm getting it out."

"This suspense is killing me."

"He wants me to send the complete manuscript! He wants to read the whole thing. Lydia, this is a top agent. If he wants to see it that means somebody will want to represent it and it will be published, and then it is going to sell. Mary's book is on its way! I'm stunned. I guess I didn't let myself think it would really happen."

"It's real, Maggie. And you will do just fine. I'll hang up now and let you tell Mary."

"I suspect she already knows."

"Is she still watching you and Michael?"

"Yes."

"Does she still want you to get together?"

"Probably. I don't know, Lydia. I can't consider that. I just have to do what feels right, one step at a time."

Early the next morning Maggie went to FedEx to overnight a copy of the manuscript. And that afternoon in the mail she found another agent's request for a full copy to read.

"Well, Mary, here we go," she said. "It's happening. I've barely finished with Amy and this starts right up. Life keeps coming."

After speaking with Michael at the end of the next Sunday's service, Maggie couldn't stop thinking about him again. Every time he looks at me, every time we talk, it is so good! Aren't we supposed to be together?

"You are together," answered Nu.

"No, we're not," objected Maggie. "Without the physical world part, it's not whole. We are physical beings, too, living in material existence. It has to be both spiritual and worldly."

"This is more than that. Like communion, it's transcendent."

"Transcendent? Nu, living is about bringing spirit into the whole of life, into the whole of being in this world. That includes making a happening connection, being together, doing life together, being partners. That includes all of it, all the way to touch and caress and being sexual. To do without worldly experience is as unbalanced as doing without spiritual experience. It's not okay to do without either part of it."

"So what are you saying, Maggie? What about Michael?"

"I love Michael. I will always love Michael. I want Michael in my life."

"But?"

"I should have a whole relationship. I shouldn't compromise on something so important. How can I can settle for this?"

Nu waited, then Maggie moaned, "But how can I turn away?"

She drove up into the mountains again, to that same river she had walked along last Christmas Day, where she had cried in the frigid cold. This time the riverbanks bloomed lush with deep pink and maroon wild rhododendron blossoms. The water sparkled and flashed under a high sun as it ran playfully, eagerly splashing and singing over, around, and between rocks, abundant from the recent rains. Maggie sat on a large boulder at the edge of the river and watched the water and sunlight dance together.

Were answers impossible? She let the current carry away questions and thought and effort. Warm sun on her skin, cool stone under her, splash and spray, delightful colors, pink and green and blue, with refracted rainbows and brilliant flashes from the water's play; damp, fresh air, loaded with smells of forest and flower and the growth and decay and fertility at water's edge; bird song, moist breeze, this place was alive with life. Maggie sat for a long time. No journaling, no inner or other level conversation, no searching, just being part of this extended, precious moment.

❧

"So," Lydia asked later, "this transcendent thing your guide is talking about, is it sort of a spiritual orgasm?"

Maggie laughed. "I don't know, Lydia. It's all pretty esoteric, isn't it?"

"Is your guide telling you to give up on sex? Is the church right? Is giving up sex really an integral part of living a spiritual life?"

"Maybe Nu is saying that being really open to this deep spiritual intimacy somehow, kind of...is sex? Sex at all levels at once, in a deep...sort of esoteric...way?" Maggie groaned.

"Personally," replied Lydia, "I want the old-fashioned, sweaty sheets, fuck me way."

"Oh, Lydia! Why'd you have to say that? Okay, yes, me too." They both laughed. "So, are we spiritually doomed?"

"Welcome to the world, Maggie."

"You've seen this all along as my being in love with a priest, as impossible."

"That's how I started out, but eventually I got it that he's not a priest, and that Protestant ministers don't do the celibacy thing. He's on his own with this, so he can change his mind."

"Because he's not Catholic? His vows, his commitment to God, only count if he is Catholic? How Catholic of you!" declared Maggie.

"Oh, I see what you mean. The old nuns' programming still works, huh?" Lydia laughed. "I should call up Sister Ana and tell her. She'll be thrilled. But, hey, listen to you defend his vows. Maybe you've got some Catholic in you, too."

"If I allow him to go against his vows it could destroy both of us. That's what it comes down to, you know," said Maggie. "After all the emotional and romantic twists and turns, there's no way around that."

"So he is a priest after all?"

"Might as well be," Maggie sighed. "This is the pits, Lydia, to find this deep love and yet not be able to have it."

"Maggie, if you take away the soul part of this, with its deep connection and amazing happenings, what have you got?"

"How can you take away the soul part?"

"Just do it for a minute. What's left?"

"Friends, I guess."

"Not even great friends, right, Maggie? Pretty cautious friends."

"Because he's so scared of getting off track."

"And you're afraid of feeling penned in."

"Right."

"So, here you are, these two hesitant, tentative friends, carrying around this massive, compelling soul connection, and not knowing what the hell to do with it."

"Crazy, huh?"

"You said it, not me."

Maggie spoke with her sister about it and Caroline said, "I'm sorry to say this, because I know you do love him, but you deserve better than this, Maggie. You deserve somebody who is so in love with you that he can't say no, who knows you are the one for him and he can't go on without you. Like you said, you should have it all, the spiritual and the being together in every other way. You are all that yourself, and you offer all that. You should get it all in return."

"So you think I should give this up? Walk away from it?"

"I haven't said this before because you seemed so determined, but I've been worried about you all along. Isn't this really a variation on what you've done before? Settling for less than you deserve?"

"Oh, please don't say that, Caroline. It's better, isn't it?"

"It is progress in that I think he really does care for you. But you haven't gotten to a whole, healthy relationship yet, have you? Isn't that what you're admitting now?"

"You're right. I'm always trying to explain away what's missing and make it seem okay. I compromise too much."

"I think it is very good that you are finally seeing this."

"It doesn't feel good."

"Of course it doesn't. But think what this means," said Caroline. "You can find someone else now, someone who will really love you, who will be much better for you than Michael is. Now you can find the real thing. Go for that, Maggie."

❧

"Do you believe in past lives?" Maggie asked as Jackie poured coffee.

"Oh, I don't know about all that. Does it matter? This right here is what we have to deal with, either way, so deal with it."

"Occasionally I run into past lives in my work with clients, but I don't know if it is there because it's real or because the client believes it's real. Do you think this urge I have to be with Michael could be left over from some past life relationship?"

"I thought Mary explained that it's because of the patterns."

"You believe that?"

"I don't know, Maggie. It doesn't matter what I believe. What do you believe?"

"I just wish everything would be clear, one way or the other."

"And it's not."

"It's all paradox and more paradox with him and me," said Maggie, letting out a big sigh.

"Shouldn't it at least be clear that you want to be with him and he wants to be with you?"

"Jackie, is he really so spiritual that this is enough for him?"

"What do you think?"

"I don't think it works that way. And I don't think it is working for him, or he wouldn't look at me the way he does."

"So, what's really going on with him?"

Maggie thought for a minute, then said, "I think the spiritual issues are real. But I also think you were right when I first told you about him. You said he's afraid to let his feelings loose, and that's why he won't open to a relationship. I think that's a significant part of this."

"And then there's your fear, too."

"We do take turns." Maggie wasn't sure whether to laugh or moan.

"The two of you are so cute!" exclaimed Jackie.

"Hey, I'm working hard to look at what's wrong, and trying to admit this is not viable. Don't tell me how cute it is. That puts me right back into it."

"It doesn't take much to do that, does it?"

"Jackie, don't I need to face the reality that this isn't going anywhere? Don't I have to turn away from it?"

"How can you do that, Maggie?"

"What if I have to? What if I'm being stupid about it, loving a man who is unavailable? What would you be saying if he were married? It's like that, isn't it? Isn't he married to God?"

"I don't think being committed to God means take yourself out of life," said Jackie. "If anything, it means be more in life, be all you can be."

Maggie stared at her, silenced. Then she said softly, "That's the kind of thing Michael would say."

"Talk to him, Maggie," said Jackie. "You're still trying to figure out what he thinks and wants. Stop guessing. Ask him."

Maggie nodded.

Chapter Twenty-two: Life with Crows and Magic

She looked at Michael, unsure how to start, and her eyes filled. He took her hand and waited. They had come out behind the church to benches under the trees, with nobody around but birds and sky and earth. Even Mary Magdalene was giving them space, watching from the other levels.

"Come sit on your boundary line with me, Michael. We need to talk there," she said.

He nodded, let go of her hand, and shifted in his seat.

"I'm going to be really honest about this," she said, "and I hope you will be, too." She paused and he watched her, waiting for her to go on. "Our friendship is very important to me," she said. "I don't want to mess it up. I hope this won't mess it up." He nodded again.

"Here's the thing," she said, and then she stopped and looked at him, not knowing what to say. He waited with that quizzical expression he often got when he gave her time to come up with the words.

"I want more," she said, diving in, watching his eyes. He didn't hide, he didn't run away, he stayed right there. She took a deep breath and went on. "Life is about living all of it. It's not just about becoming spiritual or getting closer to God. It's about being fully alive, and that means bringing ourselves into full being, that means connecting on all the levels, and that means relationship.

"I want to do that with you, Michael. I want to spend time together. I want to know your idiosyncrasies, your preferences, your fears, your joys. I want to watch your eyes light up and I want to be there when they fill with tears. I want to say good night to everybody else and still be there with you. I want you to sing to me, and try out your ideas on me. I want to plant flowers together and sit on top of a mountain together and make love together. I want it all, Michael. I want life with you."

She watched him, very aware of her breathing, relieved that she'd finally said it all. She still did not know where he would go with it. She wasn't afraid—no, that was not true, she was terrified, but she wasn't admitting it.

"You are a remarkable woman, Maggie Blume," he said. "I don't know anyone who is as honest and willing to put it all right out there as you are. I'm in awe. I feel so blessed to have you in my life." He smiled at her, then said, "Ever since you first talked to me about this I have given it a lot of thought, as you can imagine, and a lot of prayer. There's so much to consider here." He stopped and looked at her. "How honest do you really want to be?"

"Go ahead, Michael, say whatever you have to say. Let's let this be what it is."

He nodded, then said, "I talk about God bringing us surprises, and you sure have surprised me. Just when I thought everything in my life was settled into place and comfortable, here you came, challenging my understanding and expectations. I thought maybe God was testing me to see if I could hold my spiritual ground. When I did, I thought that would finish it, the test over, and you would head off in somebody else's direction. You didn't. You're still right here."

He paused for a breath, then continued. "I went out to visit my son Randy in L.A. last week. I stayed with him and his wife Evie, and the two kids. Great kids! I had a blast with the kids. But I saw something in that house. Something that really bothered me. There's so much emphasis on doing things 'right,' how things look, and what other people might think. It scared me. And the worst part was that I recognized it. Emily and I taught him that." Michael paused, holding Maggie's gaze.

"We do the best we can," she said.

He nodded, "I know. I'm not judging my past, just seeing it with a little more perspective. We looked good, Emily and the kids and I. We presented well, and it was a good life, but..."

He sat for a minute, staring down at his hands through full eyes. Maggie waited for him to go on, holding the space for him, caring so much. "But there was an emptiness," he finally said. "I see that now. It was hollow." He paused again, then added, "I didn't even know."

Maggie nodded. On the other levels she put her hand on his heart and held it there. He looked up and smiled.

"It's very different with you, with us," Michael continued. "Somehow we start in the heart of who we are. We are more there than I have ever known."

"Yes," she said silently, then out loud, "Yes."

"Did God bring you into my life to change everything? To get me to let go of the path I thought I was on and take me on a different path? Maybe trusting change is exactly the point. To deny what might come alive in my life and in me feels wrong.

"Or, am I being shown how precious it is to be fully in this world, only then to still have to choose between experiencing this or doing God's work? What if this is like Jesus' ultimate test of faith, Maggie? What if it is a test to see if I will really give over everything I am to choose this work?

He paused, looking into her eyes, then asked, "Are you sure you want to be involved in all this?"

"Do I have a choice?" she exclaimed. "I think you are built into who I am." Maggie hesitated, then asked, "Michael, if you did leave your vows and take a new path, how would you keep from doubting your choice at every difficulty or disappointment or confusion?"

"It would have to be a profoundly sound decision and incredibly strong commitment. It would have to be a choice made with all I am."

She nodded. "That's the only way to do this." Silently Maggie wondered, would that be enough?

"Pray with me," Michael said, reaching for her hands and bowing his head. "Heavenly Father, thank you for so many blessings! We are so blessed! Thank you for this wonderful woman, and this day, and this love. We are in your hands. May we have the faith and the courage to be what you have made us to be. Join with us in our holding hands, be with us, take our hands and lead us. Show us where to go. May we be open to your guidance, to your love, and to your wisdom."

Maggie added, "Thank you, God, for all we are and all we can be and whatever will be. I am profoundly grateful to be right here in this day, in this moment. May I know and trust and follow the right path, wherever it goes, wherever it takes me. And can I please—" Maggie stopped and laughed. "I want to trust and accept whatever comes, but I can't help but ask, can I please love this man, one way or another? Whatever way this works out, whatever relationship it becomes, friend, lover, brother, together or separate, can I please have him in my life and love him?"

Michael smiled and said, "Amen!" He squeezed her hands and drew her up into a hug. "How about dinner Friday?" he asked. "That will give us both some time to think, and then we need to keep talking."

❧

"That's all?" Jackie exclaimed later. "Dinner? We'll talk? You told the man you love him, that you want to make your life with him, that you want to grow old with him, and that's all he gave back?"

"For now," Maggie replied, warily eyeing Jackie. "Did you expect he'd leap out of his chair and grab me? Or burst into a love song?"

Jackie blushed and ducked her head with a sheepish smile. "I didn't know that's what I expected, but I guess I did. Now it's out. I'm a closet romantic. And I'm embarrassed about it."

Maggie laughed. "Lydia's supposed to be the one who'd want him to gallop in on a white horse, scoop me up in his arms, and carry me off to paradise. I didn't expect that from you, Jackie. Okay, yes, I admit I am disappointed. Of course I am. I can do without the horse, but it would have been thrilling to find myself in a rush of romance and excitement. Is that what you are reacting to?"

Jackie nodded, and asked, "What are you going to do, Maggie?"

"I don't know. Lydia told me to be patient, to give him time to shift gears. She said wait and see what happens on Friday."

"This is a huge decision for him," said Jackie. "He should be taking his time with it. And you, Maggie, you've got to decide what you want. Don't just leave it up to him."

Back at home in her living room Maggie asked Mary Magdalene, "I know you want Michael and me to live our lives together."

Mary nodded. "It is my deepest desire."

"But what if we don't?"

"You won't be the first." Mary sighed heavily.

"This pattern of limited relationship that you and Jesus passed on to us is such a strong, deeply entrenched pattern. What if we cannot change it? What if Michael and I can only live it as it is? Maybe, like you and Jesus, we don't get to be together in ordinary life."

"Perhaps you are right," Mary replied. "Perhaps this turns out to be more about me than anyone else. I have never let go of my regrets. I have always wanted to change this rather than allow it to be what it is."

Maggie grabbed onto what Mary had just said and nodded eagerly. "That way of responding is very familiar to me, wanting something to change instead of accepting what is. Maybe that is a key part of this pattern. Mary, let's look at this. Maybe the lesson to be learned is exactly that, to truly let go and let things be whatever they are. That means you let go of living out your life with Jesus and I let go of living out mine with Michael."

Maggie turned to Nu and said, "I have a question for you, Nu. If I do let go of the outcome with Michael, and fully accept whatever happens, then is it possible that would complete Mary's pattern and resolve it? Could everything then be freed to evolve? Could it transform to a new level and a new pattern?"

"Go on," said Nu. "There's more to what you're asking."

"Isn't it possible, then, that in the new pattern Michael and I could be together after all?"

"I am going to answer this, Maggie, because now you are wise enough to know it. Yes, you are right. You could, indeed, move into a new pattern. And in a new pattern anything is possible."

"Oh, Nu! Then we could—but no! No! I cannot even think of ending up together. I cannot consider that in the slightest. If I allow any expectation of that, if I hold any sliver of hope for that, that keeps me in the old pattern."

"Like me," said Mary.

"Exactly. So, my only choice is to absolutely, with total sincerity, allow everything to be whatever it is, and to truly, honestly, completely trust that whatever happens is sacred path and unfolding as it is meant to be."

Maggie crossed to the window, stared beyond the city to the mountains, then turned and said, "These patterns are not arbitrary. They are the framework and essence of what is. They are the substance of the divine coming into being. I want to honor them and go into and through them rather than struggle with them. I think that beyond what seems like disappointment and constraint may very well be grace and release into a new, extraordinary level of being. Whether it involves Michael or not, it is where I need to go."

Mary smiled. "Maggie, you have grown into such wisdom! Congratulations, you have learned what you needed to learn. I thank you for sharing it with me. It is what I needed, too. Of course it is. And so, it is finished now with us. I bid you farewell. May you always know that you go with God."

"Wait!" Maggie exclaimed, but Mary Magdalene was gone.

A florist delivered a long, white box to Maggie's door on Friday morning. The card said, "I'll come for you at 6. Michael." Inside were six beautiful salmon-colored roses nestled into pale yellow tissue paper.

"Roses!" exclaimed Lydia. "Maggie, he sent you roses."

"Please be careful," warned Caroline.

"Are you packing your saddlebags?" asked Jackie, laughing.

He's coming for me, thought Maggie. He's coming to my door for real this time, with roses on his mind. It's happening.

Maggie hesitated to open her door when Michael knocked. She still wasn't at all sure he would really be there. They hugged a big, long hug and she felt herself want to anchor into this moment forever. They looked into each other's eyes and all the levels of their beings opened and came together. It felt so good, so right.

Oh no, she thought, is it okay to want this? I'm supposed to not care which way this goes. How do I keep it all sorted out when so much is happening?

"Don't sort, Maggie," said Nu. "It is what is, whether you stress over it or not. Simply let it be. Let whatever happens, whatever feelings you feel, whatever the moment brings, simply be what it is. You just be you and be here."

Maggie took a deep breath and relaxed. Michael smiled, then he kissed her, and she kissed him back. She gave way to the seductive moment and let it wake deep longings in her that gathered her up and began to carry her away.

"Whoa," she exclaimed, grabbing at breath, pulling back from the embrace. Her eyes searched his bewildered face. "Are you the same man I was talking with the other day?"

Michael's confusion turned to a smile. "I think so," he said, "but I'm not sure."

"How about telling me what's going on. Talk to me."

"I'm hungry. Let's go to dinner and talk there. I made a reservation at Zambra's."

Good, she thought, a public place is safer than staying here. I sure don't want hormones to override what really matters in this.

When dinner had come and gone, and the coffee was too hot to drink, Michael took hold of her hands across the table. "Maggie," he said, "You constantly amaze me. I've never known anybody like you. I've done little else but think about this and pray about it since we last talked, and here's my answer. I can't imagine my future without you in it. I can't let you go. I can't say no again. So, my answer is yes, let's spend time together, let's see what happens."

He said yes, and he said all the words Caroline wanted to hear, but all Maggie could see were questions. She took a deep breath. "What about your vows, Michael?"

"I think the rules have changed. My life has taken on a whole new dimension with you in it, Maggie, and everything is affected. I don't know what it all means. I just know that with you here I see more, I experience more, I am more. That has to be good. Being more of what we can be is what God wants for us."

Maggie drew her hands away from his, and leaned back into her chair. "What do you want from this, Michael? From us? What do you want this to be?"

He glanced at her, then cast his eyes down for a moment's thought before he looked at her again and said, "I want to be open to what comes, to see what develops, and not have expectations."

Now Maggie looked away, confused by her mixed feelings and her mind's struggling. "Michael," she said, turning to look at him again, "you haven't said anything about love."

"I love you," he said.

"I mean big love, everything love, love that bursts out in every direction and claims life."

"You mean romantic love? Fireworks love? Aren't we beyond that?"

"Beyond? You mean too old?" she asked.

"I mean this is more profound. Isn't this soul-love? Spiritual love? Deep instead of broad?"

"Don't we get to have it all, Michael? Don't we get to have love at every level of being? Don't we get to be fully alive in every way possible?" She paused, then asked, "Michael, are you still being careful? Are you scared?"

"Of course I'm scared. Aren't you?"

"Okay, yes, I'm scared. Tell me, what are you afraid of?"

He closed his eyes and took a breath before answering. "I'm afraid I'll lose track of what matters."

"That's a big one, Michael."

His eyes searched hers and filled with tears. "Maggie, I'm afraid I'll lose God."

"But, Michael," she exclaimed, "nobody can lose God. God never leaves." Then she stopped and looked at his frightened face, and she realized that what he was saying was about him, not about God. She took a deep breath. "Damn," she said, her eyes welling up with tears now, too. "Doesn't this mean we can't do this?"

"That is what I have been afraid of all along, Maggie," he moaned.

"That fear says it all, doesn't it? You're not really here, Michael. You are back at the church, on your knees, trying to make a deal so that you can still prove your spiritual loyalty. You don't believe you can really have it all, do you, Michael? Tell me, why are you here? Why are you doing this?"

"I am here because I want to do this," he insisted.

"If this were right, neither of us would be talking about fear tonight. We would be bursting with happiness. This should be a time for blind, ecstatic, totally unrealistic joy. And look at us. Where is it? Where's the joy?"

Though silent in the restaurant, throughout the other levels Michael shouted, "But I love you!"

She answered him there, "I know you do! Your love fills my heart and everything I am. Your love lifts me up and inspires me to be all I can be. Your love feeds my soul."

"And yours does all that for me. So, how can you question this?" he implored.

Then Michael spoke out loud in the restaurant, reaching across the table toward her. "Give me your hands," he said.

When Maggie felt his hands take hers, as they had so many times on this and on the other levels, she couldn't help but respond. I know the feel of his hands so well, she thought. It is as familiar to me as breath, as heartbeat.

They looked into each other's eyes, their countenances filled with confusion and concern. They held the gaze, and continued to hold it until, finally, grace came through and wrapped around them. Their faces eased, and soft smiles emerged. The waiter moved to approach, stopped and smiled, whispered to himself, then left them alone.

Michael spoke. "Maggie, I want you in my life. I don't know what God wants from me, but I do know that you are here, and this is real, and I cannot deny it any more."

"But," she started to protest. He shook his head to silence her.

"Dear God, will you please help me," he pleaded. "How can I know what to do? How can I choose among thoughts and impressions and feelings? And how can I trust that my choice is the right one? Please, give me an answer, give me a sign."

Maggie listened, and then suddenly grinned and squeezed his hands. "A sign?" she exclaimed. "Remember the very first thing I said to you? 'If you ever doubt yourself, think of me!' There's the sign, Michael. You are doubting yourself, your feelings, your choices, your wisdom. Well, I know your strengths and beauty, Michael, even when you don't. I believe in you, even when you are confused. And now I know that God brought me here for this. How else could I have gotten here? So, trust me, Michael. What I know is that you will find the right answers. We both will."

"I love your confidence in this, Maggie, but," he began.

Maggie interrupted, rushing on. "There's more! I have been so sure that you had to come to get me. The truth is that you have been coming for me all along in all sorts of ways. And I have been coming for you, too. I came for you when I first came here to Asheville, then when I first spoke to you, and again when I told you about our soul-connection. I have come for you every time I've held your heart or brought you to your core self, a hundred times for hugs, and a thousand times to touch on our connection. And I'm coming for you right now."

He nodded as she took a breath.

"It goes both ways," she said, "both coming for the the other. Of course it goes both ways. It always does with us."

They sat in silence, looking at each other, breathing. Then Maggie smiled and said, "Michael, God has sent me to tell you and show you and share with you who you really are, and that life *is* a sacred, infinitely expansive, wonderfully paradoxical, magical, mystical, complete whole, just like you are always saying it is."

Michael grinned and squeezed her hands. "You are incredible."

"There's one more thing," she said. "Today you finally, physically came for me. You sent me that note with the flowers, and then you came to my door to get me. That's new. Things are changing."

"I agree with that," said Michael. "Things are definitely changing."

"Remember our conversation about completing a level? Maybe we have completed a level and now we are moving to the next level, where everything is new and nothing is known." She smiled and added, "Then anything can happen."

His eyes sparkled. They grinned at each other, delighted, and they laughed.

The waiter came back. "Can I get you anything else?" he asked with a cheerful lilt.

Maggie looked at Michael and smiled. He turned to the waiter and said, "No, I think we have everything we need. Thank you."

Michael dropped Maggie off in front of her apartment building, and she sat for a long time on the front steps, watching the nearly full moon rise over the city. Her breath rose and fell in the late night quiet, steady and deep. The moon's bright, inscrutable reflections offered enigmatic vistas through shadowy mountain landscapes. She gazed up at the moon, afloat in the vast, star-sparked heavens, and marveled at the fullness of life's ever-increasing possibilities.

Maggie said to herself, "I know one thing. Unless his flesh-and-blood self shouts, 'But I love you!' just as loud and strong as his soul did tonight, unless his worldly love fills my world like the bright light of this moon fills these mountains, it is not good enough. I know his soul loves me, but as long as his human love strains to reach me through doubt and fear, it's not good enough. Look how the moon shines on me now. I deserve love like this: strong and clear, bold, insistent, whole, and huge. I will not settle for less. It's hard to say this, even to myself, but unless I'm convinced things have undeniably changed, my answer has to be no."

She sat with this for a while, watching fireflies dance in the yard, then whispered into the late night stillness, "Mary, can you hear me? I really don't know what will happen with Michael and me, and I'm not going to try to guess. It could be something none of us even imagines." Maggie took a deep breath, then continued. "And that's okay with me. All I can do is be right here in this moment, every moment, living it, allowing myself to open to it, and discover what it brings. I hope that's okay with you, too."

It was late, and Maggie had weekend clients in the morning. She got to her feet to go inside, but first she paused. Looking around, she recognized that far-off high desert valley where Tiamat/God had taken her in the dream just after she and Mary finished the writing. She remembered the urge to soar down through the valley and on into the boundless path beyond.

Now she stood alone there, gazing again into the limitless, unfathomable distance ahead. Warm, rich sun on her face, wind against her body, and golden earth under her feet and between her toes, Maggie stood there, breathing, being, for as long as it lasted. And then she spread her wings, and flew.

Discuss, ask questions, and read more about this book, Mary Magdalene, and author Aliyah Schick at

www.MarysWords.com

Mary Magdalene

Sacred
Imprints

Gratitude

Thank you, Mary Magdalene, for your words, and for trusting and challenging me in so many ways.

Thank you, Rose Welchans, my soul sister, for consistently insisting I can do more than I think I can.

Thank you, Lynn Rosser, woman of so many brilliances, for your incisive and clarifying editing.

Thank you, Lucy Woodard, loving spirit, for showing me how to cherish each moment. I will never forget you.

Thank you each thoughtful and generous reader of earlier, raw versions of this book, for seeing its potential and offering encouragement.

Thank you Jubilee! Community and all who cheer and support my work and my life. Your hugs and kind words inspire and energize me more than you know.

And thank you to the short but potent list of people who have forced me to claim my strength and fly.

I am hugely grateful to be in this moment.

Aliyah Schick

www.ingramcontent.com/pod-product-compliance
Lightning Source LLC
LaVergne TN
LVHW091020080826
845145LV00002B/310